AMERICAN COUNTRY FURNITURE

PROJECTS FROM THE WORKSHOPS OF DAVID T. SMITH

by Nick Engler and Mary Jane Favorite

Rodale Press
Emmaus, Pennsylvania

If you have any questions or comments concerning this book, please write:
Rodale Press
Book Reader Service
33 East Minor Street
Emmaus, PA 18098

Editor: Jeff Day
Copy Editor: Candace Levy
Graphic Designer: Linda Watts
Graphic Artists: Tom Pickrel, Christine Vogel, Chris Walendzak
Technical Photographer: Karen Callahan
Cover and Lead Photographer: Mitch Mandel
Photograph Stylist: Janet C. Vera
Proofreader: Hue Park
Typesetting by Computer Typography, Huber Heights, Ohio
Produced by Bookworks, Inc., West Milton, Ohio

Library of Congress Cataloging-in-Publication Data

Engler, Nick
  American country furniture: projects from the Workshops of David T. Smith
by Nick Engler and Mary Jane Favorite.
      p.   cm.
  Includes bibliographical references (p.   ) and index.
  ISBN 0-87857-916-8
  1. Furniture making. 2. Country furniture—United States.
I. Favorite. Mary Jane, 1942-   . II. Workshops of David T. Smith (Firm) III. Title.
TT194.E54   1990
  684.1'04—dc20   90-8573   CIP

Distributed in the book trade by St. Martin's Press
      4 6 8 10 9 7 5 3   hardcover

THE WORKSHOPS OF DAVID T. SMITH

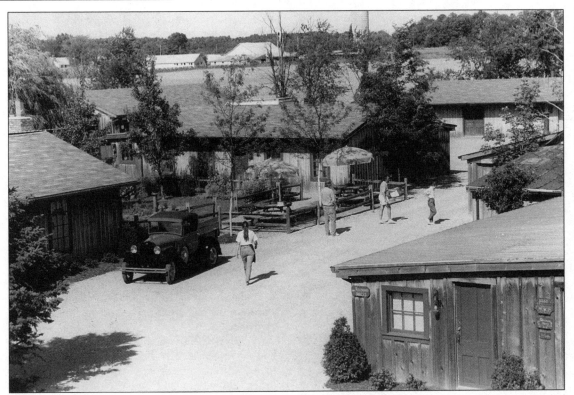

The Workshops of David T. Smith are a unique business, perhaps the only one like it in America. The craftsmen and craftswomen at the Workshops make reproductions of historical furniture, pottery, ironware, and other household items that were used by our pioneer ancestors during the eighteenth and nineteenth centuries — what we now call *American country* artifacts.

The Workshops are just that — a collection of crafts shops on a farm in Warren County, Ohio, near the village of Morrow. The area has been an important crossroads in the country furniture trade for years. Nearby are the historic towns of Lebanon and Waynesville. Waynesville supported four country cabinetmakers in the early nineteenth century; Lebanon supported over a dozen. Today, each town does a booming business in the antique trade. Just a few miles farther down the road is Cincinnati, the center of commerce (and furnituremaking) for the Midwest before the Civil War. Also nearby are the sites of three Shaker communities that flourished in the nineteenth century — Union Village and Watervaliet, Ohio, and White Water, Indiana. These communities also produced furniture. The Workshops have built their business on this rich country heritage.

David T. Smith is the founder, chief designer, and driving force behind the Workshops. He began building furniture in the 1960s when he married.

At first, he built out of necessity — he had no money to buy furniture. His father lent him a table saw, some hand tools, and a few hundred board feet of cherry lumber. With these, he began to furnish his house.

Around this same time, David attended a local auction and, at the advice of his father, picked up a table for $11. He repaired it, cleaned up the finish — and shortly thereafter a local antique dealer offered him $350 for it! He didn't sell the table (he still has it), but he did start a part-time business repairing and restoring antiques. Dealers, museums, and individuals brought him worn or broken furniture to make whole again. At first, David simply bought old wood and old furniture parts to use for restoration. Then, as he gained more experience, he purchased antiques that were only partially complete — the base of a two-piece cupboard, for example — and rebuilt them. He experimented with finishing techniques until he could match the old finishes perfectly. He also devised methods of treating new hardware to make it look old and worn. He became so adept that his customers couldn't tell what part of an antique was original and what was replaced.

As time went on, prices for antiques escalated. So did the prices for parts of antiques — or antiques with parts missing. Prices rose so high that it began to cost David more for an antique in need of restoration than he could make by restoring it. This forced him to make a decision: "I thought to myself," says David, "if I can build half of a piece of furniture, I can build all of it. So I did just that."

At first, he built furniture pieces from old wood. When old wood became scarce, he switched to new wood and perfected his finishing techniques to make the new stock look old. The new pieces were almost indistinguishable from the antiques he had restored.

In early 1980, the demand for David's furniture had grown so large, he became a full-time cabinet-maker. Almost immediately he got his first big order: 200 tables and 400 benches for a nearby recreational park. He expanded to fill this order, hiring additional craftsmen. David T. Smith became "David T. Smith and Company, Furniture Makers and Grainers." David was also interested in antique redware pottery, ironware, and other household artifacts. So he built a pottery shop, then a blacksmith shop among his cabinetmaking and finishing shops. David T. Smith and Company became "The Workshops of David T. Smith." For other items, he sought craftsmen and craftswomen who worked in the old, country manner or who made accurate reproductions of rugs, brooms, toys, woodcarvings, pewterware, decoys, and so on. Some of these people work on the premises; others work in their own shops and sell their wares through the Workshops.

Today, the Workshops employs almost three dozen people, over half of whom make furniture, pottery,

Although they use modern power tools, the craftspeople at the Workshops build accurate reproductions of American country furniture from the eighteenth and nineteenth centuries.

brooms, and ironware. This doesn't include the many associated craftspeople and cabinetmaking shops elsewhere who create everything from Windsor chairs to pewter spoons. Together, these folks have gained a countrywide reputation for highly accurate reproductions of early American artifacts. The editors of magazines and journals have praised them not only for design and workmanship, but for their "museum-quality" finishes. A curator from the Winterthur Museum in Winterthur, Delaware, after inspecting furniture and pottery from the Workshops, commented that the reproductions were "done so well [that] in some cases, we couldn't say for sure whether or not these are reproductions unless we could break them open or take them apart."

All of this has been accomplished by careful attention to details and faithfulness to history and tradition. At the Workshops, the craftspeople not only build furniture that's similar to what their great-great-grandfathers might have built, they build it in the same manner. The Workshops operate very much like the old-time cabinetmaking shops that they emulate. The craftspeople don't *manufacture* furniture; there is no assembly line. A single craftsman builds each piece, from start to finish. On large pieces, such as a corner cabinet, two craftsmen might team up.

Sometimes people with exceptional skills are called on to make certain parts of a piece — turned legs or spindles, carved moldings and ornaments, inlay and other decoration. At the Workshops, finishing has also developed into a fine skill. Some craftspeople specialize in applying museum-quality finishes. This, too, is similar to the old-time way of working. Country cabinetmakers often employed turners, carvers, inlay artists, and other specialists for specific jobs.

The unique organization of the Workshops allows them to take on both large and small jobs. The Workshops have a large enough base of craftspeople and associated shops to make 200 tables for a customer. However, they can also make one-of-a-kind pieces at a profit. This is similar to the way an eighteenth- or nineteenth-century country cabinetmaker conducted his business. He had to take his work where he could find it; no job was too small or too large. He handled small jobs himself. For large jobs, he called on his friends.

The projects in this book were developed by David T. Smith and other craftspeople at the Workshops. Some of them are one-of-a-kind pieces, made for this book or special clients. Others are "stock" pieces — popular designs that are reproduced again and again. Some are precise copies of historical pieces that can be found in museums or collections of fine furniture. Others are inspired by traditional forms. Whatever the piece, each is built as American country furniture was built centuries ago.

The Workshops are best known for their museum-quality finishes, which duplicate the worn finishes on real country antiques.

CONTENTS

❖

FINISH

INTRODUCTION: DESIGN, CONSTRUCTION, AND FINISH

As you might expect from a country craftsman, David T. Smith's woodworking philosophy is simple and straightforward: "There are three important elements to every furniture project," he maintains, "design, construction, and finish. Each of them is equally important, equally essential. You need all three — fine design, fine construction, and a fine finish — to make a fine piece of furniture. If you mess up any one element, then the entire piece may be a flop. To keep this from happening, you have to pay careful attention to the details."

This is the philosophy on which the craftsmen and craftswomen at the Workshops have built their business. Country furnituremaking is an exacting art; it requires more than an ordinary knowledge of woodworking. You must understand woodworking *history* — the kinds and styles of furniture that early American craftsmen built, the tools and materials that they used, the joinery and construction methods that were popular at the time, even the way they finished and cared for what they built. In short, you need to know the details.

For this reason, there is a great deal more to this book than project plans. To provide you with the in-depth information needed to build fine American country furniture, you will also find innovative tips, techniques, and a woodworking history of early America. In keeping with the philosophy of the Workshops, this information is divided into three categories — Design, Construction, and Finish.

Design — The American furniture tradition has deep roots in Europe. The first woodworkers to arrive in this country had learned their trade in England, Germany, and many other European countries. Consequently, their designs reflected European tastes. Europe continued to dominate American furniture design well into the nineteenth century, as the skilled cabinetmakers in the larger American cities followed the latest continental trends. But these Old World designs were tempered by the New World experience. The hard realities of life in early America contrived to create a unique body of designs that we remember as American country furniture.

These designs developed rapidly; in less than 200 years country furniture evolved from the first primitive colonial chests to the graceful, mass-produced Shaker chairs. The design section traces this development, shows the place of American country furniture in western culture, and profiles the craftsmen who made these pieces.

Construction — American country furniture was usually built by craftsmen who employed woodworking techniques and methods from all over the world. While they were skilled and had an abundance of raw materials, they were often limited by tools, time, and the wherewithal of their customers. So, their furniture was well built, yet simple and practical.

The plans for the furniture pieces in this section show complete construction details. For each project, there are also step-by-step instructions that walk you through the procedures, from cutting the raw lumber to applying the finish. The instructions include illustrated explanations of the special techniques needed to build certain projects and show how to accomplish them with contemporary tools. Innovative tips tell how to add important details, making each project look like an authentic country antique.

Finish — Finish is, perhaps, the most crucial element of a fine country furniture reproduction. When finishing a country piece, you must duplicate hundreds of years of wear — an entire *history* of use and abuse. There may, in fact, be several layers of finish that the various owners of a piece applied at different times. These must be patiently built up and worn down, layer by layer, as would have occurred in real life.

This is what the cabinetmakers at the Workshops call a "museum-quality" finish — while the piece looks well-used and worn, it also looks well-preserved and serviceable. To achieve this, the Workshops use creative combinations of chemicals and finishing techniques. This final section gives several recipes for museum-quality finishes — which chemicals to use, how to apply them, and in what order. It also shows how to duplicate popular country surface treatments, such as grain painting.

Depending on your woodworking tastes and ambitions, you may not want to try all the suggested techniques. Many woodworkers prefer *not* to make their projects look old and worn. Even David admits certain misgivings: "I really have to screw my courage up to knock the corner off a drawer or gouge the top of a table that was so hard to make."

Choose just the tips and techniques you want. Use the plans and information to build reproductions of fine American country antiques — or create fine furniture in the American country tradition. Either way, these projects will be a unique woodworking experience. They'll teach you the historical details of the craft, while helping you explore your woodworking roots.

DESIGN

THE COUNTRY CABINETMAKER

American country furniture is not just a style; it's a rich heritage.

The furniture tells the history of a young, vigorous nation — not the names, dates, and places, but the everyday life of our ancestors. Consider the dry sink: In its evolution from a simple bench that held buckets, you can discern the predicament of our great-great-great-grandparents in the American wilderness and their struggle to better themselves. Each piece of country furniture also reveals the character of the builder and how he faced a hard life in a hard land. The furniture is sometimes playful, sometimes reverent, often simple, always practical and inventive. When you build the piece, you relive a little of the maker's life.

DEFINING "COUNTRY"

Who were the builders of country furniture? They were the thousands of anonymous cabinetmakers who set up shop in the small towns and villages throughout the United States. They furnished the homes of farmers, storekeepers, tradesmen, and other common folk from 1690 to 1860. These were the years before the Industrial Revolution caught up with the woodworking trades, when furniture was still made one piece at a time. This was the country furniture era.

Despite a popular misconception, country furniture was *not* built by unskilled farmers in rural workshops. Nor was it made by cabinetmakers in the larger cities, particularly New York, Philadelphia, Boston, Newport, Baltimore, and Charleston. Most craftsmen in these cities catered to tastes of the upper class, making stylish, trendy pieces — what we now call *classic* American furniture.

Country furniture was made by skilled woodworkers, who were often trained in these large cities before moving to rural areas. Some immigrant country craftsmen were trained in the major design centers of Europe. Many were capable of making classic furniture (and sometimes did), but their clients were mostly middle and lower class. Because of this, a country cabinetmaker's work was less decorative than what the big-city craftsmen produced for rich folks. Most country designs were practical, inexpensive, simplified versions of current furniture trends.

Thomas Morgan (1820–1860) of Eaton, Ohio, was one of the few country cabinetmakers to leave us his photograph. He apparently learned the trade from his father. *From "Ohio Furniture Makers" by Jane Sikes Hageman. Courtesy of the Michaels family of Eaton, Ohio.*

There were also several groups of country cabinetmakers who worked in their own distinctive styles. For example, some German immigrants practiced woodworking traditions that dated back to medieval times. They made highly decorated furniture with distinctive fretwork and painted designs. On the other hand, the Shakers — religious refugees from England — rejected all decoration. They strived to make their furniture as plain as possible. Despite the wide differences in design, these woodworkers shared a common bond: They made little attempt to mimic current furniture trends. The work of groups such as these is often referred to as vernacular or *folk* furniture.

A HARD AND UNCERTAIN LIFE

Like the members of any profession, country cabinetmakers were a mixed lot. Some practiced for a year, some for a lifetime. Some worked for money, others for traditional or spiritual reasons. All were hardworking. They had to be — the life of a woodworker was uncertain and often nomadic. If you read their diaries and personal histories, you find that, while some cabinetmakers prospered, many didn't. They would settle in a place, set up shop, build a clientele, and be blessed with land and family — only to have it all collapse in a few years due to economic trends, poor health, or bad luck. They'd move on, usually traveling a little farther west, and begin again.

Hector Sanford, although he suffered a few more tragedies than most, was a typical itinerant cabinetmaker. He was orphaned as a boy in Fairfax, Virginia. "Charitable agents" apprenticed him to Ephraim Evans, a chairmaker. In 1797, he went to Ohio in a canoe and settled in Chillicothe. For unknown reasons, he moved to Georgetown, Virginia, in 1802, advertising that he would paint, gild, or "japan" (build up layers of lacquer on)

furniture. He also made Windsor chairs. By 1805, he was back in Chillicothe for his one moment of glory, an accomplishment that left his name in the history books: He made a set of chairs for Thomas Worthington, the governor of the new state of Ohio. He remained in Chillicothe until 1813, but then his track goes cold for more than two decades. When we last hear of him, he was a circuit-preacher in Brown County, Ohio. He died there in 1837.

Often, the only records that country cabinetmakers have left behind — other than their furniture — are the advertisements that they ran in small town newspapers. *From "Ohio Furniture Makers" by Jane Sikes Hageman.*

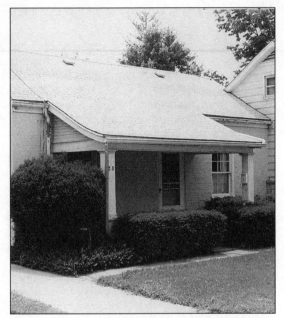

John M. Stakes made furniture in this small brick building in Bellbrook, Ohio, from 1838 until his death in 1898. Stakes was also Bellbrook's undertaker. Although there is no record of how much furniture he produced, it's said he built more than 5,000 caskets in his lifetime. *Courtesy Ruth Penewit.*

When a cabinetmaker came to a town in which he thought he might prosper, he usually set up a small shop in a rented house. He advertised his location in the local papers and hoped for the best. If business was good, he might take on an apprentice — usually a young man about 14 years old who showed some aptitude for the trade. This apprentice lived with the cabinetmaker's family, working for room, board, and — if he was lucky — a small allowance. A well-established cabinetmaker might have as many as five apprentices.

By agreement, apprenticeships usually lasted seven years, or until the young man was 21. During this time, he learned furniture design and woodworking techniques and made his first set of tools. (Until the nineteenth century, most woodworking tools were hand-made.) When he turned 21, he became a journeyman. He took his tools and went off to set up his own business.

Apprenticeships didn't always last a full seven years, however. It was common for an apprentice to run away before his full term was up. If this happened, the cabinetmaker advertised, offering a reward for the return of the apprentice. In some cases, the cabinetmaker was glad to see the apprentice go. Witness the advertisement of Tom Bereman of West Union, Ohio:

One cent reward — ran away from the subscriber on the 16th, George Welsh, an indentured apprentice to the Windsor chairmaking and painting business, 12 years old, light complexion…somewhat better clad than is usual for an apprentice to be. Whoever returns said George will be coolly treated and receive no thanks, but shall have the above reward.

If a cabinetmaker continued to prosper, he often moved his shop out of his home and into a separate building. He might even hire several journeymen cabinetmakers to work for him, if business was very good. He might also rent a "wareroom" in the town's business district, apart from his shop, to display samples of his craft. Moses Hatfield, a chairmaker in Dayton, Ohio, had three warerooms — in Dayton, Union, and Greenville.

If he didn't prosper — and many didn't — a cabinetmaker often took on other jobs to help pay the bills. There are records of cabinetmakers who worked as preachers, farmers, grocers, and justices of the peace. A fair number of them opened taverns — perhaps the hardships of the trade drove them to drink. But the most common second profession was undertaking. The cabinetmaker made the coffin, then interred the body.

Prosperous or otherwise, these craftsmen have left us with a rich legacy. Few groups of artisans have developed such a wide range of designs that have remained so practical — and so appealing — for so many centuries.

A WORLD VIEW

To better appreciate American country furniture design, you must first understand its place in world history — how the basic country forms evolved and how they were imported to America. You should also know that when America was discovered, furniture had been available to common folks — country folks — for only 200 or 300 years.

ANCIENT FURNITURE

The upper class had furniture much earlier, as you might expect. All the basic forms — chairs, tables, beds, and chests — were developed by the Egyptians between 2700 and 2200 B.C. They also built cupboards with doors and drawers, but these weren't in general use. The only known examples were apparently used by priests in the Egyptian temples.

The Egyptians invented the first furnituremaking tools — the chisel, mallet, hand saw, awl, bow-drill, and "rubber." (The rubber was an abrasive stone used with loose sand to smooth the wood, much the same way we use a sanding block and sandpaper.) With these, they made the first woodworking joints. At first, Egyptian woodworkers lashed or sewed boards together with leather thongs. But within a few hundred years, they were using sophisticated joinery, including dovetails and pegged mortises and tenons.

With the Greeks and Romans, furniture began to appear in the homes of the growing middle class. The economic benefits of civilization had created sufficient wealth for ordinary people to afford a few luxuries. The furniture owned by the middle class was sparse and limited to chairs, beds, chests, and a few small tables. Nonetheless, it was the first furniture of the common folk.

Both Greek and Roman furniture evolved from Egyptian models. Each culture adapted the basic forms to their tastes and needs. For example, the Greeks strived to make their chairs comfortable and beautiful, as the gracefully arched legs and

Bed with Foot Board

Chest

Animal-Leg Chair

Egyptian furniture, about 2200 B.C.

Tripod Table

Animal-Leg Table

"Klismos" Chair & Stool

Greek furniture, about 500 B.C.

Roman furniture, about A.D. 100

back of the *klismos* show. The Romans were more practical. Among their chair designs was the folding *curule* for their traveling magistrates to sit on when holding court. It was not particularly comfortable — it had no back — but it was stylish enough to befit the station of its owner. Better yet, it was portable.

Each culture also contributed to a growing collection of woodworking tools. The plane was introduced into Greece from the Middle East in the seventh century B.C., and they further refined it. The Greek inventor Archimedes designed the helical screw, from which came the auger. Theodorus of Samos invented the level, the carpenter's square, and the turning lathe. The Romans developed the claw hammer and several new types of saws — in particular, the frame saw.

The Romans were also the first to set the teeth on a saw, a remarkable technological advancement. Up until Roman times, a saw cut in one direction only — a craftsman had to lift his saw out of the cut on the return stroke. The set on the teeth almost doubled the efficiency of the saw. This greatly increased a craftsman's productivity and made his furniture cheaper and more affordable for common folks.

A LONG INTERRUPTION

The collapse of the Roman Empire halted the development of both furniture and tools in the West. For the next 1,000 years, only a very few of the rich and powerful in Europe had anything resembling furniture, and this was crudely built. The common people had less than that. The surfaces they needed for working, sitting, eating, and sleeping were either built into the walls of their huts or hewn from timbers.

More elaborate furniture didn't reappear again in Western Europe until medieval times. As economic ties and trades routes were slowly re-established, nobles and landowners found themselves continually on the move administering their scattered properties. They had to take their belongings with them, so they found chests extremely useful. At first, these chests were made from solid logs,

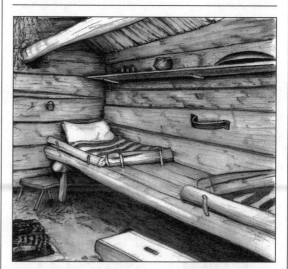

For 1,000 years, European country folks had almost no furniture at all. Beds, benches, tables, and storage shelves were all incorporated in the architecture of their homes, as shown in this artist's conception of a medieval peasant hut. The only pieces of furniture are a few crude stools.

hollowed out and fitted with lids. Later, they were assembled from boards, using simple butt joints and nails. They were often gaily painted. The traveling rulers also used folding chairs, much like those of the ancient Roman magistrates, as well as knock-down trestle tables and cupboards. All of this, while heavy by our standards, was built to be portable. The French word for furniture, *meubles,* originally meant "movables."

The central piece of medieval furniture was an open set of shelves, which the French called a *dressoir.* It displayed the noble's "plate" — his dinnerware. The number of shelves or steps showed the station of the owner. A baron commonly had just two steps, his immediate superior had three, and so on up to the royal *dressoir.* French ambassadors once gave Henry VIII a *dressoir* with twelve steps. The practice of displaying dinnerware eventually spread to the masses. The American china cabinet is a direct descendant of the *dressoir.*

Medieval furniture was crudely built, and did not last long. (There are few surviving early medieval pieces today, just some chests.) Most of it consisted of riven boards (split from logs with an axe) nailed together. There was little joinery, other than an occasional mortise and tenon, pinned with nails. However, appearance mattered little. When in use, the rough surfaces were covered with colorful cloths, tapestries, and carpets to make them comfortable and attractive. The modern tablecloth is a vestige of this practice.

THE FIRST EUROPEAN FURNITURE STYLES

During the thirteenth and fourteenth centuries, there was relative peace throughout Europe, which resulted in more trade and rapid economic growth. Cities reappeared, and with them, the middle class — common folks who could afford something as luxurious as a chair or table.

Riven Plank Chest

Trestle Table

Folding Chair

Early medieval furniture, about A.D. 1200

The invention of the sawmill in Germany in 1328 made lumber more available. Before, boards had to be riven from logs with an axe, then smoothed with an adze or plane — a time-consuming, expensive process. The sawmill increased productivity and made furniture more affordable. At the same time, medieval craftsmen called *joiners* began to use pegged mortise-and-tenon joints to make the wainscot that covered the interior of many medieval palaces and cathedrals. They soon discovered that this technique could also be used in furnituremaking, making the furniture more durable and attractive.

This new furniture style was called *Gothic.* (This was, at first, a derisive term coined by Italian designers to describe the unsophisticated designs of the north countries. It referred to the Goth barbarians that had once sacked Rome.) This furniture was massive, built like miniature buildings. Since joiners and stone masons worked side by side in raising cathedrals and palaces, the joiners borrowed many decorative elements from the

Canopy Bed

Settle Bench

Food Press

Gothic furniture, about A.D. 1400

masons — moldings, finials, pilasters, and so on. Architects had more influence on the Gothic furniture style than the woodworkers themselves.

Perhaps the most important development of the Gothic period had nothing to do with furniture design or technology, but with woodworking education and information. Craftsmen established *guilds* to train new artisans, ensure standards of workmanship, and enforce divisions of labor. As an apprentice in a guild, a young craftsman had access to the collected knowledge of the local masters who had gone before him.

The invention of printing in the fifteenth century also had a tremendous impact on furnituremaking. In 1521, an ancient Roman text, *De Architectura* by Vitruvius, was rediscovered and published in Italy. This book was extremely popular among European craftsmen, and they incorporated elements of classical Greek and Roman designs into their furniture. *De Architectura* also set an important precedent. Major architects and designers began to issue *pattern books*, helping to spread their ideas.

In the sixteenth century, the Gothic era gradually gave way to the explosion of discovery and creativity we remember as the Renaissance. Tools, joinery, hardware, and furniture all became more sophisticated. Highly trained, specialized joiners made large cupboards with drawers and glass doors, sometimes covering the surfaces with inlays or veneers of exotic woods. These were called *cabinettes* (later shortened to "cabinet"), after the word "cabin." Craftsmen who possessed the skills and knowledge to make them called themselves *cabinetmakers*. Eventually, the cabinetmakers split from the joiners to form their own guild.

During this time, the use of furniture finally spread to the lower classes. The chronicler William Harrison, in his *Description of England* (1577), said of his time that even farmers were able "to live wealthie, keep good houses, and travel to get riches" and to "garnish their cupboards with plate, their joyned beds with tapestries, and their tables with carpets."

As the Renaissance progressed, regional differences in woodworking designs and techniques became more pronounced. Each country developed its own furniture style.

Italy quickly established itself as the Western European center of fine art and design. As the direct descendants of the Romans, they had inherited the classic traditions. From Italy, design theory dispersed to other parts of Europe.

In **France,** furniture design was directly influenced by the Italians, and to a smaller extent by the Dutch. In 1550, French architect Jacques Androuet du Cerceau published a pattern book thought to have been copied from the design of a prominent Italian architect, Primaticcio. The most striking feature of these patterns was the heavy emphasis on ornament, including swags, scrolls, and mythological figures. This became known as the "Mannerist" style, and was the basis for high French design.

In **Germany,** the *Kleinmeisters* — designers of ornament — influenced furniture styles more than architects. They followed Italian examples, but often relied on their own medieval traditions, including *Fraktur* decoration. (*Fraktur* refers to the designs and motifs used by the medieval illuminators of German manuscripts and official documents.) They also used many exotic woods, metals, and gemstones in their furniture. The quality of the work was extremely high, and German craftsmen gained a reputation throughout Europe for their skill. They began to export small furniture items — particularly chests — to other countries.

In the Low Countries — **Holland** and **Flanders** — craftsmen were more creative and original than anywhere else in Europe, save Italy. They used some Italian ideas and were influenced by German craftsmanship, but they developed many of their own ideas. Architect/painter Vredeman de Vries and his sons published several pattern books of elaborately decorated Mannerist-style furniture in the late sixteenth and early seventeenth centuries. These books set the standards for Dutch and Flemish furniture for almost a century, and were highly influential in England.

Spain and **Portugal,** because they were linked to the Low Countries by their Hapsburg rulers, were also influenced by de Vries's designs. These were combined with local traditions, the *mujedar* — the decorative arts of the Moors. Moors were Moslems from North Africa who had conquered and colonized the Iberian peninsula during the Dark Ages. Although they were slowly beaten back, they left behind many distinct furniture forms.

Because **England** was isolated from the European continent, its Renaissance styles were simpler, more provincial, and more conservative than elsewhere. (In continental Europe, England was thought of as the backwaters — somewhat crude and behind the times.) If they wanted something really up-to-date, the English upper class imported Dutch, Flemish, German, and some French Renaissance furniture. Local craftsmen built furniture in the old Gothic forms, covered with a mixture of Mannerist and medieval motifs. Owing to old Norman ties, they were most influenced by Dutch and Flemish designers.

This was the state of the craft as Europe began to colonize America. In just a few hundred years, furniture had evolved from a luxury to a necessity. The well-to-do adorned their homes with stylish, highly decorated furniture. The middle class bought simpler pieces, and all but the poorest people could afford basic, utilitarian tables, chairs, chests, and beds. More important, furniture design had evolved into a unique art form that expressed both new ideas and cultural heritage.

Portable Desk (Spanish)

Table & Stools (Flemish)

"Nonsuch" Chest (English)

Renaissance furniture, about A.D. 1600

THE AMERICAN EXPERIENCE

It's impossible to overestimate the effect of the colonial experience on American furniture design. Although in many cases American woodworkers had similar training and skills as their European counterparts, they had cruder tools, a limited and uncertain supply of hardware, less time to build sophisticated furniture, and fewer clients who could afford it. Furthermore, the wilderness was a demanding environment. Many pioneer craftsmen were more concerned with survival than their craft. As Renaissance styles gave way to Baroque, and European cabinet-makers reveled in new, exuberant fantasies, Americans struggled to eke out a living in the New World. Consequently, their furniture was simpler and more practical.

At first, American immigrants longed to possess highly decorative furniture and the other refinements of European civilization. When they could afford it, they imported the latest designs from their mother countries. However, tastes change with experience. For the first generation of native-born Americans, practicality and simplicity became virtues instead of hardships.

THE FIRST AMERICAN FURNITURE — THE SOUTHWEST TRADITION

The first (documented) American furniture was made long before the Europeans came to America. Aztec and Pueblo craftsmen made *petlatls* (benches for both sleeping and sitting), *tollicpalis* (chairs), and several types of low tables. In 1521, when the Spanish conquered New Spain — the area we know as Mexico, California, Arizona, and New Mexico — they found that many natives in the area were already highly skilled woodworkers. In particular, the Pueblos and their neighbors in New Mexico had a rich woodworking tradition.

As part of the Spanish missionary efforts, immigrant *ensembladores* (joiners) taught the enslaved Indians to reproduce European furniture. The Indians found the geometric designs of the Spanish were similar to their own. They began to mix the two, producing a new furniture style. By the seventeenth century, Indian and *mestizo* (Indian/Spanish) craftsmen were making uniquely American *bancos* (benches), *sillóns* (chairs), *mesas* (tables), *arcons* (chests), and *varguenos* (writing boxes).

So quickly did the Indians master and begin to modify Old World furniture forms, that Spanish artisan guilds feared they would lose control of them. In 1598, Spain passed laws forbidding the colonists to purchase or use anything of Indian or mestizo manufacture. However, the ordinance did little to halt the spread of the new style. In the

"Palo Blanco" Table

"Trastero" Cupboard

"Sillon" Chair

Southwest American furniture, about 1700

towns of the Sante Fe and Albuquerque, far from the central government in Mexico City, craftsmen were relatively free to explore their craft. Their ethnic origin mattered little and they made Spanish furniture in the distinctive "Southwest" tradition for almost two centuries.

THE SOUTHERN TRADITION

The French began colonizing the New World in 1604, concentrating on the fur-rich lands to the north, around the Great Lakes. Although they claimed all the land drained by the Mississippi, they did little to exploit it. In the late seventeenth century, however, they realized the potential for commerce on the Mississippi and turned their attentions to the American south. They established

Armoire

Seignouret Chair

Southern American furniture, about 1800

New Orleans in 1718, making it the seat of government in "Louisiana." Owing to its location near the mouth of the largest river in North America, New Orleans quickly became a booming trade center — complete with its own furniture industry.

Louisiana was captured by Spain in 1762 and remained under Spanish rule for the rest of the century. The French won it back in the early nineteenth century, then after just a few years, sold it to the United States. Although the colony changed hands several times, the colonists continued to look to France as their cultural model throughout the eighteenth and much of the nineteenth centuries. Craftsmen made *armoires* (cupboards), tables, slat-back chairs, and other pieces based on French models.

THE EASTERN TRADITION

Although southern and southwestern design traditions are important to the history of American country furniture, their influence is minor compared to the designs of the East. The eastern tradition produced hundreds of different forms, far more than the other two combined. It eventually spread across the continent, overshadowing the others. There were three reasons that the eastern tradition was so prolific.

First, there was an abundance of raw materials east of the Mississippi. The 13 English colonies were almost completely covered with a hardwood forest containing dozens of species of trees suitable for furnituremaking. Louisiana was also well forested, but it didn't have the variety of woods found in the East. In the Southwest, there were few forests of any kind — furniture-quality lumber often had to be imported.

Second, the population — and the demand for furniture — grew much more rapidly in the East than elsewhere in America. There were just a few hundred permanent settlers in two colonies — Massachusetts and Virginia — in the early seventeenth century. Less than 50 years later, in 1650, this population had grown to 24,000 in 40 different towns all along the East Coast. Immigration was solicited by the various colonies, using "land agents." William Penn, for example, had agents throughout Europe promoting his colony of Pennsylvania. This practice continued far into the nineteenth century.

Third, there were more craftsmen and a higher caliber of skills among the eastern immigrants. This was due to several factors. The land agents who solicited immigrants looked for skilled laborers — farmers and craftsmen — not adventurers, trappers, or soldiers. Also, a curious English law, the Tunnage Acts, required that every ship leaving for America carry a carpenter. (The English wanted to ensure that these ships returned safely with their hulls, masts, and stores in good order.) Many of these carpenters decided to stay in the New World. John Alden, a member of the Plymouth colony, was one of these. Although he was not originally a member of the Pilgrim band, he elected to stay with them. He became the first furnituremaker in the eastern tradition.

Finally, the English colonized America for its trees. England was fast running out of good shipbuilding timber for its navy. In America, they found oak for hulls and pine for masts and waterproofing pitch. So the English encouraged the exploitation of American forests.

Although the East was colonized largely by the English, much of the eastern furniture tradition was derived from other sources. However, England had a relaxed attitude about colonial immigration, much more liberal than Spain or France. For instance, although the English took control of the Dutch colony in 1664, they continued to let the Dutch immigrate. After all, the Dutch were cousins to William the Conqueror.

England also had strong political ties with Germany. When the Stewart line of kings failed, Parliament looked to Germany in 1714 and imported George I. Consequently, many colonial land agents combed Germany. They had particular luck in the upper Rhine Valley, where the Thirty Years War with France had devastated the economy. Germany also went through a period of religious persecution in the seventeenth and eighteenth centuries, and many Lutherans, Moravians, Amish, Mennonites, and Schwenkfelders escaped to America.

The Swedish founded a colony in Delaware in 1638, which the Dutch captured in 1655, only to turn it over to the English nine years later. But Scandinavians continued to settle in America, contributing their furniture traditions to the colonial melting pot. The Spanish colonized Florida in 1565, and their settlements spread as far north as the Carolinas. The English took Florida in 1763, gave it up to the Spanish again in 1783, then the United States captured it early in the nineteenth century. Yet, like New Orleans, many of the woodworking traditions of the original colonists remained throughout these years.

At first, these national and ethnic groups stayed in regional pockets. The Dutch settled mostly in the Hudson Valley of New York, the Germans in the Pennsylvania counties around Philadelphia, and the Scandinavians in Delaware. The Spanish kept to themselves in Florida. Only the English colonized the entire Atlantic seaboard. The first eastern American furniture was made according to the Old World designs prevalent in the area. As time went on and craftsmen of different nationalities and beliefs traded ideas, forms began to blend and the eastern tradition took shape.

EASTERN AMERICAN COUNTRY FURNITURE

Furniture designs are never static; they're always evolving. From one period to the next, the styles in any given location may be quite different. This was the case in eastern America. The country furniture era spans several different periods and includes many different styles. Each successive style was an offshoot of the one preceding it.

THE SEVENTEENTH CENTURY

During the seventeenth century, colonial furnituremaking was not well developed, and there was little distinction between country and classic pieces. In fact, there wasn't much "country" to speak of — just a few pioneers with a tentative claim to a piece of the wilderness. Nonetheless, the designs from this time were important to the evolution of country furniture.

Primitive colonial furniture, 1607–1640

Trestle Table

Six-Board Chest

Joint Stool

Primitive Period, 1607–1640 — During this time, colonists were concerned primarily with survival. They made only the most essential, rudimentary furniture. It was as if they had stepped off their ship and back to medieval times.

There were no sawmills; planks were riven from logs. The available tools were mostly for carpentry and shipbuilding; there was little that could be used to do fine work.

Chests were important, almost indispensable to the colonists, owing to their versatility. The owners used them not only for storage, but for seating, sleeping, tables, and work surfaces. On rare occasions, they even used them for defense. During an Indian attack in Virginia, the colonists stacked chests (and any other available items) to make a breastworks.

The colonists also fashioned other basic furniture, such as stools and tables. All of it was hastily and crudely made. The chests were probably pegged or nailed together, and had leather hinges and latches. (Other than the nails in the ships' stores, metal hardware was scarce.) The stools were just legs stuck in a board seat; the tables were planks laid across sawbucks. This furniture was intended to serve only for a few years until the colonists could afford to make or buy something better. Because of this, none of these primitive pieces survive today — we know them only from written descriptions and inventories.

American Jacobean Period, 1640–1690 — By 1640, there were a small number of furniture shops in the towns and villages that were springing up on the Atlantic coast. Isolated from Europe and the development of Baroque furniture styles there, the first American cabinetmakers began building pieces based on late Renaissance English *Jacobean* designs — "court cupboards," paneled chests, and turned chairs. *Jacobean* furniture was named for King James I and II of England. In America, this is sometimes referred to as *Pilgrim* furniture.

These pieces were very heavy, often using frame-and-panel construction. Since sawmills were rare, they were made from easily-riven wood, such as oak or pine. The flat areas were often decorated with incised carvings, applied bosses and spindles, and geometric designs. Turnings, such as chair rungs or table legs, were often very intricate and exaggerated.

During this time, apprentice programs became established in America. These were loose copies of European programs. An apprentice worked with a skilled craftsman for several years, learning the craft. Upon striking out on his own, the apprentice became a journeyman. After a few years of independent practice, the journeyman called himself a master craftsman. There were no formal guidelines, however, that governed his education. American craftsmen never adopted the strict European guild system. A few Boston craftsmen tried to establish a guild, but it was short-lived.

Court
Cupboard

Paneled
Chest

Brewster
Chair

American Jacobean furniture, 1640–1690

Before the end of the century, these informal apprenticeships had graduated the first generation of native-born American cabinetmakers — technically proficient and unfettered by the rigid rules that bound their European counterparts. Not all of these woodworkers had the creativity, imagination, or good business sense to take advantage of this freedom, of course. And those that did usually took advantage only in little ways. But these little departures from the European norm sometimes made for a distinctly American piece.

THE EIGHTEENTH CENTURY

By the eighteenth century, most Americans were no longer preoccupied with survival. They had begun to build a country. Several population centers — notably New York, Boston, Philadelphia, Newport, Baltimore, and Charleston — had grown to where they could rightfully be called cities. Between them were many towns, villages, and farms — the "country." The economy had developed, too, and with distinct upper, middle, and lower classes.

In both the cities and the country, there was a well-established furniture trade. The difference between city and country life was reflected in the furniture. In the large cities, highly skilled cabinetmakers, catering to the upper class, made furniture based on the European designs — *classic* American furniture. Owing to the distance from Europe and slow-to-change provincial tastes, city pieces were often as many as ten years behind the latest European styles. Nonetheless, they were stylish. In the surrounding towns and villages, however, craftsmen made simpler, more practical furniture for less well-to-do clients. When they copied European styles, they were usually even farther behind the times.

This marked the beginning of *country* furniture — the common, everyday furniture of the time. Country furniture was usually as well constructed as classic furniture, but the design was limited by the means of the clientele — not by the skills of the craftsmen.

William and Mary Period, 1690–1725 — As life became less hard in the colonies, American craftsmen began to copy late English Baroque style, the so-called William-and-Mary designs. These were the first true American cabinet-makers, employing sophisticated woodworking techniques such as veneering, dovetail joinery, and case construction.

Water-powered sawmills appeared everywhere, and craftsmen began to use a larger variety of woods, particularly walnut and maple. They built complex pieces, such as highboys and lowboys — tall and short chests of drawers on extended legs. William-and-Mary chests and desks typically had intricate, scrolled skirts; turned pieces sometimes sported distinctive trumpet and bell shapes. The more stylish pieces were often decorated with veneering, inlay, or built-up lacquer, called "japanning." During this time, the first distinctly American furniture design appeared — the butterfly table, a drop-leaf table with wide, curved supports.

Queen Anne Period, 1725–1760 — European cabinetmakers, enamored of imported Oriental furniture, began to incorporate Japanese and Chinese design elements into their own pieces. Americans followed suit a few years later. These elements included the cabriole leg, ball-and-claw feet, and shell carvings. The cyma curve or *ogee*, which first appeared on William-and-Mary furniture, was used everywhere on Queen Anne pieces.

Lowboy

Butterfly Table

Easy Chair

William-and-Mary furniture, 1690–1725

Blockfront Desk

Side Chair

Drop-Leaf Table

Queen Anne furniture, 1725–1760

Overall, the designs were less cluttered, lighter, and more graceful than previous styles.

Craftsmen of different areas began to work predominantly in certain types of wood. In New England, many cabinetmakers built furniture of maple. In Connecticut, they preferred cherry, and in Pennsylvania, walnut. In the Carolinas, it was cypress. In port cities, particularly centers of classic furnituremaking, craftsmen used imported mahogany. These regional preferences remained throughout the remainder of the country era.

During the Queen Anne period, there were several important innovations in furniture design and construction. For the first time, cabinetmakers made lipped drawers and mounted large pieces on casters. They invented the rule joint for drop-leaf tables. Americans also made another original contribution to furniture design. The cabinetmakers of Newport, Rhode Island, developed *blockfront* chests and desks.

Chippendale Period, 1760–1780 — In 1754, Thomas Chippendale published *The Gentleman and Cabinet-Maker's Director,* a pattern book of ornate designs. His designs used many basic Queen Anne forms, but they were heavier and added decoration such as carved finials and pierced fretwork. He also reintroduced the straight line as a design element; many Chippendale pieces had square, untapered legs or geometric "Chinese" fretwork. This was one of the most durable furniture styles ever conceived. Although Chippendale built furniture for only a few decades, his designs were used by cabinetmakers on both sides of the Atlantic long into the nineteenth century. Some furniture manufacturers have continued to use Chippendale designs to this day.

As you might expect, the American interpretations of Chippendale's designs were much more restrained than the English. In the country shops, there was little change from the Queen Anne style — country cabinetmakers and their clients could not afford Chippendale ornament.

Chippendale furniture, 1760–1780

Meanwhile, American furnituremakers made another important contribution. This time, however, it wasn't just a design, but an innovative furniture form — the *rocking chair.* Tradition has it that the first rockers were designed to give old folks some simple exercise, but this can't be confirmed. Whatever the original reasons, the rocker quickly became popular in the colonies and, by the nineteenth century, had spread to Europe.

THE NINETEENTH CENTURY

In the late eighteenth century, several large cabinetmaking businesses experimented with a new "shop method" of manufacture — what we now call an assembly line. Each craftsman or apprentice specialized in making one part of a larger assembly. In 1793, Sir Samuel Bentham, an English engineer, designed and patented a remarkable collection of woodworking equipment for sawing, planing, cutting joints, and shaping surfaces. Designed to be run by the newly-invented steam engine, they were the first "power" tools. Seven years later, American inventor Eli Whitney introduced a line of muskets with standardized, interchangeable parts.

These three innovations — the assembly line, power tools, and standardized parts — changed the nature of manufacturing forever. The small shops began to *industrialize*. Production went up, profits went up, and more shops industrialized to keep up. Cabinetmakers were among the last to change to the new system. (When they did, they were slow to adopt power tools — even those who worked for large furniture manufacturers preferred to use hand tools.) However, by the time of the American Civil War, the individual craftsman — and a way of working that had lasted for more than 4,000 years — became a curiosity.

The final days of the individual cabinetmaker were his best. Although clients were buying more and more of their everyday furniture from industrialized factories, many small shops reached their zenith in the early nineteenth century. This was the golden age of American country furniture.

Federal Period, 1780–1820 — Immediately after the American Revolution, there was a brief backlash against all things English — including furniture designs. For the first time, American cabinetmakers looked to France for inspiration, and adopted the neoclassic *Directoire* styles. These were more functional designs based on actual Greek or Roman forms. Americans were also influenced by two French-inspired English designers. In 1788, George Hepplewhite published a pattern book, *The Cabinet-maker's and Upholster's Guide*. This was followed quickly by Thomas Sheraton's *The Cabinet-Maker's and Upholster's Drawing Book* in 1791. Ironically, both men were only minor craftsmen, although their books had enormous impact on American furniture.

Federal furniture, 1780–1820

Hepplewhite and Sheraton furniture followed the neoclassic design trend that began in the late eighteenth century. The shapes of their furniture were simple, light, and graceful. They used more straight lines than previous designers — their tapered legs were their hallmark. The flat surfaces were often veneered with exotic woods and decorated with intricate inlay, particularly on Hepplewhite-inspired pieces. In America, these decorations often had patriotic themes.

Because they were simpler, these designs were much more widely imitated than Chippendale, especially in the country. Country cabinetmakers, however, still could not afford the exotic veneers used in neoclassic furniture. So they developed techniques of painting their furniture to look as if it were veneered. *Grain-painted* furniture became popular among country folks.

Ante-Bellum Period, 1820–1860 — This era coincides with the *Empire* period in France (after the French Empire of Napoleon), and is often called *American Empire* since American cabinetmakers continued to copy French designs. The neoclassic style continued to evolve, becoming heavier, more severe, and geometric. Surfaces were often left plain, with little ornament. In France, Roman forms were copied directly, as Napoleon longed to identify himself with the great Roman emperors.

During this time, Duncan Phyfe became the first internationally known American furniture designer. Phyfe had been New York's leading craftsman since the late eighteenth century, employing over 100 men in his shops. He blended both French and English styles in his designs, but added his own touches. He also used patriotic motifs, such as eagles and shields. This created the first (and only) uniquely American classic style — Duncan Phyfe furniture.

Although he earned a worldwide reputation, Phyfe's forms were not widely copied outside of the New York area, particularly in the country — possibly because he never published a pattern book. Country craftsmen continued to make furniture in Federal styles, sometimes with a few Empire elements. During this time, their technical excellence reached its peak, then fell quickly as they struggled to compete with industrialized shops.

FOLK FURNITURE

Several popular styles appeared in America that belong to no particular period and were not greatly affected by prevailing trends. These were *folk* furniture styles. For religious, cultural, or sometimes just plain practical reasons, the craftsmen who made this furniture developed their own body of forms and designs, and stuck to them. The best

Washstand

Side Chair

Canopy Bed

Ante-Bellum furniture, 1820–1860

Settee

Rocking Chair

Continuous Arm Windsor

American Windsor chairs, 1725–1830

known examples are Windsor chairs, Pennsylvania German furniture, and Shaker furniture.

Windsor Chairs, 1725–1830 — American Windsor chairs were adapted from a country form made throughout England (not just Windsor) in the sixteenth and seventeenth centuries. The basic design probably developed from a simple country stool, because the chief characteristics are a carved "saddle" seat and turned legs. This chairmaking style was part of the *turner's* woodworking tradition. In England, turners were a separate trade from the joiners. Turners who specialized in chairmaking were called "bodgers."

American turners began making Windsor chairs around 1725, and quickly made the style their own. They developed dozens of different forms, including the rocking chair mentioned previously. American Windsors are distinguished by a thick seat, legs set at pronounced angles, and spindle backs. The parts were usually made from different types of wood, so the craftsmen painted their chairs a single color to disguise this.

More than other folk styles, Windsor chairs were sometimes influenced by design trends. In rare instances, American Windsor made during the Queen Anne and Chippendale periods have cabriole legs. In the nineteenth century, craftsmen painted them with patriotic designs and other Ante-Bellum motifs — these were called *fancy chairs.*

Pennsylvania German Furniture, 1730–1840 — This was once mistakenly called "Pennsylvania Dutch," a mispronunciation of *deutsche* (the German word for "German"). The craftsmen who made it were immigrants from Switzerland and Germany. They settled in Pennsylvania, but banded together in tight, conservative communities that preserved their Old World traditions. From the early eighteenth century (and possibly before) until well into the nineteenth century, they built furniture in distinctive German medieval and Gothic forms — large wardrobes called *schranks,* dower chests, chests of drawers, trestle tables, plank chairs, and so on.

The most striking characteristic of this furniture was its intricate, brightly colored painted decorations. These were related to *Fraktur,* the German medieval style of manuscript illumination. It included traditional German and Swiss designs that are now synonymous with country furniture — tulips, finches (called *distelfinks*), unicorns, stars and other geometric shapes, and especially hearts. Heart shapes have been popular in most European folk designs since before medieval times.

After several generations, Pennsylvania German furniture became more and more Americanized. The old German forms blended with other designs, and by the nineteenth century, much of it looked like English furniture with *Fraktur* decoration. Later Pennsylvania German craftsmen were influenced by Federal and Ante-Bellum styles — their painted decorations sometimes included eagles and other patriotic motifs.

Plank Chair

Schrank (Wardrobe)

Dower Chest

Pennsylvania German furniture, 1730–1840

Shaker Furniture, 1790–1935 — "Shaker" furniture was developed by a strict religious order, the United Society of Believers in Christ's Second Appearing. The sect was founded on the principles of celibacy, equality of the sexes, communal living, separation from "the world," and asceticism. Led by Mother Ann Lee, a group of nine believers journeyed from England to America in 1774. (They had visions that their works would take root and flourish in the New World.) They bought a farm on the Hudson River (which later became the Watervaliet Shaker community) and set out on a missionary tour of New England. By 1800, they had 1,000 believers. Fifty years later, there were 6,000 believers living in 19 communities throughout the East and Midwest.

As the sect grew, they began to make their own furniture, based on traditional English forms. However, because the Shakers believed "beauty rests on utility," they stripped these pieces of almost all ornament. In doing so, they created a style whose forms rested purely on function.

Cupboard-on-Chest

Sewing Stand

Rocking Chair

Shaker furniture, 1790–1935

Shakers also believed that good craftsmanship was a form of worship. The integrity of one's work expressed the love of God. Because of this, Shaker furniture was exceptionally well made. Although their furniture was plain even by country standards, the quality of their craftsmanship quickly earned the Shakers a good reputation in neighboring communities. Soon, the "world's people" were asking to buy Shaker furniture.

The Shakers began to operate their communal cabinetmaking shops as commercial enterprises. They did their best work between the years of 1820 and 1860 — the Ante-Bellum period. During this time, Shaker craftsmen and craftswomen produced all manner of furniture for sale, from small, oval wood boxes to large cupboards. They are, however, best remembered for their ladderback chairs and rockers.

The Shakers embraced progress. (The sect eventually owned over 100 patents and produced hundreds of other innovations, such as the circular saw.) They viewed labor-saving devices as an aid to worship — the quicker and better you could do your work, the more time was available for spiritual contemplation. So when small cabinetmaking shops began to give way to large factories, they industrialized. Shaker furniture designs, because they were devoid of ornament, were well suited to mass production. Consequently, Shaker furniture was the only pure American country furniture form to survive the Industrial Revolution.

The Shaker community of New Lebanon, New York, continued to manufacture chairs well into the twentieth century. It finally declined, not for lack of customers, but for lack of Shakers. By the mid-1930s, there were only two Shaker chairmakers at New Lebanon — Sister Lillian Barlow, who built the frames, and Sister Sarah Collins, who wove the seats. Sister Lillian died in 1942, and Sister Sarah died in 1947. Their passing marked the end of the old-time American country furniture tradition.

CONTEMPORARY COUNTRY FURNITURE DESIGN

As country cabinetmakers slowly disappeared, country furniture was used up, thrown out, or stored in attics and barns. Nonetheless, Americans have remained interested in country artifacts. Perhaps because we have such a short history compared to our European ancestors, Americans have always treasured what we do have. With few exceptions, no people on earth are so passionate about collecting antiques.

Drive through almost any small country town or village, and you'll find a junk store or antique shop. Or witness the auctions at Sack's or Sotheby's in New York: In 1989, a mid-eighteenth century blockfront desk made by John Townsend of Newport, Rhode Island sold for $12.1 million — the highest price ever paid for a piece of antique furniture, anywhere! The irony of this is that, by world standards, Americans don't have any antiques. The oldest piece of American furniture on record — a chest made by Thomas Mulliner in New Haven, Connecticut — could *possibly* date to 1639. To our European cousins, that barely qualifies as being old.

Besides our passion for history, there is a second reason country artifacts interest us: Mankind has a habit of recollecting the good old days, no matter how bad they might have been. Life was easier and simpler in times gone by. We take mental and spiritual refuge from today's stress by remembering — or inventing — a less demanding, happier yesterday.

Whatever the reason, interest in American country furniture is at an all-time high. We are in the midst of a country furniture *revival*. Most enthusiasts trace this development to the success of Mary Ellisor Emmerling's book, *American Country: A Style and Source Book* (Clarkson N. Potter, New York, 1980). Once again, history repeats itself: Like so many design trends of past centuries, the current country furniture vogue was promoted by a pattern book.

But this isn't the first time that the old country styles have been all the rage in home decorating. We are actually riding the crest of the *third* country furniture revival.

COTTAGE AND COLONIAL FURNITURE

The first revival began as country cabinetmakers were disappearing. Fashionable men and women began purchasing *Cottage* furniture. This was inexpensive, mass-produced furniture, gaily painted with fruits and flowers derived from then-current Victorian motifs. (These decorations were not consciously contrived to imitate the painted folk furniture of the Pennsylvania Dutch, though they sometimes had the same visual effect.) Although the wood was covered with painted Victoriana, the materials were cheap, and the construction was often poor, the furniture designs were inspired by traditional country furniture from a half-century before.

The second revival overlapped the first, beginning in the last years of the nineteenth century with the introduction of *Colonial* (also called *Colonial Revival*) furniture. Again, the basic

Victorian Cottage furniture, 1860–1910

designs for these pieces were based on traditional country forms from both the seventeenth and eighteenth centuries. Some were decorated with elaborate turnings, in a parody of the William and Mary and Windsor styles. Like the Cottage furniture before it, Colonial furniture was designed to be mass produced. Although the forms were traditional, the joinery, materials, and finishes often were not.

THE COUNTRY REVIVAL

The events leading to this latest revival began long before Mary Emmerling published her book. As America approached her bicentennial, our interest in history and tradition waxed stronger. We rediscovered *folk* — folk music, folk tales, folk art, and folk crafts. As this took place, interest in antique furniture — particularly early American furniture — also grew. Mary Emmerling's book didn't start the third revival; it simply focused it and gave it a name: *American Country*.

The marked difference between this revival and the previous two is its focus on *authentic* country designs. In most revivals, old styles are adapted to new tastes. For example, the Greek and Roman designs revived during the Federal and Ante-Bellum periods were incorporated into nineteenth century pieces such as sideboards and dressing tables. Today's craftsmen and craftswomen sometimes make similar accommodations in contemporary American country furniture design. They convert Pennsylvania German *schranks* into entertainment centers, modify rope beds to fit standard-size mattresses, and scale down floor-to-ceiling cabinets to fit modern homes.

People who are serious about country furniture, however, insist that contemporary designs remain as historically correct as practical. The intense interest in history and folk arts that preceded this revival helped educate both the craftsman and the consumer. Both have come to appreciate the value of hand-made, traditional furniture. They may

Colonial Revival furniture, 1890–1925

change the dimensions of the piece, or use it differently than it was originally intended, but they pride themselves on the *authenticity* (historical roots) of a reproduction. For both the maker and the user, keeping faith with the past is a source of personal satisfaction.

The furniture produced by the Workshops of David T. Smith and featured in this book are all faithful reproductions of country forms from the eighteenth and nineteenth centuries. There are three distinct types, as distinguished by the degree to which one adheres to tradition. Some pieces are *historical* designs — accurate copies of original antiques, now kept in museums or private collections. Others are *inspired* designs — combinations or modifications of design elements that have historical precedent, even though the actual piece may not. In a few cases, the craftsmen have *updated* certain designs, making concessions to current trends. This has been done judiciously and sparingly, only to make an historical form more useful in a modern setting. For the most part, the furniture in this book falls into the first two categories — furniture that our pioneer ancestors might have built.

The following pages show examples of all three types of contemporary country furniture — historical, inspired, and updated. You can find the plans for these pieces in the Construction section.

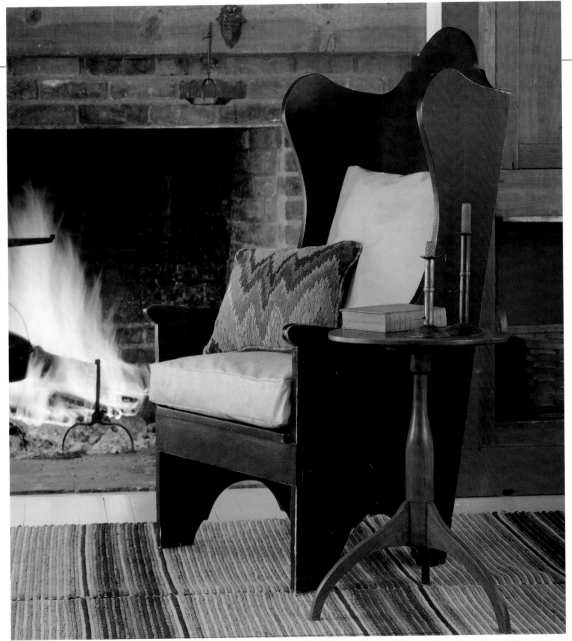

American country furniture was made from about 1690 to 1860 — you can see both the beginning and the end in these two pieces. The Wing-and-Arm Chair is one of the earliest designs, made by colonists from the early eighteenth century on. The Shaker Candle-stand is one of the latest. This is a reproduction of a stand made at the New Lebanon community in New York during the first half of the nineteenth century. The original is now in the American Wing of the Metropolitan Museum of Art in New York City.

Many of the designs in this book are historically accurate reproductions. This Sofa Table was copied from a serving table made by the Moon family in Hope Township, Northumberland County, Pennsylvania, around 1825. The original is now in a private collection.

The Porringer Table, with its "country cabriole" legs, was copied from an antique made in Newport, Rhode Island. The original is now in the Winterthur Museum in Winterthur, Delaware.

The Pie Safe was a traditional ventilated cupboard made to store baked goods. This cupboard is a reproduction of a piece from Laurens County, Georgia. The original was built around 1840, and is now in a private collection.

The original model for this Settle Table was made in New England in the eighteenth century, and can now be seen in Old Sturbridge Village in Massachusetts. Settle tables were popular with tavern owners in England, and were used by all manner of people in the American colonies. The top was mounted on a pivot, so the piece could be used as a chair when the top was vertical *(below, left)* or a table when the top was horizontal *(below, right)*. In addition, there was a storage chest under the settle seat.

Several historical Shaker designs are collected in this book. The originals were all made during the early nineteenth century. The Lap Desk *(upper left)* was made at the New Lebanon Shaker community in New York. The original is kept at the Shaker Museum in Old Chatham, New York. This table and bench are both reproductions of Shaker originals. The Trestle Table was made at the Union Village Shaker community in Ohio, and is now displayed at the Warren County Historical Society Museum in Lebanon, Ohio. The Shaker Dining Bench was made at the Hancock, Massachusetts, community and now resides in the American Wing of the Metropolitan Museum of Art in New York.

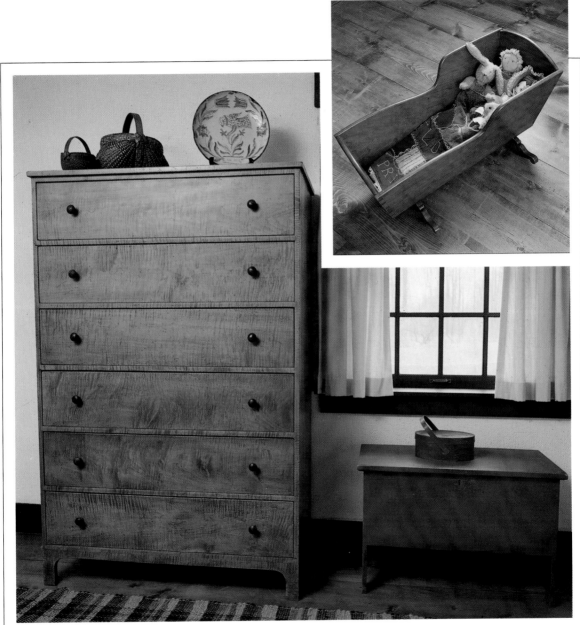

The origin of this Cradle *(upper right)* design is unknown, but it's thought to be Shaker. The original is now at the Shaker Museum in Old Chatham, New York. This Chest of Drawers was patterned after one designed and built by the Shakers of Union Village, Ohio. The original is in the Warren County Historical Society Museum, in Lebanon, Ohio.

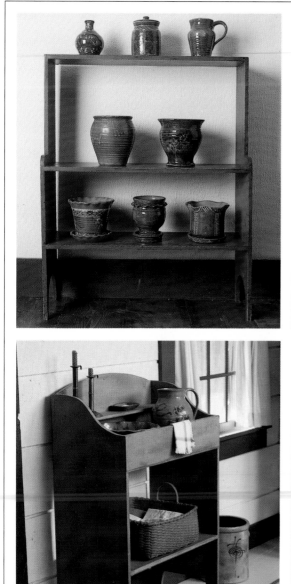

Some pieces are more than historical reproductions; they reveal the history of early America. The Bucket Bench *(left)* is one example: When folks built their first cabins in the wilderness, they also built a bench to set outside the back door. This held buckets of water, hauled from a nearby spring. As the land became more settled and life less hard, the pioneers refined their old bucket bench by enclosing the top shelf with splashboards, making a sink. They called this a Water Bench *(lower left)*. As the rigors of pioneer life gave way to the less demanding routine of farm life, furniture became more sophisticated. Folks enclosed the base of their water bench with cupboard doors, moved it into the kitchen, and called it a Dry Sink *(lower right)*.

You can see the same sort of evolution looking at the Pewter Bench. This was a simple design, patterned after medieval *dressoirs,* that gave the earliest settlers a place to store their dinnerware.

As America grew more tame and prosperous, simplicity gave way to more and more refinement. Craftsmen began to build doors and drawers, enclosing the open shelving units. By the time the great-grandchildren of the first pioneers inherited the dinnerware, they were storing it in furniture like this Step-Back Cabinet.

Not all of the designs shown are precise reproductions of historic antiques. Many pieces — particularly the smaller ones — are *inspired* by American country originals. They are not copied from any one piece, but combine historical elements from several. The Five-Board Bench *(left)*, for example, is typical of many benches built in the eighteenth and nineteenth centuries. This Bookshelf *(lower left)* is another piece inspired by historical design. The design is similar to many early American hanging plate racks and shelving units.

Paging through books of antique furniture, you can find many different adjustable candlestands. The design for the Ratchet Candlestand *(below)* combines several of them.

This Step-Down Windsor Chair is representative of many that were made in America during the early years of the nineteenth century. It's not, however, copied from any particular one.

This Shaker Herb Cupboard walks the line between an inspired and historical piece. The design is based on an actual cupboard made by the Shakers of Pleasant Hill, Kentucky, in the nineteenth century. However, the craftsmen at the Workshops changed the dimensions and the number of pegs to give the piece a more pleasing appearance.

Historical and inspired designs are comprised strictly of country elements. In some cases, however, it's necessary to update a piece with one or two contemporary details. Wherever possible, these should be hidden from view. This Wardrobe, for instance, is historically correct on the outside. But the inside has been adapted to house audio/visual components.

The updating on this Oval Tea Table is subtle and not immediately obvious: The legs have been shortened to coffee-table height. Other than workbenches, there were no low tables in country homes.

Two of the pieces shown in this country study have been updated. The Meal Bin (left, against the wall) is adapted to hold hanging files. The Plantation Desk has several modern elements, such as adjustable shelves. It can be further updated by changing the dimensions of the top to hold a personal computer.

Although both of the beds in this book are patterned after historical country antiques, they have been updated to hold box springs and inner-spring mattresses. (The originals had rope supports for feather or straw mattresses. They were also very short by modern standards — folks in the eighteenth and early nineteenth centuries slept sitting up.) As shown, the Turned-Post Bed accommodates a standard-size twin mattress…

…and the Pencil-Post Bed holds a queen-size mattress. You can easily adapt either bed to hold any size mattress.

Whether historical, inspired, or updated, good country design depends on careful attention to the details. Study the dovetails used to join the parts of this Keeping Box. The tails are very wide, while the pins are narrow — this was the prevailing style on much country furniture. Notice, too, the scribe lines at the corners of the box and tray. Cabinetmakers laid out their dovetails with a marking gauge, leaving lines like these.

Decorative details, such as the cove molding atop the Pie Safe, have to be carefully thought out. Could a country cabinetmaker shape these with the tools available to him? This particular molding might have been made with a round-bottom or "hollow" plane.

The bead molding that holds the tin panels to the Pie Safe could have been made with a scratch stock, a scraper shaped to the profile of the bead. In addition to knowing antique tools, you must also consider what kinds of marks these tools left on the wood. If necessary, scrape the surface to remove any evidence of having been machined, then make a few hand-tool marks.

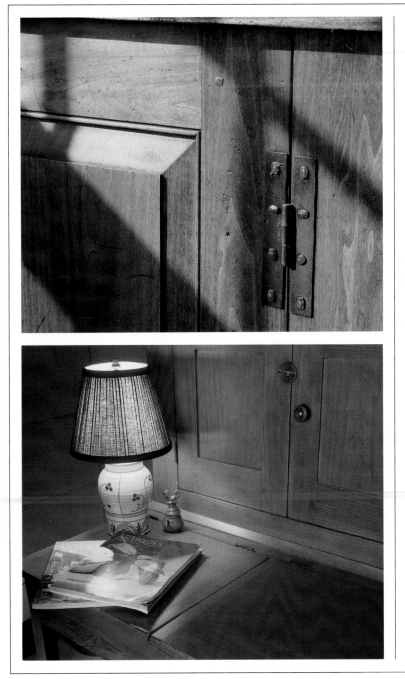

Where possible, use the same joinery that a country cabinet-maker might have used. The frame of this door, for example, is held together with pegged mortises and tenons. The pegs are plainly visible.

In a very few cases, it may *not* be advisable to use authentic joinery — country craftsmen didn't always use the best techniques. For instance, the manner in which they attached breadboards to tabletops and desk tops often caused the wood to split. To correct this, the breadboards on this Plantation Desk are fastened with modern hardware. However, to preserve the old-time appearance, the hardware is disguised to look like the traditional joinery.

Carefully consider the type of wood and finish in a piece. Different combinations produce different effects. This Spice Cupboard *(upper left)* was made from curly maple, then finished with a dark stain and varnish. This gives it a formal appearance. A piece like this might grace a dining room or living room.

The same Spice Cupboard *(upper right)*, made from poplar and painted blue, looks utilitarian and informal. This piece might be more at home in a kitchen. In some cases, country cabinetmakers *grain-painted* furniture made of cheap wood to make them look more formal. This, too, has a distinct effect — "folk formal." The grain painting on the door frame of the Step-Back Cabinet *(left)* mimics curly maple, and the painting on the panels suggests a mahogany or walnut crotch.

The last — and perhaps the most important — details that you must ponder when designing country furniture have to do with *surface wear*. A piece that has been around for over a hundred years would show some signs of age. For example, the paint on the Spoon Rack *(right)* has been carefully scraped away where fingers would have rubbed against it.

The drawer on this Ohio Corner Cabinet *(lower left)* has been stained and glazed, to imitate the dirt that would have accumulated around the edges. In addition, the wood surface is *slightly* dinged and gouged, the way a real antique might be. Be careful when you do this dinging; it's very easy to over-do. The wear must be *believable*.
  Finally, contemplate how the finish itself might have aged. Old finishes often dry out and shrink, leaving a cracked surface *(lower right)*. You can duplicate this effect with special chemicals and finishing techniques.

DESIGNING YOUR OWN

If you design your own contemporary American country furniture, or modify the designs in this book, pay careful attention to the details. It's the little things that distinguish a fine reproduction. The best way to address these details is through careful research.

Begin your research by visiting the furniture sections of museums or looking through books of antique furniture for *historical precedents*. You may find a piece to copy, or several that you can combine. In particular, there are four books that you may want to consult first, just for the sheer numbers of examples they contain:

- *The Heritage of Upper Canadian Furniture* by Howard Pain (Key Porter Books, Ltd., 1984). Despite the misleading title, this book contains photographs of country furniture antiques from all over North America.
- *Furniture Treasury* by Wallace Nutting (Macmillan, 1928). This work is comprised of several volumes. The photography is not always first rate, but there are thousands of examples of country furniture. The sheer numbers make browsing through this book well worth your time.
- *Three Centuries of American Furniture* by Oscar P. Fitzgerald (Gramercy Publishing Company, 1982). The author focuses on classic furniture, but there are many examples of country designs as well. The book also clearly explains the evolution of styles.
- *The Book of Shaker Furniture* by John Kassay (University of Massachusetts Press, 1980). The author shows many examples of Shaker furniture and how they were constructed. This is, perhaps, the best reference for country joinery.

For additional titles of books, magazines, and catalogs, refer to the Sources section.

When you have discovered one or more historical examples that come close to the project you want to design, read about the *period* or era in which they were built — William and Mary, Queen Anne, Chippendale, and so on. Study the prevalent styles of the time, and understand how these might have been employed by a country cabinetmaker. If you're making a folk piece, such as a Shaker chair or Pennsylvania German chest, explore the culture, its distinctive forms, and design motifs. Don't combine styles or forms that are too widely separated by time or cultural beliefs. It would be unlikely to find an antique that combined elements of the American Jacobean and the Federal periods — there is a century between the two. Likewise, you couldn't find a piece that combined both Shaker and Pennsylvania German designs — their philosophies concerning ornament were worlds apart. Your design must be historically possible.

If you must update a design to use it for a modern purpose, do it discreetly. When you can, hide the updated elements on the inside or behind it. Avoid unnecessary updates, such as adding electrical lighting to a cabinet.

Finally, decide who might have made this piece and to what purpose. Was he a pioneer, more concerned about crops and Indians than he was about craftsmanship? Was he a Shaker brother, who believed his craftsmanship was a form of prayer? Or a German immigrant, who used his craftsmanship to preserve his Old World cultural heritage? Or a small-town cabinetmaker, whose craftsmanship was an uncertain livelihood for himself and his family? When you can fill in these biographies, the details of the design come much easier.

CONSTRUCTION

TOOLS, MATERIALS, AND TECHNIQUES

The construction of American Country furniture, while not particularly difficult, is exacting, detailed work. This comes as no great surprise to most woodworkers; all fine furnituremaking is exacting. However, there are several special details to keep in mind when making country furniture. You must use the same wood and hardware that a country cabinetmaker might have used, assemble the piece with the same joinery, and make it look as if you had used the same tools.

SELECTING LUMBER AND HARDWARE

There were more species of wood in Colonial eastern American forests suitable for furnituremaking than any other place in the world. Country cabinetmakers found that certain woods worked better for specific kinds of projects. They also found that different woods — or combinations of woods — produced different aesthetic effects.

Some were considered attractive, *formal* woods to be used for special projects. Because their wood grain was especially beautiful, these were usually finished with clear oil, beeswax, varnish, shellac, or lacquer. Others were common, *utilitarian* woods for projects that saw everyday use. These were often painted, since the wood grains weren't considered appealing. Utilitarian woods were also used as *secondary* woods (for inside, unseen parts) on large, formal case pieces. Here's a brief profile of a dozen common country furniture woods:

White Pine — Initial color is white, becoming light brown as it ages. The settlers found American white pine was soft, lightweight, easy to work, and surprisingly strong. Once it had been properly dried, it was fairly stable and durable. It has a subtle to moderate grain pattern. They used pine mostly for scooped chair seats, carved boxes or panels, and utilitarian furniture, especially painted benches, chests, and cupboards. It was also used as a secondary wood.

The pine lumber from 150 years ago and what you buy today are almost two different species. Old pine was cut from virgin timber and had small, tightly spaced growth rings. Because of this, it was very stable. Today's pine is harvested from fast-growing, hybrid trees. The growth rings are extremely wide, sometimes 1/4" or more. This makes the wood very unstable — not well suited for furniture. If you must use pine for a project, look for old lumber or lumber with small growth rings. If not, use poplar instead.

Yellow Poplar — Initial color is a light yellow, becoming streaked with various shades of brown as it ages. Poplar has an extremely subtle grain pattern. It's slightly harder, more durable, and more stable than pine, but much more difficult to carve. Because of the tulip-shaped flowers on the trees, poplar was called *tulipwood* by the settlers, and was used as a utilitarian or secondary wood, like pine. If you need wide planks for a project, poplar is often your best choice. You can still find boards up to 18" wide.

Walnut — Initial color is deep purple-brown, lightening somewhat as it ages. Walnut is handsome, soft, durable, and easily worked wood. It has a moderate grain pattern, but lumber cut from a crotch or the tap root of the tree is often highly figured. Country cabinetmakers used it for formal pieces. They often made panels of figured walnut. Because they could easily carve it, they sometimes substituted walnut for imported mahogany on classic furniture with shell carving, ball-and-claw feet, and so on.

If you can, purchase *air-dried* walnut. Most kiln-dried walnut is steamed to disperse the brown color throughout the light-colored sapwood. This makes more of the lumber usable, but the color isn't as rich.

Cherry — Initial color is light pink, becoming a dark red-brown as it ages. Cherry has a subtle to moderate grain pattern and develops a rich patina in just a few years. It's not as hard as walnut, not as easily worked, but many woodworkers consider it easier to finish. However, it was used much like walnut, as a formal wood. You can sometimes find curly or figured cherry. The figuring isn't as pronounced as walnut or maple figuring, but it was highly regarded by country cabinetmakers.

Elm — Initial color is light red-brown, becoming darker with age. The wood is hard, not particularly strong, but it bends well. The grain pattern is subtle to moderate. The wood is considered a formal wood, but it was used little by cabinetmakers. It's not very stable — it expands and contracts more than other species. It was, however, popular with chairmakers, who used it both for seats and bent parts.

Hard Maple — Initial color is white, becoming light brown as it ages. The grain is sometimes figured, showing jewel-like curls, burls, or bird's-eyes. These become more prominent as the wood ages. It's extremely hard but moderately easy to work. Settlers used it for both utilitarian and formal furniture and sometimes as a secondary wood. It was a favorite of chairmakers, who used it to make long, slender spindles, legs, and rungs. It was commonly used to make objects that were expected to see a lot of wear, such as tabletops, bowls, pivots, and bentwood boxes. Tool handles and plane stocks in a country cabinetmaker's shop were often made of hard maple.

Soft Maple — Initial color is white, becoming light brown as it ages. Like hard maple, the grain is sometimes figured. The lumber is moderately soft and only moderately stable. Maple with ordinary grain was used as both a utilitarian and secondary wood; maple with figured grain was used as a formal wood.

Note: Highly figured woods often have to be worked down slowly with hand planes and sanders.

Power planers and jointers sometimes tear the grain.

Birch — Initial color is white, becoming light brown as it ages. This wood has many of the same characteristics and grain pattern as hard maple, but it's not as easy to work with hand tools. Consequently, cabinetmakers used it little, and only as a utilitarian or secondary wood. Chairmakers sometimes used it for turning. After birch has been aged a few years, it's indistinguishable from maple without microscopic analysis.

Oak — Initial color is white or light pink, becoming a deep brown as it ages. There are several species of oak, but they all have similar properties and uses. Oak is very hard, flexible, and has a very prominent grain pattern. Because of its large, open pores, it's not very stable. Up until the eighteenth century, oak (especially white oak) was considered a formal wood, but it fell out of favor with fine cabinetmakers. The grain pattern was too strong to be used with the intricate, flowing designs of the Queen Anne and Chippendale periods. During the country-furniture era, oak was used mostly as a utilitarian wood, although it was sometimes used in formal Pennsylvania German pieces. Chairmakers used oak for both turned and bent parts.

Ash — Initially a light tan color, becoming only slightly darker as it ages. Ash is lightweight, strong, flexible, and fairly easy to work. Depending on the species, it's hard to moderately hard, and has a moderate grain pattern. It was considered a utilitarian wood by cabinetmakers, who also used it for tool handles. It was more often used by chairmakers, who found it could be easily bent.

Chestnut — Initially a light brown color, becoming a rich nut-brown with age. It's a very soft wood, but flexible and highly resistant to rot. It has a prominent grain pattern. Chestnut was used as a formal wood up until the early eighteenth century, then fell out of favor for the same reason as oak. However, it continued to be a popular utilitarian wood throughout the country-furniture era, because it was so easy to work. It was used by chairmakers for both turning and bending.

Although there are no lumber-size living chestnut trees today, you can still purchase chestnut lumber. A blight killed the trees in the early part of this century, but because the wood is so rot resistant, many of the standing dead trees are still sound.

Hickory — Initially light reddish brown, becomes darker with age. Hickory has a moderate grain pattern. It's not particularly stable, but it is extremely hard — much harder than any other wood on this list. For this reason, it was often used for pegs and "tree nails," pinning wooden parts together. As such, it was primarily a utilitarian wood. Despite its hardness, it also bends easily. Chairmakers used hickory for both turning and bending.

For an authentic reproduction, do not use plywood or particleboard, even for the backs of cupboards and cabinets. Plywood was not commercially available until the late nineteenth century, and particleboard not until the twentieth century.

In addition to wood, country cabinetmakers also used metal hardware. The type (and the amount) of hardware depended on when the furniture was made.

In rural eighteenth-century America, hardware was used sparingly, because it was expensive and added needlessly to the cost of the project. Pulls and latches were almost always fashioned from wood; the only metal parts in a typical country furniture piece were locks, hinges, nails, and perhaps a few blunt-end screws. These were usually made of iron by a local blacksmith. Brass hardware, while it was readily available in the larger American cities, had to be imported into rural areas. This extra transportation cost made *brasses,* as they were called, much more expensive than iron hardware.

The most visible pieces of hardware on an eighteenth-century piece were the hinges. The most common were surface mounted — butterfly, rat-tail, and various other shapes. These had been used since medieval times not just as hinges, but as metal gussets to strengthen a project. A cabinetmaker often mounted them to straddle the joints of a door frame and help hold it together. He usually attached these surface hinges with nails, driving them through the wood and clinching them over on the back side.

Mortised or *butt* hinges — the type that we take for granted nowadays — were less common. They were harder to make and install. However, like brasses, they were considered the mark of a fine piece of furniture. For a special project in which appearance was paramount, the cabinetmaker spent the extra money and effort for butt hinges, brasses, and screws to mount them.

During the early country-furniture era, the most common types of hinge were all surface-mounted. Shown here are three popular styles: rat-tail hinge (*a*), butterfly hinge (*b*), and H-hinge (*c*).

The late eighteenth century saw rapid advances in metallurgy, including new technologies for working both iron and brass. As America was industrialized, hardware became less expensive, and country furniture used more of it. By the early nineteenth century, country cabinetmakers used manufactured brasses regularly — pulls, latches, and escutcheons as well as locks and latches. At the same time, screws began to replace nails as common fasteners.

Hardware designs — particularly brasses — evolved over time, like furniture. Hardware styles went in and out of vogue with furniture styles. For example, ornate "cloud-form" drawer pulls were popular only during the Queen Anne and Chippendale periods. By the Federal period, brass pulls had become simple ovals and shields. Consult the chart to see what hardware styles were popular during what periods.

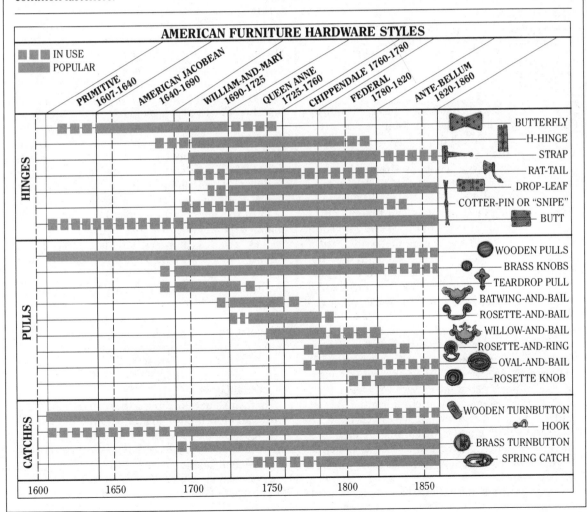

AMERICAN FURNITURE HARDWARE STYLES

To help select the proper materials for a country piece, give some thought to its history. How, where, and when was the furniture used? What period was it built? Did the cabinetmaker intend it as a formal or utilitarian piece? Would he have painted it or finished it naturally? Would he have used ordinary iron hardware or spent the money for fancy brasses? The answers to these questions will help you select the appropriate wood and hardware.

COUNTRY CONSTRUCTION TECHNIQUES

If you study a well-constructed piece of country furniture, you'll see that it's built like a three-dimensional puzzle. All the wood and hardware fit together in such a way that, even if the glue fails, the piece will remain whole. A Shaker chair is a prime example: All the wooden parts — legs, rungs, posts, stretchers, and slats — were assembled with round mortises and tenons, glued together. The top slat was mortised *and* pegged in the back posts, and the seating material — rush, reed, or cloth tape — was woven around the stretchers. Even if the glue failed in all the joints, the pegs and woven seat held the chair together.

Good construction also lets the wood "breathe." Wood breathes in moisture during hot, humid weather, expanding slightly. During cold, dry weather, it exhales this moisture and contracts. Furthermore, because of the way in which wood cells are shaped, wood swells and shrinks approximately ten times more *across* the grain than *with* it. For instance, if you cut a board 12" wide and 12" long in the winter, it may swell to 12¼" wide and 12¹/₆₄" long in the summer. This movement isn't noticeable when the wood is under 3" wide, but it becomes an important consideration on large panels.

Good country joinery allowed for the movement of wide boards. Where possible, the wood grain was oriented so all the parts would swell and shrink in the same direction. When this couldn't be arranged, cabinetmakers "floated" the wide parts in the assembly or cut them up into smaller parts. In a frame-and-panel door, for instance, the wide panel floats in the grooved edges of the frame members. On a table, the top floats on the aprons. The wide backs of cabinets and cupboards were cut into narrow, overlapping boards, so each could expand and contract separately.

In some cases, hardware helped compensate for the movement of the wood. Small nails and screws are flexible — they will bend slightly with the movement of the wood. When the grain directions of two parts opposed each other, cabinetmakers sometimes nailed (but did *not* glue) the parts together. For example, moldings were sometimes nailed to the sides of cupboards and cabinets. The grain of the molding was horizontal, while that of the sides was vertical. But as the broad sides expanded and contracted, the nails holding the moldings flexed slightly. The moldings remained in place without restricting the wood movement.

All of the joinery was simple, no different than many of the joints we use today — rabbets, dadoes, grooves, mortises, tenons, and dovetails. Country cabinetmakers kept their construction simple because they used simple tools. You can duplicate most of these joints with contemporary power tools. Modern tools can also make some joints that weren't possible in an old-time cabinetry shop. A country cabinetmaker couldn't make dowel joints or "biscuit" joints. He didn't have a doweling jig, power drill, or plate joiner. If you do use modern tools, be careful not to add modern touches.

There are a few operations that can *only* be done with hand tools. For instance, you must use hand methods to make dovetail joints with narrow pins and wide tails — the style that was popular during the last half of the country-furniture era. There are commercial router jigs that will cut many different types of dovetail, but none that will cut pins narrow enough to duplicate those in many fine country antiques.

This isn't to say that you shouldn't use power tools when making country furniture. Most professional craftsmen couldn't survive in today's economy without using power tools to speed up woodworking operations. And most amateurs can't invest the time necessary to become proficient with hand tools. Use whatever tools do the best job for you. However, to preserve the accuracy of a reproduction, use the same joinery and construction techniques that a country cabinetmaker might have used.

A COUNTRY CABINETMAKER'S TOOLS

A fine reproduction should also look as if it were built with hand tools, even if you don't use them. Hand tools and power tools work very differently. Power tools arrive at the desired shape in a different manner from hand tools, and leave a different set of marks upon the surface. As you build, consider how an old-time cabinetmaker's tools cut or shaped the wood.

What sorts of tools did this cabinetmaker use? You would be surprised at how short the list is. Even the best cabinetmakers of Philadelphia, New York, or Newport had fewer tools than a well-equipped amateur, by today's standards. Consider the shop of John Hedges, a successful cabinetmaker in Circleville, Ohio, during the first part of the nineteenth century. Hedges ran a busy shop, employing four apprentices. When he died at age 49, at the peak of his career, the inventory of his estate listed these tools:

- 5 workbenches (one for himself, and one for each apprentice)
- 10 handscrew clamps and other miscellaneous clamps
- 1 grindstone
- 1 lathe
- 1 set of lathe chisels
- 1 hand saw
- 1 saw buck and ax
- 1 lot miscellaneous cabinetmaker's tools (valued at $5.00)
- 1 lot miscellaneous carpenter's tools (also valued at $5.00)
- 5 gallons of varnish

The lots of miscellaneous tools probably included a dozen or more planes, several chisels and gouges, some scrapers, two or three different gauges, one or two rules, a try square, a mallet, a drawknife or spokeshave, a rasp or a file, perhaps a hammer and a frame saw, and some nails and hardware. In addition, some of the apprentices probably had their own tools, and these weren't listed in the inventory. Even so, there weren't a great many tools for a busy shop.

This is a re-creation of a typical early nineteenth-century country cabinetmaker's shop at Ohio Historical Village in Columbus, Ohio. Craftsmen from the country era worked almost exclusively with hand tools. *Courtesy Ohio Historical Society.*

The most abundant tool in a country cabinetmaker's shop were his planes. There were usually at least a dozen, and often more than thirty, all handmade by the cabinetmaker himself. He used these to plane, joint, trim, smooth, and shape stock — operations we now perform mostly with power tools. *Courtesy Ohio Historical Society and Thomas Clark.*

The only tools in a country cabinetmaking shop that worked with a rotary motion were the gimlets, augers, brace and bits, and lathe *(not shown)*. All other tools worked with a linear motion. Each type of motion leaves distinctive marks on the wood.

However, the most important difference between nineteenth- and twentieth-century woodworking shops is not the relative number of tools, but *how these tools worked*. Almost all the tools in the Hedges inventory operated with a *linear* motion. For example, the most abundant tool in an old-time cabinetmaker's shop were his planes. He often had thirty or more, and used them during all phases of construction to plane, smooth, joint, trim, or shape the wood. All of these cut in a *straight line*. Only the lathe and the drilling tools (augers, gimlets, braces and bits) shaped the wood with a *rotary* motion. Today, all our power tools, (except the band saw, jigsaw, and saber saw) *rotate*.

These two cutting motions — linear and rotary — each produce a distinct surface on the stock. Hand saws leave uneven, straight lines; circular saws leave consistent, arched lines. When properly sharpened and adjusted, a hand plane leaves a glass-smooth surface. Most rotary power tools, including the jointer, planer, shaper, and router, leave wavelike *mill marks*.

For a truly accurate country-furniture reproduction, you must reproduce the effects of hand tools — or, at least, disguise the effects of power tools. If the cut surface is to be left rough, use a band saw or reciprocating saw instead of a circular saw. After planing, jointing, shaping, or routing surfaces that will be seen on the finished piece, carefully sand and scrape away the mill marks. If you wish, make a few passes with a hand plane to thoroughly disguise the machined surface. This doesn't take a lot of extra time — just some extra thought.

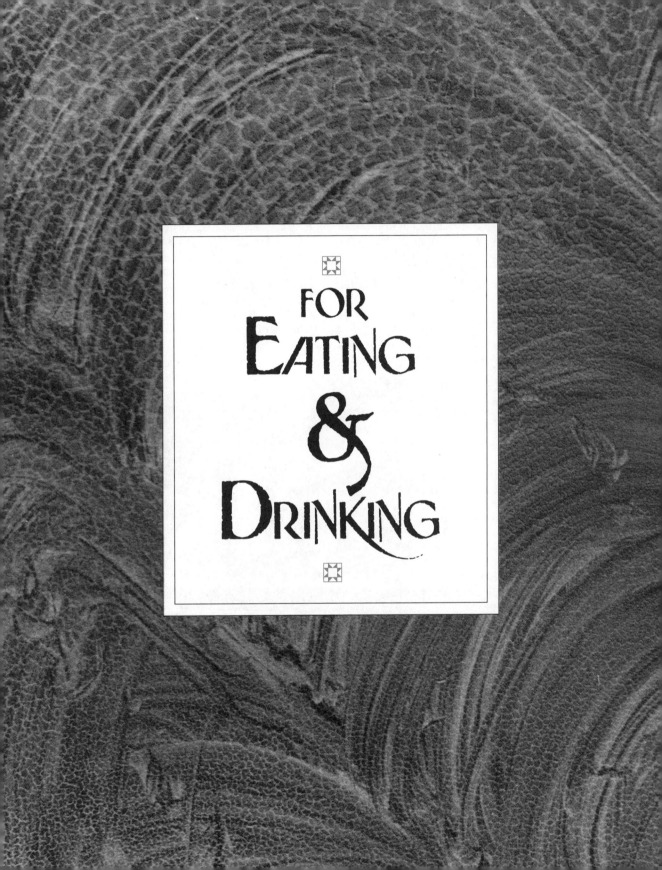

FOR
EATING
&
DRINKING

TRESTLE TABLE

For hundreds of years before the discovery of America, European country folk made tables by placing a long, thick board across two or more trestle supports. (A medieval trestle was a horizontal beam supported by legs, much like a modern sawhorse.) In the sixteenth century, joiners (medieval woodworkers) began to fasten the boards permanently to the trestles. By using the trestle to hold the board flat, they could make the tabletops much thinner. They also simplified the trestles, building flat assemblies joined by long stretchers. Today, we remember this design as the trestle table.

Trestle tables continued to be used by country folk on both sides of the Atlantic. Because space was so precious in a pioneer home, most seventeenth- and eighteenth-century trestles and boards were disassembled and stored away when not in use. But as America became more settled and homes grew larger, trestle tables followed the European lead — they were built to stay assembled.

In the nineteenth century, the United Society of Believers in Christ's Second Appearing — the Shakers — used trestle tables for communal dining.

They often built tables 20 feet long or more! The table shown is a shortened version of a table built by Shaker cabinetmakers in Union Village, Ohio.

It's interesting that these trestle dining tables were one of the few pieces of Shaker furniture (other than chairs) that had stretchers. Shakers discouraged stretchers because folks were tempted to put their feet on them. This, in turn, caused the furniture to wear prematurely. Note that the stretcher on this table is placed too high to comfortably rest your feet on.

EXPLODED VIEW

BILL OF MATERIALS

WOODEN PARTS/*FINISHED DIMENSIONS*

A.	Top boards (3)	$7/8$" x 12" x $75^1/2$"
B.	Breadboards (2)	$7/8$" x $1^1/4$" x 36"
C.	Breadboard caps (12)	$3/8$" x $1/2$" x $1^1/4$"
D.	Trestle tops (2)	$7/8$" x $3^1/2$" x $33^1/2$"
E.	Braces (2)	2" x 2" x $28^3/4$"
F.	Posts (2)	2" x 6" x $20^1/4$"
G.	Feet (2)	2" x 7" x $25^1/2$"

H.	Stretcher	2" x 6" x $49^1/2$"
J.	Pins (2)	$5/8$" dia. x 6"
K.	Pegs (20)	$3/8$" x $3/8$" x $1^1/4$"

HARDWARE

#8 x $1^3/4$" Flathead wood screws (8)
#12 x $1^1/2$" Roundhead wood screws and washers (12)

PLAN OF PROCEDURE

1

Plane, rip, and cut the parts to the sizes shown in the Bill of Materials.

2

Cut the joinery needed to assemble the table:

- 1"-wide, 4"-long mortises through the posts, as shown in the *Post Layout/End View*

- 1"-wide, 1"-deep, 4"-long mortises in the braces and feet, as shown in the *Brace Layout* and *Foot Layout*
- 1"-thick, 2"-long, 4"-wide tenons on the ends of the stretcher, as shown in the *Stretcher Layout*
- 1"-thick, 1"-long, 4"-wide tenons on the ends of the posts, as shown in the *Post Layout*

- 3/8"-wide, 3/4"-deep, 1 1/4"-long mortises in the outside edges of the bread-boards, as shown in the *Breadboard Joinery Detail* and *Breadboard Layout/ End View*

TOP VIEW

TOP VIEW

Mortise for Post

END VIEW
BRACE LAYOUT

END VIEW
POST LAYOUT

SIDE VIEW
STRETCHER LAYOUT

END VIEW

3

Notch the edges of the post and stretcher tenons, creating "shoulders." Fit the tenons to their respective mortises.

4

Lay out the shape of the feet on the stock and cut the shapes. Sand the sawed edges.

5

Round over the ends of the braces and trestle tops, as shown in the *End View* and *Brace Layout/End View*.

6

Finish sand the feet, posts, braces, trestle tops, and stretcher. Join the feet, posts, braces, and trestle tops with glue to make two trestle assemblies. Reinforce the glue joints between the braces and trestle tops with #8 x 1¾" flathead wood screws. Countersink the heads of the screws.

7

Joint both edges of the top boards. Lightly chamfer or "break" the hard corners along the edges, as shown in the *Tabletop Joinery Detail*. Glue the boards together, edge to edge, so the end grains cup up.

END VIEW
BREADBOARD LAYOUT

Mortise for Post

TOP VIEW

10¼" Rad

8¼" Rad

END VIEW
FOOT LAYOUT

Chamfer or "Break" Corner

TABLETOP JOINERY DETAIL

³⁄₁₆" Wd x ½" Lg Slot

⅜" Wd x ¾" Dp x 1¼" Lg Mortise

#12 x 1½" RHWS & Washer

BREADBOARD JOINERY DETAIL

PLAN OF PROCEDURE

8

While the glue is drying on the tabletop assembly, position the trestles on each end of the stretcher. Glue the stretcher to the posts, then drill a 5/8"-diameter hole through the mortise-and-tenon joint in each post, as shown in the *Side View*. Glue a 5/8"-diameter dowel in each hole to peg each tenon in its mortise. Sand the dowel ends flush with the edges of the posts, and the tenon ends flush with the faces.

9

Finish sand the tabletop assembly, then lay it across the trestles. Center it and make sure the end grain cups up.

10

Round the bottom portion of the pegs, as shown in the *Peg Detail*. Drill 3/8"-diameter, 1 1/4"-deep holes through the top boards where shown in the *Top View*. Drive a peg into each hole. Do *not* glue the tabletop to the trestles.

11

Attach the breadboards to the ends of the tabletop with #12 x 1 1/2" roundhead wood screws and flat washers, as shown in the *Breadboard Joinery Detail*.

Glue breadboard caps in the breadboard mortises to hide the screw heads. Sand the caps flush with the edges of the breadboards.

12

Do any necessary touch-up sanding, then apply a finish to *all* sides — top and bottom — of the entire table.

PEG DETAIL
(Make from *very* hard wood.)

▨ **SECTION A**

◐ **SECTION B**

● **SECTION C**

END VIEW

78"

75½"

1¼"
(Typ)

12"
(Typ)

⅜" Pegs
(Typ)

13½"
(Typ)

3½"

TOP VIEW

78"

⅞"

⅝" Dia x
6" Lg Dowel

2"

2"

49½"

SIDE VIEW

COUNTRY CRAFTSMAN'S
KNOW-HOW: JOINING BREADBOARD ENDS

To prevent wide boards from cupping, cabinet-makers often attached "breadboards" to the ends. While these controlled cupping, they sometimes created other problems. Because the boards were fastened so the wood grains were perpendicular, the breadboards restricted the normal movement of the wider board. As it expanded and contracted with changes in humidity, it often split or popped the joints.

To correct this, use the following *nontraditional* method for joining breadboards to tabletops and other wide parts. It controls cupping *and* allows the wide boards to shrink and swell. You can disguise the hardware used in this joinery to look like traditional mortises and tenons.

Splits and checks develop here.

Tenons sometimes break here.

Breadboard

1 There were several traditional methods for joining breadboards, but one of the most common was mortise-and-tenon joints. The cabinetmaker cut tenons in the wide board and fit them to mortises in the breadboards. In some cases, the joints were pegged. This restricted the movement of the wide board, eventually causing the board to split or the tenons to break.

Slot

Plug

Mortise

Breadboard

RHWS & Washer

2 To prevent this from happening, attach the breadboards with roundhead screws. Drive these screws through slots in the breadboards. As the wide board shrinks and swells, the screws move slightly in the slots. The breadboards, however, remain securely fastened.

3 Mortise the edge of the breadboard for screws by drilling a line of overlapping holes. These holes should be about twice the diameter of the head of the screw. Clean up the edges of the mortise with a chisel.

4 Cut the screw slots in the same manner — drill a line of holes in the bottom of each mortise. The diameter of the holes should be the same size as or slightly larger than the screw shaft.

5 When you have made the mortises and slots, clamp the breadboard to the end of the wider board. Drill pilot holes, then put flat washers over the screw shanks and drive the screws through the slots and into the board. Tighten each screw so it's snug, but not so tight that it presses the washer into the wood.

6 Make wooden plugs for the mortises to hide the screws and washers. Glue each plug in place so the end grain faces *out*.

7 After the glue dries, sand the plug flush with the edge of the breadboard. The breadboard will appear as if it's held to the wider board with mortises and tenons.

SHAKER DINING BENCH

There were more than 100 religious experiments in communism — communal ownership and living — in eighteenth- and nineteenth-century America. One of the most successful was the United Society of Believers in Christ's Second Appearing, better known as the *Shakers*. From just eleven followers, newly arrived from England in 1774, the sect had over 1,000 members in eleven separate communities by 1800 and 6,000 in eighteen communities by 1850.

Because Shaker life was communal, they designed and built many pieces of furniture for group activities. Among them was this *dining bench*, used by several communities in their dining halls and schoolrooms. It was an original invention, a variation on a traditional five-board bench. The Shaker craftsmen extended the legs to support a slender backrest. The result was a piece that was more comfortable — and more elegant — than an ordinary bench.

The design for this dining bench was inspired by a similar bench built at the Shaker community in Hancock, Connecticut, and used in their dining room. It's now on display at the Metropolitan Museum of Art in New York City.

EXPLODED VIEW

BILL OF MATERIALS

WOODEN PARTS/*FINISHED DIMENSIONS*

A. Seat $^7/_8$" x $11^3/_4$" x 78"
B. Legs (3) $^7/_8$" x $15^1/_4$" x $34^1/_4$"
C. Rail $^7/_8$" x 4" x 74"
D. Backrest $^7/_8$" x 4" x 78"

HARDWARE

#12 x $1^3/_4$" Flathead wood screws (12)

PLAN OF PROCEDURE

1

If necessary, glue up wide stock for the legs and seat. Plane, rip, and cut the parts to the sizes shown in the Bill of Materials.

2

Lay out and cut the shape of the legs, as shown in the *End View*. Sand the sawed edges.

3

Miter the ends of the rails at 60°, as shown in the *Front View*.

4

Cut three ⁷/₈"-wide, 2"-long notches in the bottom edge of the rail and cut matching notches in the top ends of the legs, where the seat attaches, as shown in the *Rail-to-Leg Joinery Detail*.

FRONT VIEW

5

Rout or cut beads in the front face of the backrest, near the edges, as shown in the *Backrest Profile*.

6

Finish sand the parts of the bench and dry assemble them to check the fit of the joints. Reassemble the parts with glue and flathead wood screws. Counterbore and countersink the screws, then cover their heads with putty.

7

Do any necessary touch-up sanding and apply a finish to the completed project.

BACKREST PROFILE

END VIEW

RAIL-TO-LEG JOINERY DETAIL

PORRINGER TABLE

The word *porringer* is a combination and corruption of two old words: the French *potage* (meaning soup) and the English *porridge* (as in the breakfast cereal). "Porringer" was used to describe a small soup bowl with an oversize handle. Tradition has it that the *potage* bowl was a French invention and the English adopted it to feed their children their daily porridge. The porringer was a common item in every English — and colonial — nursery.

In the eighteenth century, a few country cabinetmakers made small tables with rounded, protruding corners. The reason for these corners is lost to us. Some scholars speculate that the protrusions were used to hold serving plates, but the more probable explanation is that some cabinetmakers rounded the corners of their tables so their customers wouldn't bang their hips on them. Whatever the reason, the cabinetmakers exaggerated the round corners, making them very prominent. These reminded their clientele of the handles on their porringers, and the name stuck. Since then, these unique pieces have been known as porringer tables.

EXPLODED VIEW

BILL OF MATERIALS

WOODEN PARTS/*FINISHED DIMENSIONS*

A.	Tabletop	$7/8$" x 25" x 38"
B.	Legs (4)	2" x 2" x $25^{1}/8$"
C.	Front/back aprons (2)	$3/4$" x 4" x $23^{1}/2$"
D.	Side aprons (2)	$3/4$" x 4" x $13^{1}/2$"
E.	Pegs (16)	$5/16$" x $5/16$" x $1^{1}/4$"

HARDWARE

#8 x $1^{1}/4$" Flathead wood screws (10)

PLAN OF PROCEDURE

1

If necessary, glue up the stock to make the tabletop. Then plane, rip, and cut the parts to the sizes shown in the Bill of Materials, except the legs. Leave them 1"–2" longer than called for.

2

Cut 1/4"-wide, 3/4"-deep, 3"-long mortises in the inside surfaces of each leg, as shown in the *Leg Layout*.

3

Turn the legs on a lathe. When making each leg, mount the stock so the bottom end is offset toward the inside corner, as shown in the *Leg Offset Detail*. Shape the tapered shaft and flared ankles. Center the bottom end of the stock, then turn the foot, as explained in Making a Turned Cabriole Leg on page 68.

LEG OFFSET DETAIL
BOTTOM VIEW

LEG LAYOUT

4

Drill two screw pockets in the inside face of each side apron and three pockets in the front and back aprons, as shown in the *Top View.*

5

Cut ¼"-wide, ¾"-long tenons in the ends of the apron, using a dado cutter or router. Notch the tenons, as shown in the *Front/Back Apron Layout* and *Side Apron Layout,* so they are 3" from edge to edge.

6

Lay out and cut the shapes of the front, back, and side aprons, as shown in the *Front/Back Apron Layout* and *Side Apron Layout.*

7

Lay out and cut the shape of the top, as shown in the *Top View.* Sand the sawed edges, and round them over slightly with a rasp or file.

FRONT VIEW
SIDE APRON LAYOUT

END VIEW

FRONT VIEW
FRONT/BACK APRON LAYOUT

END VIEW

PLAN OF PROCEDURE

8

Dry assemble the legs and aprons to check the fit of the joints. Finish sand all the parts of the table, then assemble the legs and aprons with glue.

TOP-TO-APRON JOINERY DETAIL

Top

#8 × 1¼" FHWS

¾" Dia Screw Pocket

¼" Dia Pilot Hole

Apron

APRON-TO-LEG JOINERY DETAIL

¼"

¼"

¾"

2"

¾"

½"

¼"

2"

9

Round the bottom portion of the pegs, as shown in the *Peg Detail.*

10

Drill two 5/16"-diameter, 1¼"-deep holes through each joint in the legs and then drive the pegs into the holes from the outside. Leave about 1/16" of each peg protruding.

11

Attach the top to the aprons with flathead wood screws, as shown in the *Top-to-Apron Joinery Detail.* Do *not* glue the top to the aprons or legs; this would restrict the wood movement.

12

Do any necessary touch-up sanding on the table. Then apply a finish to the completed project.

25"

4½" 2" 12" 2" 4½"

⅞"

5" 4"

26"

20⅛"

SIDE VIEW

TOP VIEW

1 Square = 1"

SECTION A

SECTION B

SECTION C

FRONT VIEW

Pegs

3/8"

3/8"

A A

1¼" B B

C C

PEG DETAIL

(Make from *very* hard wood.)

COUNTRY CRAFTSMAN'S
KNOW-HOW: MAKING A TURNED CABRIOLE LEG

In the eighteenth century, during the Queen Anne and Chippendale periods, craftsmen began making cabriole (S-shaped) legs for the tables and chairs of their upper-class clientele. These were difficult and time-consuming to make — the curves had to be rough-cut with a frame saw, then carefully shaped with a drawknife. Country folks could rarely afford true cabriole legs. In their place, craftsmen substituted *turned cabriole* legs — sometimes called "country cabrioles." These were straight instead of curved, so they could be shaped quickly on a lathe. However, they had some elements of true cabriole legs — a graceful taper and a pad foot.

1 Before turning the country cabriole shape — while the stock is still square — cut the mortises and any other joinery in each leg. It's very difficult to make accurate joints in a leg after it's been shaped.

Inside Corner

Offset Axis

Center Axis

Outside Corner

Bottom View of Leg Stock

2 You must actually turn each country cabriole leg *twice* — first with the bottom end of the stock slightly offset, and then with it centered. Mark the two turning axes on the bottom end of the leg stock. The centered axis should be equidistant from all four corners. The other axis should be offset toward the *inside* corner, along a diagonal drawn between the inside and outside corners.

3 For the first turning, mount the stock on the lathe with the bottom end offset. Before starting the lathe, swing the stock through several complete revolutions — make sure it won't hit the tool rest!

4 Turn on the lathe at a *very low* speed and cut the tapered shaft and flared ankle. As you remove more and more stock from the leg, gradually speed up the lathe. If it starts to vibrate excessively, slow it down. Do *not* shape the foot yet — leave the stock square. However, finish sand the shaft and ankle.

5 Dismount the leg, then mount it again so the bottom end is centered.

6 Turn on the lathe at low speed. (The leg will be un-balanced again, and if you turn it too fast, it may vibrate loose.) Shape the pad foot, then finish sand it.

7 You may have to do some handwork to complete the leg, particularly where the foot and ankle meet. If so, finish shaping it with a rasp and file.

KNIFE BOX

Knives, like all metal implements, were in short supply during the first years of the colonies. The earliest settlers revived an old medieval custom requiring each person to bring his own knife to a meal. This became unnecessary as the colonies prospered and households acquired more tableware. Soon, there was abundance of knives, and cooks needed a place to keep them between meals. By the late eighteenth century, craftsmen were building *knife boxes* to display and store this newly acquired wealth of cutlery.

The boxes were made in all shapes and sizes. Most had slots or notches to hold the knife blades, some had lids that covered the handles. During the Federal period, in the early nineteenth century, some craftsmen created boxes in complex shapes with intricate veneer inlays. Most boxes, however, were plain and practical. The knife box shown is typical of many built by country craftsmen. The blades of the knives are inserted in the slots, and their handles are exposed so they can be drawn out again easily. You can hang the box on a wall, set it on a shelf, or even lay it in a drawer.

EXPLODED VIEW

BILL OF MATERIALS

WOODEN PARTS/*FINISHED DIMENSIONS*

A.	Back	$1/2$" x $9^3/4$" x 17"
B.	Sides (2)	$1/2$" x $3^1/2$" x $12^1/2$"
C.	Front	$1/2$" x $8^1/2$" x $9^3/4$"
D.	Top/bottom	$1/2$" x $2^1/2$" x $8^3/4$"

HARDWARE

1" Square-cut headless brads (20–24)

PLAN OF PROCEDURE

1

Plane, rip, and cut the parts to the sizes shown in the Bill of Materials.

2

Lay out the shapes of the sides as shown in the *Side View,* and cut them. Sand the sawed edges.

3

Lay out the shape of the back as shown in the *Front View,* and cut it. Sand the sawed edges.

4

Drill a ¼"-diameter hole through the back, near the top end, as shown in the *Front View.*

5

Using a table saw, cut two ⅛"-wide, 7¾"-long slots in the top, as shown in the *Top View.* To make these cuts, first lower the blade below the surface of the table. Then place the stock over the blade, using the fence to align it. Hold it in place with a pushstick or push block. Turn the saw on, and carefully raise the saw so it pierces the stock.

6

Finish sand the parts of the knife box. Assemble them with glue and square-cut brads. Do *not* glue the top or bottom to the front or back — just nail these parts together.

7

Set the nails and cover the heads with putty.

⅛" Slot (Typ)

3½" 2½" ½" 1¾" ½" 7¾" 9¾"

TOP VIEW

8

Do any necessary touch-up sanding and apply a finish to the completed project.

9

Drive a nail or install a Molly anchor in the wall where you want to hang the knife box.

10

Place the box over the head of the anchor or the nail.

4⅞" Rad

¼" Dia Thru

1 Square=½"

17"

8½"

12½"

½" 8¾" ½"

9¾"

½" 3½" ½"

FRONT VIEW

SIDE VIEW

SHOE-FOOT SETTLE TABLE

During the Middle Ages, a unique piece of furniture began to appear in English taverns. It combined several medieval furniture forms — settle, chest, and trestle table — to provide extra seating, storage, or table space, depending on the needs of the innkeeper. Two trestles supported a chest and a pivoting top piece. When the top was vertical, folks could sit on the chest or put things in it. When it was horizontal, it became a large table. These settle tables, or "monk's chairs," were among the earliest examples of convertible furniture.

The popularity of the piece gradually declined in England, but in the seventeenth and eighteenth centuries, American colonists revived and refined it. They found it was a useful design not just for taverns and inns but for many country homes where space was at a premium. Between meals, when a table was not needed, the top tilted up and the settle table was stored against a wall. This freed the room to be used for other purposes.

The settle table shown is similar to one now on display at Old Sturbridge Village in Massachusetts. The chest and seat are supported by distinctive shoe-shaped feet. As on many tables that survive from this period, the base is painted, while the top is natural wood. Originally, the entire piece may have been painted. However, years of scrubbing and scouring removed the paint from the top.

EXPLODED VIEW

BILL OF MATERIALS

WOODEN PARTS/*FINISHED DIMENSIONS*

A.	Trestles (2)	$7/8"$ x $15"$ x $26^{1}/8"$
B.	Shoe feet (2)	$2"$ x $2"$ x $22"$
C.	Armrests (2)	$2"$ x $2"$ x $20"$
D.	Chest front/back	$7/8"$ x $9^{1}/8"$ x $21^{3}/4"$
E.	Chest bottom	$7/8"$ x $13^{1}/4"$ x $20^{3}/4"$
F.	Seat	$7/8"$ x $3^{1}/2"$ x $20"$
G.	Seat lid	$7/8"$ x $12^{1}/2"$ x $19^{7}/8"$
H.	Lid supports (2)	$7/8"$ x $1^{1}/2"$ x $13^{1}/4"$
J.	Braces (2)	$7/8"$ x $3^{7}/16"$ x $41^{5}/8"$
K.	Top boards (4)	$7/8"$ x $12^{3}/8"$ x $48"$
L.	Pivots (4)	$1^{3}/8"$ dia. x $4"$
M.	Long pegs (10)	$3/8"$ x $3/8"$ x $1^{3}/4"$
N.	Short pegs (16)	$3/8"$ x $3/8"$ x $1^{1}/4"$

HARDWARE

#10 x $1^{1}/2"$ Flathead wood screws (8)
$1^{3}/4"$ x $3"$ Butt hinges and mounting screws (1 pair)
6d Square-cut nails (16–20)

PLAN OF PROCEDURE

1

If necessary, glue up wide stock to make the trestles and other parts. Plane, rip, and cut the parts to the sizes shown in the Bill of Materials, except the pivots. Cut these 1"–2" longer than specified.

2

Lay out the shape of the trestle, feet, and armrest, as shown in the *Trestle Layout, Shoe Foot Layout,* and *Armrest Layout.* However, don't cut the shapes yet.

3

Cut or rout the joinery necessary to build the base:

- 7/8"-wide, 3/8"-deep, 13¼"-long double-blind dadoes in the inside faces of the trestles, as shown in the *Trestle Layout/Side View*
- 3/8"-wide, 1"-deep, 7"-long mortises in the top surfaces of the feet, as shown in the *Shoe Foot Layout/Top View*

15"

2"   11"   2"

75° Shoulder
for Dovetail
(Typ)

7/8" Wd x
3/8" Dp
Double-Blind
Dado
Inside
Trestle

26⅛"

13¼"

3" Rad

1"   7"   1"

9"

SIDE VIEW

1"

8"   7/8"

9⅛"

75°

7"

1" (Typ)

¼"   3/8"

END VIEW

TRESTLE LAYOUT

4

Using a band saw or saber saw, cut the shapes of the trestles. Notch the tenons so they fit their respective mortises.

- 3/8"-wide, 1"-deep, 11"-long mortises in the bottom surfaces of the armrests, as shown in the *Armrest Layout/Bottom View*
- 3/8"-thick, 1"-long tenons along the entire width of the top and bottom ends of the trestles

5

Using a band saw, remove as much waste as possible from the dovetail notches. Cut the angled shoulders of the notches with a chisel, as shown in the *Trestle Layout/End View.* Sand the sawed edges.

6

Lay out and cut the chest front and back, as shown in the *Chest Front/Back Layout,* to fit in the dovetail notches.

CHEST FRONT/BACK LAYOUT

TOP VIEW

SIDE VIEW

SIDE VIEW
SHOE FOOT LAYOUT

BOTTOM VIEW
ARMREST LAYOUT

PLAN OF PROCEDURE

7

Drill 17/32"-diameter holes through the armrest, as shown in the *Armrest Layout/Side View.*

8

Cut the shapes of the feet and armrests. Sand the sawed edges.

9

Finish sand the trestles, feet, armrests, chest bottom, front, and back. Dry assemble the parts to check the fit of the joints, then reassemble the trestles, feet, and armrest with glue.

10

Round the bottom portion of the long pegs, as shown in the *Peg Detail.*

11

Drill 3/8"-diameter, 13/4"-deep holes through the mortise-and-tenon joints that hold the feet and armrests to the trestles, as shown in the *Side View.* Drive the long pegs into the holes from the outside. Leave about 1/16" of each peg protruding.

12

Glue the chest bottom in the dadoes in the trestle assemblies and glue the front and back to the bottom. Do *not* glue the front and back to the trestles. (The trestles' grain direction opposes that of the front and back. Glue joints would keep the front and back from expanding and contracting properly.) Instead, attach the front and back to the trestles with square-cut nails.

SECTION C

SECTION D

SECTION E

PEG DETAIL
(Make from *very* hard wood.)

SIDE VIEW

TOP VIEW

- 24"
- ⅞"
- 48" Dia
- Pegs
- 41⅝"
- 12" (Typ)
- ⅜" Wd × ⅜" Lg Tongue & Groove (Typ)
- ⅞" Wd × ⁷⁄₁₆" Dp Dovetail Slot & Tenon

FRONT VIEW

- 48"
- 11⅛" (Typ)
- ⅞" (Typ)
- 2"
- ⅞"
- ⅞"
- 10"
- 1½"
- 29"
- 9"
- 2"
- 2"
- 21¾"
- ⅞"
- 2"
- 22⅞"

PLAN OF PROCEDURE

13

Finish sand the lid supports and fasten them to the inside surfaces of the trestles with flathead wood screws. Countersink the screws, so the heads are flush with the surface of the supports. Do *not* glue the supports to the trestles — the grain directions oppose each other.

14

Cut off the front corners of the lid, as shown in the *Lid Layout*. Sand the sawed edges.

15

Mortise the adjoining edges of the lid and seat for hinges.

16

Finish sand the lid and seat, then fasten the seat to the back and lid supports with glue and nails. Mount the lid to the seat.

17

Set all the nails, then cover the heads with putty.

18

Cut a 3/8"-wide, 3/8"-deep groove in one edge of each top board and a matching 3/8"-thick, 3/8"-long tongue in the other edge. Clamp the boards together, edge to edge, with the tongues fitted in the grooves. However, do *not* glue them up.

19

With a string or a beam compass, lay out the circular shape of the top and the positions of the braces, as shown in the *Top View*.

LID LAYOUT

SECTION A

20

Rout two ⅞"-wide, ⁷⁄₁₆"-deep dovetail grooves across all four boards (perpendicular to the tongue-and-groove joints), where you wish to mount the braces. Using a table-mounted router, rout matching dovetails in each brace.

21

Miter the ends of the braces at 60°, as shown in the *Top Brace Layout/Side View.*

22

Disassemble the top boards. Finish sand the boards and the braces. Clamp the boards back together, edge to edge, lining up the dovetail slots. Slide the braces into the slots. *Do not apply glue.*

23

Turn the top assembly over, so the top side faces up. Saw the circular shape and sand the sawed edges.

24

Place the top assembly on the settle, so the braces straddle the armrests. Center the top on the settle, then reach through the holes in the armrests with a pencil or an awl to mark the inside surface of the braces.

SECTION B

SIDE VIEW

END VIEW

TOP BRACE LAYOUT

PLAN OF PROCEDURE

25

Remove the top and disassemble it. Drill $^{17}/_{32}$"-diameter holes through the braces at each of the marks, then reassemble the top.

Note: There should be two holes in each brace, front and back. The back hole should be $13^{1}/_{2}$" from the back end, and the front hole should be $10^{1}/_{2}$" from the front end.

26

Turn the shapes of the pivots, as shown in the *Pivot Layout*.

27

Reposition the top assembly on the settle, lining up the front and back holes in the braces with those in the armrests. Slide the pivots through the braces and into the armrests.

28

Round the bottom portion of the short pegs, as shown in the *Peg Detail*.

29

Drill $^{3}/_{8}$"-diameter, $1^{1}/_{4}$"-deep holes through the top boards into the braces. Drive the short pegs into the holes, leaving about $^{1}/_{16}$" of each peg protruding.

30

Check the tilting action of the top. Remove the front pivots and tilt the top up until it's vertical. It should move easily and remain vertical with no need to brace it. Make any necessary adjustments.

31

Remove all the pivots and take the top off the base. Also remove the lid and the hinges. Do any necessary touch-up sanding, then apply a finish to the completed settle table. After the finish dries, replace the lid and the top.

PIVOT LAYOUT

SPOON RACK

At the country table, spoons were the most important utensils. The early settlers rarely used forks and employed knives just for cutting and spearing. Most of the actual eating was accomplished with spoons.

Consequently, the cook kept the spoons ready. Many plate racks, pewter benches, and cupboards had notches in the front edges of the shelves to hold the spoons where they could be easily reached. It was also common to find the spoons arranged on their own special rack, hung on the kitchen or eating room wall.

The spoon rack shown is a copy of an old country design. Three notched bars hold a dozen spoons — a king's ransom in spoons for many pioneer families.

EXPLODED VIEW

BILL OF MATERIALS

WOODEN PARTS/*FINISHED DIMENSIONS*

A. Backboard $1/2" \times 91/4" \times 211/2"$
B. Holders (3) $1/2" \times 11/4" \times 91/4"$

HARDWARE

6d Square-cut nails (9)

PLAN OF PROCEDURE

1

Plane, rip, and cut the parts to the sizes shown in the Bill of Materials.

2

Cut 1"-wide, 1/2"-deep notches in the holders, as shown in the *Holder Detail*.

3

Lay out and cut the *Backboard Pattern*. Sand the sawed edges.

4

Finish sand the parts of the spoon rack, then glue the holders to the backboard.

5

Let the glue dry, then drill pilot holes for square-cut nails. Drive the nails through the holders and into the backboards, but don't set or cover the heads — let them show.

6

Do any necessary touch-up sanding and apply a finish to the completed project.

HOLDER DETAIL

FRONT VIEW **SIDE VIEW** **BACKBOARD PATTERN**

KNIFE CADDY

ountry folks made all sorts of carryalls and containers to help them organize their lives. This "knife caddy" was one of the most common. It was not unusual for a family to have a dozen or more of these carriers, which they used to hold everything from dinnerware to sewing notions to gardening tools.

The knife caddy looks like a small, contemporary toolbox or "tote." It's made in much the same way — just a shallow box with a handle that also serves as a divider. Like most utilitarian pieces, it's fairly plain. The only decorative feature is the heart-shaped handle cutout. Hearts have been a common folk ornament since medieval times.

EXPLODED VIEW

BILL OF MATERIALS

WOODEN PARTS/*FINISHED DIMENSIONS*

A.	Sides (2)	3/8" x 21/4" x 14"
B.	Ends (2)	3/8" x 21/4" x 7"
C.	Divider	3/8" x 47/8" x 131/4"
D.	Bottom	1/4" x 7" x 131/4"

HARDWARE

11/4" Headless brads (24–30)

PLAN OF PROCEDURE

1

Plane, rip, and cut the parts to the sizes shown in the Bill of Materials.

2

Lay out and cut the shape of the divider, as shown in the *Divider Pattern*. Sand the sawed edges.

3

Finish sand the parts of the knife caddy and dry assemble them to check the fit. Reassemble the parts with glue and headless brads. Set the heads of the brads and cover them with putty.

4

Do any necessary touch-up sanding and apply a finish to the completed project.

1 Square = ½"

DIVIDER PATTERN

FRONT VIEW

SIDE VIEW

OVAL TEA TABLE

One of the distinguishing features of the nineteenth century was its pomp and ceremony. The new American republic embraced ritual with the same enthusiasm that it had only recently rejected it. After the Revolution, people reinstituted old traditions and created new ones. One of these customs was "tea."

Tea was a light meal, served in the afternoon, often on a small "tea table." It was a popular custom in Europe, begun in the eighteenth century. It slowly gained acceptance here, and American cabinetmakers began to make tea tables for upper-class clients. By the nineteenth century, the custom had spread to the growing middle class, and tea tables were a common sight in country homes.

Early tea tables had round or square tops. The oval shape became common later, in the Federal period. Many of the better tables had "galleries" — a small railing around the perimeter of the top. The plain top shown was more common in the country. All tea tables, city or country, were about 30" tall, the same as an ordinary table. The legs on this table have been shortened as a concession to contemporary needs and tastes.

EXPLODED VIEW

BILL OF MATERIALS

WOODEN PARTS/*FINISHED DIMENSIONS*

A. Top · · · · · · · · · · · ³/₄" x 26" x 36"
B. Legs (4) · · · · · · · · · · 2" x 2" x 19¹/₄"
C. Front/back aprons (2) · · · · ³/₄" x 4" x 23¹/₂"
D. Side aprons (2) · · · · · · ³/₄" x 4" x 13¹/₂"
E. Pegs (16) · · · · · · · · ⁵/₁₆" x ⁵/₁₆" x 1¹/₄"

HARDWARE

#8 x 1¹/₄" Flathead wood screws (10)

PLAN OF PROCEDURE

1

If necessary, glue up stock to make the tabletop. Then plane, rip, and cut the parts to the sizes shown in the Bill of Materials.

2

Cut 1/4"-wide, 3/4"-deep, 3"-long mortises in the inside surfaces of each leg, as shown in the *Leg Layout*.

3

Turn the legs on a lathe. When making each leg, mount the stock so the bottom end is offset toward the inside corner, as shown in the *Leg Offset Detail/Bottom View*. Shape the tapered shaft and flared ankles. Center the bottom end of the stock, then turn the foot, as explained in Making a Turned Cabriole Leg on page 68.

4

Drill two screw pockets in the inside face of each side apron and three pockets in the front and back aprons, as shown in the *Front View* and *Side View*.

5

Cut 1/4"-wide, 3/4"-long tenons in the ends of the aprons, using a dado cutter or router. Notch the top and bottom of the tenons, as shown in the *Apron Layout*.

LEG LAYOUT

LEG OFFSET DETAIL
BOTTOM VIEW

END VIEW   **FRONT VIEW**

APRON LAYOUT

Plan of Procedure

6

Lay out and cut the shapes of the front, back, and side aprons, as shown in the *Apron Layout*.

7

Lay out the shape of the top, as shown in the *Top Layout*. Draw the major and minor axes of the oval on the stock, marking points A through F. Drive two small brads at the foci, points B and C. Tie a loop of string twice as long as the distance from A to C (52¹⁄₈"), and put the loop around the brads. Insert the point of a pencil through the knot in the string loop. Pull the loop taut and mark the oval, dragging the string around the brads. The pencil line should pass through points A, D, E, and F.

8

Cut the oval shape of the top. Sand the sawed edges and round them over slightly with a rasp or file.

9

Dry assemble the legs and aprons to check the fit of the joints. Finish sand all the parts of the table, then assemble the legs and aprons with glue.

SECTION A   **SECTION B**   **SECTION C**

10

Round the bottom portion of the pegs, as shown in the *Peg Detail*.

PEG DETAIL
(Make from *very* hard wood.)

APRON-TO-LEG JOINERY DETAIL

TOP LAYOUT

11

Drill two 5/16"-diameter, 1¼"-deep holes through each joint in the legs and then drive the pegs into the holes from the outside. Leave about 1/16" of each peg protruding.

12

Attach the top to the aprons with flathead wood screws, as shown in the *Top-to-Apron Joinery Detail*. Do *not* glue the top to the aprons or legs; this would restrict the wood movement.

13

Do any necessary touch-up sanding on the table. Then apply a finish to the completed project.

TOP VIEW

26"

Top

#8×1¼" FHWS

3/16" Dia Pilot Hole

Screw Pocket

Apron

TOP-TO-APRON JOINERY DETAIL

36"

5" 2" 22" 2" 5"

¾"

26"

5" 2" 12" 2" 5"

Pegs

4"

5"

4"

Screw Pockets

Screw Pockets

20"

14¼"

FRONT VIEW

SIDE VIEW

HARVEST TABLE

Throughout the seventeenth and eighteenth centuries, there were few large dining tables. Early country homes were small and had no formal dining areas. There was little space for a large table. So most tables were small, seating no more than six people. When folks needed a larger table, they simply laid long boards across sawbucks.

By the mid-nineteenth century, small-town and rural Americans were enjoying relative prosperity. They had tamed the wilderness east of the Mississippi and were reaping the benefits of industrialization. They began to build larger homes or add on to their small ones. Imitating their big-city cousins, they set aside areas or entire rooms for dining. Country craftsmen began to make large, simple dining tables, such as the harvest table shown. ("Harvest" is a modern title; nineteenth-century folks knew this as a drop-leaf, or folding, table.)

The table shown has a rectangular top with two leaves. These leaves fold down when the table isn't in use, saving space. Despite their larger homes, folks were still space conscious — old habits die hard. And the leaves serve another, equally important purpose. In the sixteenth century, when drop-leaf tables first appeared, craftsmen discovered that when a thin table surface was hung in a vertical position, it was less likely to warp. Wide table-tops that were permanently horizontal had to be made very thick or had to be braced with strong battens and breadboards. By making drop leaves, craftsmen could make larger tables using less lumber.

EXPLODED VIEW

BILL OF MATERIALS

WOODEN PARTS/*FINISHED DIMENSIONS*

A.	Legs (4)	2" x 2" x 28¹/4"
B.	Side aprons (2)	³/4" x 6¹/2" x 52"
C.	End aprons (2)	³/4" x 6¹/2" x 18"
D.	Top	³/4" x 22" x 78"
E.	Leaves (2)	³/4" x 10" x 78"
F.	Slides (4)	³/4" x 2¹/2" x 19¹/4"
G.	Slide supports (2)	³/4" x 2³/8" x 18¹/2"
H.	Slide housing (4)	³/4" x 3¹/16" x 18¹/2"
J.	Stop dowels (4)	¹/4" dia. x 1¹/4"
K.	Pegs (16)	⁵/16" x ⁵/16" x 1¹/4"

HARDWARE

#8 x 1¹/4" Flathead wood screws (12)
6d Square-cut nails (16)
Drop-leaf hinges and mounting screws (4 pairs)
Small pulls (4)

PLAN OF PROCEDURE

1

If necessary, glue up stock to make the wide tabletop. Plane, rip, and cut the parts to the sizes shown in the Bill of Materials, except the leaves. Leave these 1"–2" wider than specified until *after* you cut the rule joints.

2

Cut 3/8"-wide, 3/4"-deep, 2¼"-long mortises in the inside surfaces of each leg, as shown in the *Leg Layout*.

3

Turn the legs on a lathe. When making each leg, mount the stock so the bottom end is offset toward the inside corner, as shown in the *Leg Offset Detail/Bottom View*. Turn the tapered shaft and flared ankles. Center the bottom end of the stock, then turn the foot, as explained in Making a Turned Cabriole Leg on page 68.

LEG OFFSET DETAIL
BOTTOM VIEW

LEG LAYOUT

END VIEW

TOP VIEW

SIDE VIEW

PLAN OF PROCEDURE

4

Drill two screw pockets in the inside face of each end apron and four pockets in each side apron, as shown in the *End Apron Layout* and *Side Apron Layout.*

5

Cut 3/8"-wide, 3/4"-long tenons in the ends of the apron, using a dado cutter or router. Notch the tenons, as shown in the *End Apron Layout* and *Side Apron Layout,* so they are 2 1/4" from shoulder to shoulder. Fit these tenons to the mortises in the legs.

6

Cut 3/16"-diameter beads in the outside faces of the aprons, near the bottom edge, as shown in the *Apron Profile.*

7

Cut the joinery needed for the slides and housings:

- 13/16"-wide, 2 9/16"-long notches in each side apron, as shown in the *Side Apron Layout*
- 1 1/16"-wide, 1/4"-deep rabbets in the top face of each slide support, as shown in the *Slide Support Detail*

- 5/16"-wide, 9"-long slots in the slide supports
- 1/4"-wide, 1/4"-deep rabbets in the bottom face of each slide support
- 1/4"-wide, 1/4"-deep grooves in the inside face of each slide housing, as shown in *Section A*

8

Drill a 1/4"-wide, 3/4"-deep hole in the bottom edge of each slide, as shown in the *Slide Layout.*

FACE VIEW   **END VIEW**   **APRON PROFILE**

END APRON LAYOUT

FACE VIEW   **END VIEW**

SIDE APRON LAYOUT

9

Chamfer the outside ends of the slides, as shown in the *Slide Layout*.

10

Joint the adjoining edges of the tabletop and leaves, then cut rule joints in these edges, as shown in the *Rule Joint Detail*.

11

Mortise the bottom faces of the top and leaves for hinges. Attach the hinges.

12

Rip the leaves to their proper width. Joint the sawed edges.

RULE JOINT DETAIL

SLIDE LAYOUT

END VIEW **FACE VIEW**

SECTION A

END VIEW **TOP VIEW**
SLIDE SUPPORT DETAIL

PLAN OF PROCEDURE

13

Dry assemble the legs and aprons to check the fit of the joints. Finish sand all the parts of the table, then assemble the legs and aprons with glue.

14

Round the bottom portion of the pegs, as shown in the *Peg Detail*.

15

Drill two 5/16"-diameter, 1¼"-deep holes through each joint in the legs and then drive the pegs into the holes from the outside. Leave about 1/16" of each peg protruding.

16

Glue dowels in the holes in the slides and attach pulls to the outside ends.

17

Assemble the slide supports and slide housings with glue. Then attach the slide housing assemblies between the side aprons, fastening them in place with nails. Set the heads of the nails and cover them with putty.

18

Lay the slides in place in the housings. The dowels should fit into the grooves in the slide supports. Test the sliding action. If the slides bind, plane or sand the faces of the slides until they move smoothly.

19

Attach the top to the aprons with flathead wood screws, as shown in the *Screw Pocket Detail*. Do *not* glue the top to the aprons or legs; this would restrict the wood movement. Test the action of the leaves and slides.

20

Remove the top from the table and take the slides from their housings. Remove all hardware. Do any necessary touch-up sanding on the table parts. Apply a finish, then reassemble the parts and hardware.

PEG DETAIL
(Make from *very* hard wood.)

APRON-TO-LEG JOINERY DETAIL

Tabletop

3/16" Dia Pilot Hole
#8 × 1¼" FHWS & Washer
Apron
Screw Pocket

SCREW POCKET DETAIL

▨ SECTION B

▨ SECTION C

◉ SECTION D

FOR
READING
&
WRITING

LAP DESK

During the Middle Ages, the few literate folks in western Europe who could read and write often used a *writing box* — a small chest with a flat, slanted lid. The writing box was a storage chest, a tabletop desk, and a book stand all in one. The box had compartments for paper, pens, and ink. The lid provided a writing surface or supported books at a comfortable angle for reading.

This basic design continued to be used through the eighteenth century in England and longer in her colonies. In America, folks called it a *lap desk,* although they rarely used it on their laps. They rested the box on a table when it was needed and set it aside on a shelf or in a cabinet when it wasn't. As the American public became more and more schooled and reading and writing became a part of everyday life, the lap desk gave way to larger desks with legs attached to them.

The lap desk shown is patterned after one made in the Shaker community in New Lebanon, New York, during the first part of the nineteenth century. It has several clever features: A small drawer on the right side serves as an inkwell and a larger drawer on the left holds extra paper. Under the lid, there is space for books or additional writing materials and a ledge or *till* for pens, pencils, and nibs.

EXPLODED VIEW

BILL OF MATERIALS

WOODEN PARTS/*FINISHED DIMENSIONS*

A.	Lid	$5/16$" x $13^{1}/8$" x $17^{3}/8$"
B.	Breadboards (2)	$5/16$" x $1^{3}/16$" x $13^{1}/8$"
C.	Left side	$3/8$" x $3^{5}/8$" x $12^{3}/4$"
D.	Right side	$3/8$" x $5^{5}/8$" x $12^{3}/4$"
E.	Front	$3/8$" x $3^{15}/16$" x $18^{3}/4$"
F.	Back	$3/8$" x $5^{5}/8$" x $18^{3}/4$"
G.	Bottom	$3/16$" x 13" x 19"
H.	Shelf	$1/4$" x $12^{3}/8$" x $18^{3}/16$"
J.	Side bead moldings (2)	$1/8$" x $9/16$" x 2"
K.	Top bead molding	$1/8$" x $9/16$" x $12^{1}/4$"
L.	Paper drawer front	$3/8$" x $1^{13}/16$" x $11^{15}/16$"
M.	Paper drawer sides (2)	$1/4$" x $1^{13}/16$" x $18^{3}/16$"
N.	Paper drawer back	$1/4$" x $1^{7}/16$" x $11^{15}/16$"
P.	Paper drawer bottom	$1/4$" x $11^{5}/8$" x $18^{1}/8$"
Q.	Ink drawer front	$3/8$" x $2^{1}/8$" x $2^{5}/8$"

R.	Front ink drawer side	$1/8$" x $1^{13}/16$" x $2^{5}/8$"
S.	Back ink drawer side	$1/8$" x $1^{13}/16$" x $5^{5}/8$"
T.	Ink drawer back	$1/8$" x $1^{11}/16$" x $2^{1}/16$"
U.	Ink drawer bottom	$1/8$" x $2^{1}/16$" x $2^{5}/8$"
V.	Ink drawer keeper	$5/16$" x $5/16$" x $1^{1}/2$"
W.	Pencil till bottom	$1/8$" x $2^{5}/16$" x 12"
X.	Pencil till lip	$1/8$" x $3/4$" x 12"
Y.	Pencil till glue blocks (2)	$5/16$" x $5/16$" x $2^{7}/16$"

HARDWARE

$1/2$"-dia. Brass drawer pulls (2)
Small lock and latch
Escutcheon
$7/8$" Wire or headless brads (24–36)
#6 x $5/8$" Roundhead wood screw
#6 Flat washer

PLAN OF PROCEDURE

1

Plane, rip, and cut the front, back, sides, bottom, lid, breadboards, and shelf to the sizes shown in the Bill of Materials. Bevel the top edges of the front and back at 8°, as shown in *Section A*. Plane and rip the bead molding stock to the specified thickness and width, but don't cut it to length yet. You can plane the stock needed for the other parts, but don't cut them to length or width.

Note: The smaller assemblies in this project — the paper drawer, ink drawer, and pencil till — should be fitted to the desk *after* it's built. If the dimensions of the desk change slightly from what's shown as you assemble it, the size of these smaller pieces must change also.

2

Cut the opening for the ink drawer in the right side, as shown in the *Right Side Layout*.

3

Lay out and cut the dovetails that join the front, back, and sides. For instructions on how to cut these dovetails, refer to Making Hand-Cut Dovetails, page 112.

12¾"

8°

3⅝"

1¹⁵⁄₁₆"

LEFT SIDE LAYOUT
(BEFORE CUTTING DOVETAILS)

12¾"

8°

2⅞"

⅞"

1⅞"

5⅝"

2⅞"

3¹⁵⁄₁₆"

RIGHT SIDE LAYOUT
(BEFORE CUTTING DOVETAILS)

⅜"

¾"

¾"

¹⁄₁₆"

10°

LARGE DOVETAIL DETAIL

Miter at 8° (Typ)

5/16"

3/8" (Typ)

13 1/8"

Round Over

1/4"

5 5/8"

1/8" Wd. Molding (Typ)

6 1/8"

1/8" Bead

1 7/8" Opening

3/16"

3/8" (Typ)

1/8" (Typ)

12" Opening

1/8" (Typ)

13"

LEFT SIDE VIEW

Mortise for Hinges

13 1/8"

B

5/16"

2 1/8" Door Front

6 1/8"

1/4"

5 5/8"

2 5/8" Door Front

1/4"

B

3/8" (Typ)

12"

1/8" (Typ)

3/16"

13"

RIGHT SIDE VIEW

PLAN OF PROCEDURE

4

Cut or rout the remaining joinery necessary to assemble the desk:

- 1/4"-wide, 3/16"-deep double-blind grooves in the front, back, and right side to hold the shelf, as shown in *Section A* and *Section B* (stop these grooves 3/16" from the ends of the parts; do *not* cut through to the ends)
- 1/2"-wide, 1/8"-deep, 2"-long blind rabbets in the left ends of the front and back to hold the bead molding, as shown in the *Left Side/ Molding Detail*
- 1/8"-wide, 1/8"-deep rabbet in the left edge of the shelf, to house the bead molding

- 1/8"-wide, 3/16"-deep grooves in the ends of the lid, to hold the breadboards, as shown in the *Breadboard Joinery Detail*
- 1/8"-wide, 3/16"-long tenons in the inside edges of the breadboards, to fit the grooves in the lid

- Mortises in the front, back, and lid for the hinges and lock (the dimensions of these mortises will depend on the hardware)

3/32
5/16
3/16
1/8
3/16
1 3/16

BREADBOARD JOINERY DETAIL

8° Bevel
1/16
3/4
1 1/8
4 1/4
1 7/8 1/4
3/16

8° Bevel
Back
Glue Block
1/4" Wd × 3/16" Dp Groove

12"
Pencil Tray
Shelf
Front
Bottom

SECTION A
(WITHOUT LID AND PAPER DRAWER)

5

Drill a hole in the front so you can insert the key in the lock.

6

Assemble the lid and breadboards with glue. Let the glue dry, then sand the surfaces clean and flush.

LEFT
SIDE/
MOLDING
DETAIL

SECTION B
(WITHOUT LID AND PAPER DRAWER)

PLAN OF PROCEDURE

13⅛"

1" · 17⅜" · 1"

19⅜"

Mortise Bottom of
Lid for Latch

TOP VIEW

A

19⅜"

Round
Over
Edge

⅜"

Mortise Inside of
Front for Lock

⅛"

18"

19"

A

FRONT VIEW

7

Round over the outside edge of the bead molding stock, the side and front edges of the lid assembly, and all four edges of the bottom.

8

Dry assemble the front, back, sides, and shelf to test the fit of the joints. Adjust the fit as necessary, then cut the moldings to length. Miter the adjoining edges.

9

Finish sand all the parts you've made so far. Assemble the front, back, sides, shelf, and moldings. Glue all parts except the shelf. Let it float in its grooves.

10

Attach the bottom to the front, back, and right side with brads. You may glue the bottom to the front and back, but do *not* glue it to the right side. Set the heads of the brads.

11

Attach the lid to the desk assembly.

12

Install the lock and escutcheon. When the lock is installed, measure the location of the latch on the lid.

13

Cut a mortise for the latch, and install it in the lid.

TOP VIEW

FRONT VIEW

SIDE VIEW

PAPER DRAWER

PLAN OF PROCEDURE

14

Measure the opening for the paper drawer and determine the proper dimensions for the drawer. (It should be approximately 1/16" smaller than the width and height of the opening when finished. You may wish to build it slightly large, then plane or sand it to fit.) Cut the paper drawer parts to size.

15

Lay out and cut the dovetails that join the drawer front, back, and sides. Note that the dovetails that join the front to the sides are *half-blind,* so they can't be seen when the drawer is closed.

16

Rout or cut 3/16"-wide, 1/8"-deep grooves in the inside surfaces of the drawer front and sides to hold the drawer bottom, as shown in the *Paper Drawer/ Side View.*

17

Dry assemble the drawer to test the fit of the joints, and adjust them as necessary.

18

Finish sand the parts of the paper drawer, then assemble the front, back, and sides with glue. Using a handplane, "relieve" the edges and front ends of the drawer bottom so the bottom tapers to 3/16" thick, as shown on the *Paper Drawer Joinery Detail.* Slide the bottom into its grooves and tack it to the back with brads. Do *not* glue the bottom in place; let it float in the grooves. Sand the drawer joinery clean and flush.

19

Install one of the drawer pulls on the front and test its fit in the desk. If it binds, sand or plane stock from the drawer parts to adjust the fit.

20

Measure the ink drawer opening and determine the proper dimensions for the drawer, as you did with the paper drawer. Cut the ink drawer parts to size.

21

Rout or cut 9/32"-wide, 3/16"-deep rabbets in the ends and bottom edge of the drawer front. Cut a 5/32"-wide, 3/16"-deep rabbet in the top edge, as shown in the *Ink Drawer/Side View* and *Ink Drawer/Top View.*

22

Rout or cut a 9/16"-wide, 2 1/2"-long groove in the back side, as shown in the *Ink Drawer/Side View.*

PAPER DRAWER JOINERY DETAIL

GLUE BLOCK DETAIL

23

Cut the keeper to fit the groove in the ink drawer side, as shown in the *Ink Drawer Keeper Detail.* Drill a ⅛"-diameter hole through the keeper.

24

Finish sand the ink drawer parts, then assemble them with glue and brads. Sand the joints clean and flush and install the remaining drawer pull on the front.

25

Slide the drawer into the opening to check the fit. If necessary, sand or plane the drawer until it slides smoothly in and out of the desk. Then install the keeper on the inside face of the back, holding it in place with a roundhead wood screw and flat washer. Do *not* glue the keeper in place, in case you want to remove it to repair the drawer.

26

Measure the space for the pencil till and cut the parts accordingly. Bevel the edges of the glue blocks, as shown in the *Glue Block Detail.*

27

Finish sand the parts of the pencil till. Glue the blocks inside the desk and glue the till lid to the till bottom. When the glue dries, attach the till inside the desk, gluing it to the blocks and the left side.

28

Remove the drawers from the desk and detach all hardware — hinges, pulls, lock, latch, and escutcheon. Apply a finish to the desk, then replace the drawers and hardware.

INK DRAWER KEEPER DETAIL

TOP VIEW

FRONT VIEW **SIDE VIEW**

INK DRAWER

COUNTRY CRAFTSMAN'S
KNOW-HOW: MAKING HAND-CUT DOVETAILS

When assembling boxes — plank chests, cases, and drawers — cabinetmakers often used dovetails to join the front, back, and sides. These are extremely durable joints — the *pins* lock between the *tails,* so the joint holds tight even without glue or metal fasteners.

Old-time craftsmen cut these joints by hand, employing a chisel and a saw. Today, there are several commercial router jigs that will cut the dovetails with a machine, but so far, no one has produced a jig that can reproduce the slender pins and wide tails favored by eighteenth- and nineteenth-century cabinetmakers. The best way to make these dovetails is still by hand. With a little practice, you can cut them manually as easily as with a router.

In addition to a chisel and a saw, you'll also need a small mallet (to strike the chisel), a marking gauge, a marking knife or scratch awl, and a template (to lay out the dovetails). You can purchase commercially made dovetail templates, make your own, or substitute a sliding T-bevel. The homemade template shown offers an advantage over commercial templates and T-bevels: You can also use it to guide the saw.

Dovetail Template and Guide (make from a very hard wood, such as maple or hickory)

1 You can start with either the pins or the tails — most craftsmen prefer the tails. Using the marking gauge, scribe two lines — one on each face — near the end of the board. These lines indicate the length of the tails and are called "baselines." Through tails are as long as the adjoining board is thick; half-lap tails are half to two-thirds as long.

2 Using the template and a marking knife, draw the angled lines that mark the sides or "cheeks" of the tails. Once again, mark *both* sides of the board. Shade the area between the tails — the waste to be removed — with a pencil. Note that the tails are noticeably wider than the waste. This is not necessary, but, as mentioned previously, it's traditional.

3 Saw the cheeks of the tails down to the baselines, cutting on the waste side of the marks. If you wish, guide the saw with the template. Use a small, fine-toothed saw, such as a dovetail saw or a Dozuki saw, to do the cutting.

(Continued)

COUNTRY CRAFTSMAN'S
KNOW-HOW: MAKING HAND-CUT DOVETAILS — *CONT.*

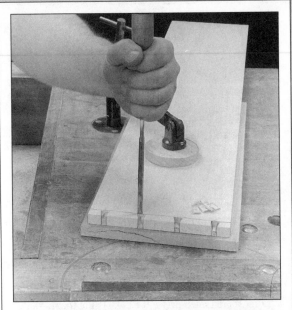

4 Once you have cut the cheeks, remove the waste between the tails with a *very* sharp chisel. Remove each bit of waste in two steps: First, use the chisel as a cutting tool. Hold it vertically and place the edge on the baseline. Strike it with a mallet, cutting 1/16"–1/8" deep all along the line.

5 Next, use the chisel as a wedge. Hold it horizontally and put the edge against the waste at the end of the board, 1/16"–1/8" below the face. Strike it with a mallet, lifting a small amount of waste.

6 Repeat this procedure until you've cut halfway through the board. Then turn the board over and remove waste from the other side. Continue until you have removed all the waste between the tails.

7 Scribe baselines on both sides of the adjoining board, then mark the pins. Use the completed tails as a template. (If you chose to make the pins first, you can use the completed pins to mark the tails.) Once again, shade the waste area.

8 Saw the cheeks of the pins down to the baselines, cutting on the waste side of the marks. (This prevents you from removing too much stock.) If you wish, guide the saw with the template.

9 Remove the waste with a chisel, using the same cutting and wedging technique as before. Cut halfway through the board, turn it over, and remove the remaining waste.

10 Test the fit of the joint. Because you cut on the waste side of the marks when making both the tails and the pins, the fit is likely to be tight. If it's too tight, shave a little bit of stock from the pins with the chisel.

BOOKSHELF

Until the mid-nineteenth century, the "library" of a typical country home would fit in a small box. Most families had but a single book — a Bible. Books, after all, were a luxury, and most country folks didn't know how to read.

In the early nineteenth century, two events changed that forever. The newly developed American system of public education, in little more than a generation, taught most of the nation's children to read, write, and cipher. For the first time in history, literacy became the rule rather than the exception. At the same time, the riot of innovation and invention that we remember as the Industrial Revolution spawned a parade of fast, efficient printing presses. A tidal wave of inexpensive books washed over a literate public hungry for things to read. Almost overnight, home libraries expanded from one book to dozens.

This, in turn, created an inevitable problem — where to store the books? Country folks, with typical inventiveness, began to modify existing cupboards and racks — most of which had been used to keep cooking and eating utensils — to hold books. The bookshelf shown is an example. It's built in the same manner as a plate rack, but with wider shelves.

EXPLODED VIEW

BILL OF MATERIALS

WOODEN PARTS/*FINISHED DIMENSIONS*

A.	Sides (2)	3/4" x 10 3/4" x 39 1/4"
B.	Top	3/4" x 11 3/4" x 58"
C.	Shelves (2)	3/4" x 10 3/4" x 55 1/4"
D.	Top/middle rails (2)	3/4" x 2" x 56"
E.	Bottom rail	3/4" x 3" x 56"
F.	Pegs (7)	1 3/8" dia. x 1 1/8"

HARDWARE

#8 x 1 1/2" Flathead wood screws (7)
6d Square-cut nails (24–30)

PLAN OF PROCEDURE

1

Plane, rip, and cut the parts to the sizes shown in the Bill of Materials. You can purchase pegs similar to those shown from some woodworking suppliers, or substitute Shaker pegs, which are handled by most suppliers. If you plan to turn these pegs, cut turning stock for each peg about 1" longer than specified.

2

Cut the joinery necessary to assemble the project:

- 3/4"-wide, 3/8"-deep dadoes in the sides, as shown in the *Front View*, to hold the shelves
- 3/4"-wide, 2"-long notches in the back edges of the sides, to hold the top and middle rails, as shown in the *Side View*
- 3/4"-wide, 3"-long notch in the back edges of the sides to hold the bottom rail

3

Lay out and cut the shape of the sides, as shown in the *Side View*.

4

Rout or cut the molded shapes:

- 5/16"-diameter beads in the front face of the rails, near the bottom edge, as shown in the *Rail Profile*. This bead runs the full length of the rails.
- 1/2"-radius cove in the front edge and ends of the top, as shown in the *Top Profile*

5

If you're turning your own pegs, turn them to the profile shown in the *Peg Detail*.

6

Drill 1/8"-diameter, 1"-deep pilot holes, centered in the back ends of the pegs. Also drill 1/8"-diameter pilot holes through the bottom rail where you wish to mount these pegs. Countersink the pilot holes on the back surface of the rail.

SIDE VIEW

TOP PROFILE

PEG DETAIL

7

Finish sand the parts of the bookshelf and dry assemble them to check the fit of the joints. Reassemble the sides, shelves, top, and rails with glue and square-cut nails.

8

Set the nails and cover the heads with putty.

9

Attach the pegs to the bottom rail with flathead wood screws. Drive the screws from the back of the rail into the pegs.

10

Do any necessary touch-up sanding and apply a finish to the completed project.

11

Hang the finished bookshelves on a wall by driving screws or Molly anchors through the top rail.

Note: To support the weight of the books safely, fasten the shelves to *two* or more studs in the wall.

3/4" Wd × 3/8" Dp Dado (Typ)

5/16" Bead

3/4"

RAIL PROFILE

58"

40"

1¼"

6¼" — 7" — 7"

3/4"

3/4"

56"

FRONT VIEW

SHAKER CANDLE LEDGE

The United Society of Believers in Christ's Second Appearing — better known as the Shakers — developed an entire storage *system* around the simple peg. They lined the rooms in their community buildings with peg rails, then made clothes hangers, shelves, cupboards, and other small furniture pieces that could be hung on them.

This candle ledge is an example. It's patterned after a ledge made by the Shakers of Pleasant Hill, Kentucky. It's designed to be easily moved. If necessary, the Shakers could carry the candle ledge from room to room, hanging it on the wall wherever they wished.

They could also move the candle ledge around within a single room. Because they could place it anywhere there was a peg, and hang it at several different heights, a Shaker brother or sister could set the candle where its light was most needed. They might also use the ledge to hold other small items — kitchen utensils, sewing notions, tools, a water glass, or the personal effects that folks collect in their pockets.

The ledge is made in the same manner as Shaker bentwood boxes. The outside lip is a single piece of thin hardwood, bent into a hoop and pegged to a round bottom.

EXPLODED VIEW

BILL OF MATERIALS

WOODEN PARTS/*FINISHED DIMENSIONS*

A. Bottom   9" dia. x $5/8$"
B. Lip $3/32$" x $13/4$" x $301/4$"
C. Post $1/2$" x 2" x $283/4$"
D. Pegs (16–18) $1/16$" dia. x $1/2$"

HARDWARE

#6 x 1" Flathead wood screws (2)
#2 Copper tacks* (6)

You can purchase these tacks from:
W. W. Cross Nail Company
P.O. Box 365
Jeffery, NH 03452

PLAN OF PROCEDURE

1

Plane, rip, and cut the parts to the sizes shown in the Bill of Materials.

Note: Most planers will only plane wood to 1/8" thick. To make the 3/32"-thick stock for the lip, rip a thin slice from a wider board.

2

Mark the locations of the 1¼"-diameter holes on the post, as shown in the *Front View,* and drill them through the stock.

3

Miter the top of the post at 45°, so it comes to a point.

4

Bend the lip to form a 9"-diameter hoop, following the technique in Making Bentwood Boxes on page 124.

5

Cut the round bottom, beveling the edge at 5°, as shown in *Section A.* Fit the bottom to the lip, as described in Making Bentwood Boxes.

6

Remove the bottom from the lip and cut a 2"-wide, ½"-deep notch in the bottom, as shown in the *Top View.*

7

Finish sand the post and bottom. Fasten the post in the notch with flathead wood screws and glue. The end of the post should be flush with the bottom surface of the bottom.

8

Fit the lip to the bottom again, so it laps behind the post. Peg the bottom to the lip, as described in Making Bentwood Boxes. Sand the pegs flush with the surface of the lip.

EDGING DETAIL

9

Finish sand the lip and do any necessary touch up sanding to the other parts of the candle ledge. Apply a finish to the completed project.

3/32"
Lip
Bevel Edge at 5°
1 3/4"
1/16" Dia × 1/2" Lg Peg
Bottom

SECTION A

1/2"
3/32"
9" Dia

TOP VIEW

Bevel End Under Overlap
Post
Lip
#2 Copper Tacks
Peg
1/16" Dia × 1/2" Dp Hole (Typ)

LIP DETAIL

2"
2"
45°
1 1/4" Dia (Typ)
3" (Typ)
28 3/4"
5/8"
1 3/4"

FRONT VIEW

COUNTRY CRAFTSMAN'S
KNOW-HOW: MAKING BENTWOOD BOXES

Sometime in the seventeenth century — perhaps earlier — craftsmen began to make round and oval bentwood boxes. These curved boxes, made from thin stock, were much lighter than rectangular boxes made from thicker boards. Yet, because the sides were curved, they were just as strong and durable. Country folks found many uses for these boxes — they made them into storage containers, shipping crates, trays, carryalls, and hanging shelves, such as the Shaker Candle Ledge. There are even records of these boxes being used as spitoons!

The box maker was a specialist, like the turner or chair bodger. As such, he had special tools. The most important were a steamer, or *poacher,* to make the wood pliable and bending forms (called *box molds*) to bend the wood to the proper shape. He also used a special *clinch anvil* to bend the points of the tiny tacks that held the wood together. Finally, he needed *dryers* to hold the shape of the wood until it cooled and dried. You can make all of these tools from scraps of hardwood, metal pipe, and metal guttering, as shown in the drawings.

Aluminum End Caps (2 Read'd)

¾" (Typ)

Aluminum Gutter (40" Long)

3"

2"

Note: Attach end caps to gutter with solder or heat resistant sealant.

Width of Gutter

Note: Adjust height of poacher support to hold gutter just above hot plate camp stove, or other heat source.

Variable

6d Finishing Nails

Poacher Support (Make 2)

Poacher, Exploded View

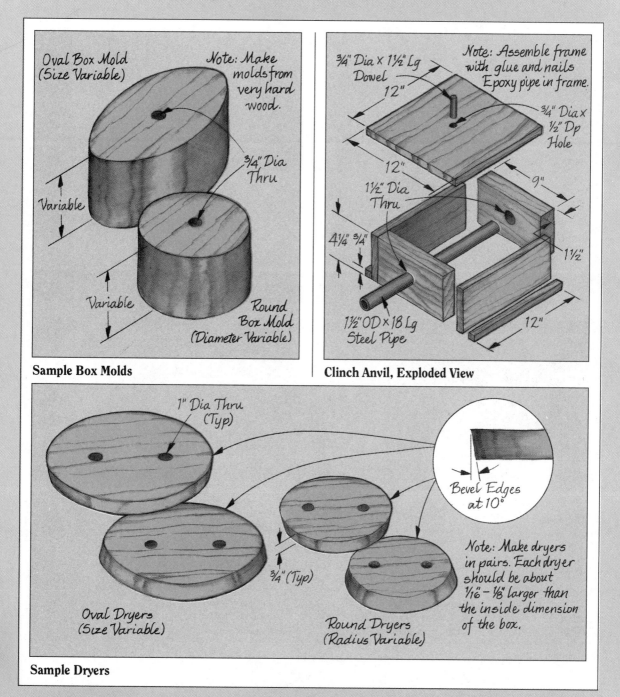

Oval Box Mold
(Size Variable)

Note: Make molds from very hard wood.

¾" Dia Thru

Variable

Variable

Round Box Mold
(Diameter Variable)

Sample Box Molds

¾" Dia × 1½" Lg Dowel

12"

Note: Assemble frame with glue and nails Epoxy pipe in frame.

¾" Dia × ½" Dp Hole

12"

1½" Dia Thru

9"

4¼" ¾"

1½"

1½" OD × 18 Lg Steel Pipe

12"

Clinch Anvil, Exploded View

1" Dia Thru (Typ)

Bevel Edges at 10°

¾" (Typ)

Note: Make dryers in pairs. Each dryer should be about ⅟₁₆ – ⅛ larger than the inside dimension of the box.

Oval Dryers
(Size Variable)

Round Dryers
(Radius Variable)

Sample Dryers

(Continued)

COUNTRY CRAFTSMAN'S
KNOW-HOW: MAKING BENTWOOD BOXES — *CONT.*

1 First, cut the thin stock that forms the sides, or *bands,* of the boxes. You can use almost any stock, but box makers traditionally used maple. Depending on the size of the box, these bands should be 3/64"–3/32" thick — the bigger the box, the thicker the band. Since most planers only plane to 1/8" thick, cut the bands with a table saw and a hollow-ground planer blade.

2 Where each band laps over itself, you must cut tapering fingers or *swallowtail joints* in the outside end. These swallowtails keep the band from splitting as the wood expands and contracts. Drill 3/64"-diameter holes for the tacks in the swallowtails — this makes the tacks easier to drive.

3 If you wish, chamfer the edges of the swallowtails with a bench knife. This is not necessary, but it does make a more attractive joint.

4 Taper the other end (opposite the swallowtails) with a belt sander. Use a thin scrap to press the inside surface of the wood against the abrasive belt, as shown. This protects your fingers from the heat generated by the friction of sanding. After making the taper, lightly sand the entire band to remove the saw marks.

5 Heat water in the poacher until it's as hot as you can get it without boiling. Let the band soak for 15–25 minutes, then take it out with a pair of tongs.

6 Before the wood cools, wrap it around the box mold as tightly as you can. If you're making an oval box, position the lapped portion of the band over the "side," where the elliptical curve is flattest. The swallowtails must end up on the outside, with the chamfers facing out.

(Continued)

COUNTRY CRAFTSMAN'S
KNOW-HOW: MAKING BENTWOOD BOXES — *CONT.*

7 Mark the edges of the band across the lapped portion, near the base of the swallowtails. Loosen the band *slightly* and take it off the mold.

8 Put the band back together, so the marks on the edges line up. Place the band over the end of the anvil, then drive tacks through the swallowtails. The tacks will clinch over when the points hit the metal anvil. This, in turn, will hold the band together.

9 Press the dryers into the assembled band as you'd press a cork in a bottle. Use two dryers for each band, one in the top and one in the bottom. Leave the dryers in place while the band dries.

10 If you want to make a lid for the box, bend the lid band around the box band in the same manner that you bent the box band around the mold. Mark the lapped edges, tack the lid band together, and put it back over the box band to dry.

11 Cut the box bottom and lid from stock ¼" thick or thicker. You may want to use a softwood for these parts — box makers traditionally used white pine. Cut the part a little large, then sand it to size on a disk sander. As you sand, bevel the edge at 5° by tilting the sander's worktable.

12 Remove the dryers from the band and test the fit of the bottom (or lid). Place the edge of the stock against the lapped portion of the band. Let it swing into place, as if you were closing a door. The fit should be snug, but not too tight — you shouldn't have to force it. If the fit is too tight, remove a little stock from the bottom with the disk sander.

13 Adjust the bottom so it's flush with the edge of the band. Drill ¹⁄₁₆"-diameter, ½"-deep holes, spaced every 2"–3" around the circumference, through the band and into the bottom. (If you're making an oval box, do *not* drill holes at the points of the ellipse — this will weaken the box.) Dip round toothpicks in glue and insert the ends into the holes. Let the glue dry, then trim the toothpick pegs flush with the band.

RATCHET CANDLESTAND

One disadvantage of candlelight is that as a candle burns, it becomes shorter and the light gets lower. It strikes the page of the book — or whatever you're trying to see — at a more oblique angle, making the object harder to see. Because of this, the country folks who used candles invented several ingenious devices to raise the candle easily from time to time.

One of their favorite devices was a *ratchet candlestand*. This is a small table mounted on a telescoping pedestal. The sliding portion of the pedestal — the *ratchet* — has several teeth that point down. These engage a hinged *pawl* on the stationary part. This simple mechanism allows you to raise the stand a few inches at a time without having to loosen or tighten anything. Simply lift the top until the pawl drops under the next tooth on the ratchet — the pawl will prevent the top from sliding back down. To lower the top, lift the ratchet and let it slide back down.

EXPLODED VIEW

BILL OF MATERIALS

WOODEN PARTS/*FINISHED DIMENSIONS*

A.	Top	$1/2$" x 14" x 14"
B.	Top trim (4)	$1/4$" x 1" x $14\frac{1}{2}$"
C.	Top mounting block	1" x 5" x 5"
D.	Ratchet	$3/4$" x $1\frac{1}{2}$" x $20\frac{3}{4}$"
E.	Legs (2)	$3/4$" x $1\frac{1}{2}$" x $21\frac{1}{2}$"
F.	Stretcher	$3/4$" x $1\frac{3}{4}$" x 10"
G.	Guide	$3/4$" x $1\frac{3}{4}$" x $5\frac{1}{4}$"
H.	Pawl	$3/4$" x $1\frac{3}{4}$" x $5\frac{5}{8}$"
J.	Dowel	$1/4$" dia. x $1\frac{3}{4}$"
K.	Base	$1\frac{3}{4}$" x $10\frac{3}{4}$" x $11\frac{1}{2}$"

HARDWARE

$7/8$" Square-cut headless brads (12–16)

PLAN OF PROCEDURE

1

If necessary, glue up stock to make the top. Then plane, rip, and cut the parts to the sizes shown in the Bill of Materials, except the top trim. Cut the trim 1/2"–1" longer than specified.

2

With a dado cutter or a table-mounted router, cut tenons in the ends of the rachet and legs, as shown in the *Ratchet Layout* and *Leg Layout*. Note that although the tenons are all the same thickness and width, their lengths differ.

3

Cut the mortises in the top mounting block, stretcher, guide, and base, as shown in the *Top Mounting Block Layout, Stretcher Layout, Guide Layout,* and *Base Layout*. As you cut, carefully fit the tenons on the ratchet and legs to the appropriate mortises. Note that all of these mortises go completely through the parts.

4

Chamfer the bottom edges of the top mounting block and the top edges of the base, as shown in the *Top Mounting Block Layout* and *Base Layout*.

5

Lay out the teeth on the ratchet, as shown in the *Ratchet Layout,* and cut them with a band saw or scroll saw. Sand the sawed edges.

LEG LAYOUT

RATCHET LAYOUT

TOP VIEW

SIDE VIEW

STRETCHER LAYOUT

TOP VIEW

SIDE VIEW

TOP MOUNTING BLOCK LAYOUT

TOP VIEW

SIDE VIEW

BASE LAYOUT

TOP VIEW

SIDE VIEW

GUIDE LAYOUT

PLAN OF PROCEDURE

6

Lay out the shape of the pawl, as shown in the *Pawl Layout,* and cut it on a band saw. First, cut the point with the pawl stock resting on its edge. Then cut the notch, with the stock resting on its face. Sand the sawed edges.

7

Lay out and cut the notches in the guide, and shown in the *Guide Layout.*

8

Finish sand all the parts of the stand. Position the top mounting block and the top so the grain of both parts are parallel, then glue them together.

9

When the glue dries, fit the trim around the circumference of the top. Miter the adjoining ends, as shown in the *Top View.* Attach the trim with brads or finishing nails and set the heads. Do *not* glue the trim to the top.

10

Drill a 5/16"-diameter hole in one of the legs, as shown in the *Leg Layout.* Then attach the pawl to the leg with the dowel. Glue the dowel in the pawl, but *not* in the leg. The pawl must pivot freely in the leg.

11

Dry assemble the stand and check the ratchet action. The ratchet should slide up and down easily, and the weight of the pawl should keep it against the ratchet teeth. Make any necessary adjustments. When you're satisfied the parts fit and work properly, disassemble the stand.

12

Assemble the legs, stretcher, and base with glue. Let the glue dry, then sand the leg tenons flush with the surfaces of the base and stretcher.

13

Assemble the ratchet and the top assembly, gluing the 1"-long tenon in the top mounting block.

14

Place the guide so the notches straddle the legs. Pivot the pawl so it points up, and insert the ratchet through the stretcher. Glue the ratchet in the guide. When the glue dries, file the bottom ratchet tenon flush with the bottom surface of the guide.

TOP VIEW   **SIDE VIEW**

PAWL LAYOUT

15

Once again, check the ratchet action to be sure it operates properly. Do any necessary touch-up sanding on the stand, then apply a finish.

5" (Typ)

4⅜" (Typ)

¼" (Typ)

14"

TOP VIEW

14½"

14"

¼"

1"

1"

½"

45° Chamfer (Typ)

5"

¾"

10"

¾"

¼" Dia × 1¾" Lg Dowel

19"

21½"

1½" (Typ)

¾"

¾"

½" Wd × 1¼" Lg Mortise (Typ)

5¼"

4¼"

1¾"

1¾"

11½"

10¾"

FRONT VIEW   **SIDE VIEW**

MEAL BIN FILING CABINET

Country cooks often stored their flour in a meal bin. They mixed bread dough and let it rise in a similar bin called a "dough box." Both the meal bin and dough box were wooden chests with legs. When they weren't being used to make bread, these bins and boxes provided extra work surfaces. The lids were often split so the cook could move the items on them to one side, then open the other side of the lid.

As more and more Americans bought their bread from bakers and grocery stores, meal bins and dough boxes became less common. However, the general design remained useful. Bins and boxes were converted to store linens, records, wine, and many other small items.

Outwardly, this meal bin is a copy of an old country piece. However, the inside has been adapted to hold hanging letter-size files. These are suspended from pairs of metal rods that run side to side in the bin. Like all traditional meal bins, the lid is split. You can reach the files by raising one or the other half-lid. If you've placed something on top of the bin, simply move it aside to the portion of the lid you don't need to open.

EXPLODED VIEW

BILL OF MATERIALS

WOODEN PARTS/*FINISHED DIMENSIONS*

A.	Sides (2)	$3/4$" x 14" x $31^{3}/4$"
B.	Front/back (2)	$3/4$" x 12" x 54"
C.	Bin bottom	$3/4$" x $12^{1}/2$" x $53^{1}/4$"
D.	Bottom shelf	$3/4$" x 14" x $53^{1}/4$"
E.	Lids (2)	$3/4$" x $14^{1}/16$" x $26^{1}/8$"
F.	Front outside moldings (2)	$7/8$" x 1" x $27^{7}/8$"
G.	Right/left outside moldings (2)	$7/8$" x 1" x $14^{15}/16$"
H.	Right/left inside moldings (2)	$3/4$" x $7/8$" x $14^{1}/16$"
J.	Pegs (8)	$5/16$" x $5/16$" x $1^{1}/4$"
K.	Caps (12)	$3/8$" x $1/2$" x $1^{1}/4$"

HARDWARE

#12 x $1^{1}/4$" Roundhead wood screws and flat washers (12)

$1^{1}/2$" x 2" Butt hinges and mounting screws (2 pairs)

$1/4$"-dia. x $13^{1}/4$" Metal rods (8)

6d Square-cut nails (24–30)

PLAN OF PROCEDURE

1

Plane, rip, and cut the parts to the sizes shown in the Bill of Materials, except the moldings. Cut these to the proper thickness and width, but wait to cut them to length. They must be fitted to the lids.

2

Cut 3/4"-wide, 3/8"-deep dadoes in the sides, as shown in the *Side Layout*.

3

Lay out and cut the shapes of the sides. Sand the sawed edges.

4

Drill 1/4"-diameter, 3/8"-deep holes in the *inside* face of the front and back, as shown in the *Front/Back Layout/Inside View*. These holes will hold the file suspension rods.

5

Finish sand the sides, front, back, bin bottom, and bottom shelf. Glue the sides, bin bottom, and shelf together. Reinforce the joints with nails.

6

Check that the assembly is square. Glue the back to the bin bottom, then nail the back to the sides. Do *not* glue the back to the sides.

7

Insert the metal rods into the holes in the back. Glue the front to the bin bottom, inserting the rods into the holes in the front. Nail the front to the sides.

8

Sand the ends of the front and back flush with the sides. Set the heads of all the nails and cover them with putty.

OUTSIDE MOLDING PROFILE

SIDE LAYOUT

SIDE VIEW

INSIDE VIEW
FRONT/BACK LAYOUT

54"
1¼"   12¼"   12 ¼   12¼"   12¼"   1¼"
¾"   1"   ¾"
¼" Dia × ⅜" Dp
Hole (Typ)
1½"
12"

⅞"   26⅛"   ⅞"   ¾"
¼" Dia
Metal
Rod
12½"   14"
⅞"
¾"
45° Miter   **TOP VIEW**

⅞"   55 13/16"   ⅞"
54"
1/16" Gap   ¾"
⅞"   53¼"
¾" Wd × ⅜" Dp
Dado
¾" (Typ)
FRONT VIEW

PLAN OF PROCEDURE

9

Chamfer the lower corner of the outside molding stock, as shown in the *Outside Molding Profile*.

10

Miter the moldings to fit the lids and make 3/8"-wide, 3/4"-deep, 1¼"-long mortises in the right and left moldings, as shown in the *Side View* and *Right/Left Molding Joinery Detail*. Cut a 3/16"-wide, 1/2"-long slot at the base of each mortise.

11

Attach the right and left moldings to the ends of the lids with #12 x 1¼" roundhead wood screws and flat washers, as shown in the *Right/Left Molding Joinery Detail*. Do *not* glue the right or left moldings to the lids. Glue caps in the mortises to hide the screw heads. Sand the caps flush with the edges of the moldings.

12

Glue the front outside molding to the lids.

13

Round the bottom portion of the pegs, as shown in the *Peg Detail*. Drill four 5/16"-diameter, 1¼"-deep holes through each of the front moldings, as shown in the *Front View*. Drive a peg into each hole.

14

Finish sand the lids. Cut mortises for the hinges and mount the lids to the bin.

15

Remove the lids from the bin and the hinges from the lids. Do any necessary touch-up sanding, then apply a finish to the completed meal bin. When the finish dries, reassemble the lids and bin.

RIGHT/LEFT MOLDING JOINERY DETAIL

PEG DETAIL
(Make from *very* hard wood.)

SECTION A

SECTION B

SECTION C

SHAKER CANDLESTAND

Small, portable pieces of country furniture, particularly stools and tables, often had just three legs. The reason was threefold: First, a tripod always sets solidly, no matter how uneven the floor or ground might be. Second, the economy of legs makes the piece lighter and easier to move. Finally, when not in use, a three-legged piece can be conveniently stored in an out-of-the-way corner.

The tripod design is ancient — archaeologists have found three-legged furniture in Egyptian tombs dating back to the third millennium B.C. But it became particularly popular in the late eighteenth and early nineteenth centuries. Craftsmen on both sides of the Atlantic turned out thousands of *pedestal tables* — small tables with a turned central support and three spreading feet. These small stands were used for everything from serving wine to supports for lamps and candles. Perhaps the best remembered are the "candlestands" made by United Society of Believers in Christ's Second Appearing — also known as the Shakers.

Shaker candlestands were without decoration, since the beliefs of the religious order forbid unnecessary ornament. Nonetheless, the simple, Spartan lines were often strikingly elegant. Because of this, many historians and collectors consider these pedestal tables to be among the best examples of American country furniture. The crescent legs and urn-shaped pedestal of this small table is typical of many that were made in the Shaker furniture shops of New Lebanon, New York, during the first half of the nineteenth century.

EXPLODED VIEW

BILL OF MATERIALS

WOODEN PARTS/*FINISHED DIMENSIONS*

A. Tabletop   20" dia. x $^3/_4$"
B. Brace $^3/_4$" x 5" x 13$^3/_4$"
C. Pedestal   2$^3/_4$" dia. x 18$^3/_4$"
D. Feet (3) $^3/_4$" x 5" x 14$^3/_4$"
E. Wedges (2) $^5/_{32}$" x $^3/_4$" x 1"

HARDWARE

#8 x 1$^1/_4$" Flathead wood screws (4)

PLAN OF PROCEDURE

1

If necessary, glue up wide stock for the top. Plane, rip, and cut the parts to the sizes shown in the Bill of Materials, except the pedestal. Make this about 1/4" thicker and wider than shown. Cut the wedges from a piece of very hard wood, such as maple or hickory, tapering them from 5/32" at the top to about 1/16" at the bottom.

2

Turn the pedestal stock to a simple cylinder, 23/4" in diameter. Then turn the bottom portion of the cylinder to 21/2" in diameter, creating a 1/8" step, as shown in the *Pedestal Layout*. Finish sand the 21/2"-diameter portion.

3

Rout three 3/4"-wide, 5/8"-deep, 31/2"-long dovetail grooves in the bottom end of the cylinder, as shown in *Section B;* see Routing Dovetail Mortises and Tenons on page 146.

4

Enlarge the foot pattern, as shown in the *Side View,* and trace it on the stock. Cut the tenon faces *only* — the flat ends that attach to the pedestal.

5

Rout dovetail tenons in the top ends of the legs, fitting them to the mortises.

6

Turn the upper half of the pedestal and finish sand the completed pedestal on the lathe. Do *not* sand the bottom 21/2"-diameter portion of the pedestal, where the feet will be attached.

7

Mount the top on the lathe, making sure the end grain curves up, as shown in the *Top Section.* Turn the top, as shown in *Section C.* If your lathe doesn't have a 20" swing, rout the recess in the top with a core-box bit. Shape the bottom edge with a quarter-round bit. Finish sand the top.

Round Over Edge
1/8" 3/4"
1" Rad

SECTION C

3/4"
1/2"
21/2" Dia
3/4"
5/8"
120° (Typ)

SECTION B

Growth Rings Must Curve Up
Wedge (2 Req)
Top
Brace
Pedestal

TOP SECTION

PLAN OF PROCEDURE

8

Chamfer the edges of the brace at 15°, as shown in the *Brace Detail*.

9

Drill a 1"-diameter round mortise in the brace to attach it to the pedestal.

10

Cut two 1/8"-wide, 3/4"-deep slots in the tenon at the top of the pedestal.

11

Cut the shape of the feet and sand the sawed edges.

12

Finish sand the feet and brace. Glue the pedestal to the brace and drive the wedges into the slots at the top of the tenon.

Note: The wedges and slots must be *perpendicular* to the wood grain of the brace.

13

Glue the feet to the pedestal. Sand or file the bottom of the pedestal and the dovetail tenons clean and flush.

14

Turn the top upside down, and position the brace on it. Fasten the brace to the top with flathead wood screws, countersinking the heads. Do *not* glue the brace to the top.

15

Using a file, round over the edges of the feet, as shown in *Section A*. Do any necessary touch up sanding to the table, and apply a finish.

WEDGE DETAIL

BRACE DETAIL

SECTION A

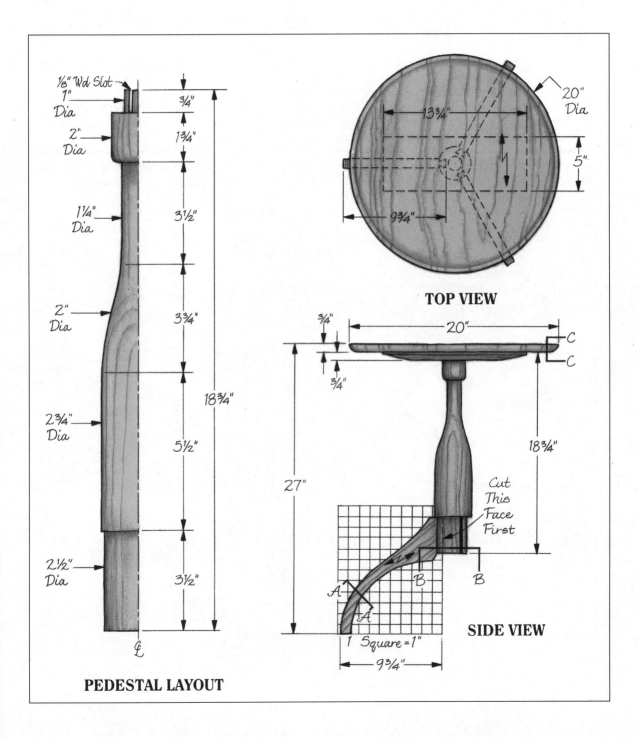

TOP VIEW

SIDE VIEW

1 Square = 1"

PEDESTAL LAYOUT

COUNTRY CRAFTSMAN'S KNOW-HOW: ROUTING DOVETAIL MORTISES AND TENONS

Country craftsmen often used dovetail mortises and tenons. These were also called sliding dovetails (because the parts slid together) or, less commonly, French dovetails (for reasons that are lost to history). They cut these joints with a small saw and chisel — same tools they employed for making dovetails in drawers and boxes. You can duplicate these joints with a router and a dovetail bit.

The technique for routing a dovetail mortise and tenon in square stock is straightforward: Rout the mortise in the same manner you might rout a dado or groove, but use a dovetail bit instead of a straight bit. Then rout the tenon with the same dovetail bit.

The technique for routing these joints in round stock is more involved. You need a way to hold the round stock while you rout it and a way to guide the router. Some craftsmen use their lathe to hold the stock, then make a routing jig that mounts on the lathe. Others mount the stock in a V-block, then cut the mortises with an overhead routing jig, as shown in the drawings.

V-block

Overhead Routing Jig

1 Before mounting the stock, carefully measure where you want to cut the mortises and mark them on the end of the stock — several straight lines through the diameter. Place the stock loosely in the V-block, and place the jig on your workbench. Rest a try square on the bench near the marked end, and turn the stock until the first mortise line is parallel to the edge of the square. Tighten the straps.

2 With a dovetail bit in the router, adjust the overhead routing jig to the proper height. Clamp a straightedge under the jig to guide the stock and clamp a block to the straightedge to stop the cut when the mortise is the proper length. Turn the router on and feed the stock slowly, keeping the V-block pressed against the straightedge. Repeat for each mortise.

3 When using an overhead routing jig, observe the same precautions that apply to a table-mounted router. Place the straightedge so the rotation of the bit helps to keep the V-block against the fence as you cut.

(Continued)

COUNTRY CRAFTSMAN'S
KNOW-HOW: ROUTING DOVETAIL MORTISES AND TENONS — *CONT.*

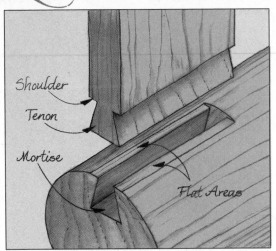

4 A dovetail tenon, like any other tenon, has flat shoulders. Because of this, you must cut flat areas on the cylinder, on either side of the dovetail mortises. Otherwise, the tenons won't mate properly with the mortises.

5 Cut these flats with the same setup used to make the mortise, but mount a straight bit in the router instead of a dovetail bit. After routing the flats, square them off with a chisel, if necessary.

6 Rout the dovetail tenons with a table-mounted router and the *same* dovetail bit used to make the mortises. Clamp a straightedge to the table to guide the stock. Cut each tenon in two passes — rout one face of the stock, then turn it over and rout the other.

7 Slide the tenon into the mortise to test the fit. It should be snug, but not too tight. You may have to make several practice tenons until you cut one that fits just right.

PLANTATION DESK

Although well-to-do folks had desks as early as the sixteenth century, desks for country folks are a fairly recent development. Until the beginning of the nineteenth century, the typical country family could keep all of its important papers, letters, writing materials — its entire *library* — in a small box. The first country desks were, in fact, boxes like the Lap Desk and Keeping Box.

However, education was nurtured and encouraged in the years following the American Revolution. The public quickly became more literate, and families outgrew their desk boxes. At first, they simply made these boxes larger and put legs on them. Then they began to add shelves and dividers to help organize their paperwork.

A popular early desk was a simple cupboard placed on a table. Country folks favored this design because it was practical and easy to build. Often, they simply joined two furniture pieces they already had on hand — a worktable and a wall cupboard. They sometimes added either a drawer or a compartment beneath the tabletop to provide extra storage space. Inside the cupboard, they added vertical dividers between the shelves, creating pigeonholes.

This marriage between a table and a cupboard was especially common in the rural South — Kentucky, Tennessee, and Georgia. For that reason, we remember it as a "plantation" desk.

**DESK
EXPLODED VIEW**

BILL OF MATERIALS

WOODEN PARTS/*FINISHED DIMENSIONS*

Desk

A.	Desk top	$3/4" \times 15^3/4" \times 38"$
B.	Lids (2)	$3/4" \times 16^1/4" \times 15^7/16"$
C.	Breadboards (4)	$3/4" \times 1^1/4" \times 16^1/4"$
D.	Breadboard caps (12)	$3/8" \times 1/2" \times 1^1/4"$
E.	Foot molding (total)	$1" \times 1" \times 68"$
F.	Legs (4)	$1^3/4" \times 1^3/4" \times 28^1/4"$
G.	Front/back aprons (2)	$7/8" \times 5" \times 34"$
H.	Side aprons (2)	$7/8" \times 5" \times 29"$
J.	Desk bottom	$1/2" \times 29^1/4" \times 34^1/4"$
K.	Small glue blocks (28)	$3/4" \times 3/4" \times 2^1/2"$
L.	Front-to-back divider	$3/4" \times 3^3/4" \times 29^1/4"$
M.	Side-to-side divider	$3/4" \times 3^3/4" \times 16^5/8"$
N.	Stiffeners (2)	$7/8" \times 3^3/4" \times 27^1/2"$
P.	Small pegs (16)	$5/16" \times 5/16" \times 1"*$

Cabinet

P.	Small pegs (4)	$1/4" \times 1/4" \times 1"*$
Q.	Sides (2)	$3/4" \times 12^1/4" \times 39"$
R.	Top/shelves (4)	$3/4" \times 11^3/4" \times 35^1/4"$
S.	Narrow backboard	$1/2" \times 6^3/4" \times 39"$
T.	Wide backboards (4)	$1/2" \times 7^1/2" \times 39"$
U.	Center shelf support	$3/4" \times 11^3/4" \times 23^5/8"$
V.	Pigeonhole dividers (8)	$1/2" \times 5^3/4" \times 11^3/4"$
W.	Adjustable shelves (2–4)	$3/4" \times 11^3/4" \times 16^3/4"$
X.	Face frame stiles (2)	$3/4" \times 4" \times 39"$

**CABINET
EXPLODED VIEW**

Y.	Face frame top rail	$3/4$" x 4" x 30"
Z.	Face bottom rail	$3/4$" x 3" x 30"
AA.	Crown molding (total)	$3/4$" x $35/8$" x 74"
BB.	Large glue blocks (14)	$17/16$" x $17/16$" x $21/2$"
CC.	Door stiles (4)	$3/4$" x 3" x $317/8$"
DD.	Top/middle door rails (4)	$3/4$" x 3" x $101/4$"
EE.	Bottom door rails (2)	$3/4$" x 4" x $101/4$"
FF.	Door panels (4)	$1/2$" x $87/8$" x $115/8$"
GG.	Large pegs (12)	$3/8$" x $3/8$" x $11/4$"*
HH.	Shelving support pegs (8–16)	$1/4$" dia. x $3/4$"

HARDWARE

6d Square-cut nails ($1/4$ lb.)
4d Finishing nails ($1/4$ lb.)
#12 x $11/2$" Roundhead wood screws and washers (12)
#10 x $11/4$" Flathead wood screws (6)
$11/2$" x 2" Butt hinges and mounting screws (4 pairs)
Door latch
Door catch
Door pull

*Make the pegs at least this long, then trim them after
you install them.*

PLAN OF PROCEDURE

To help this project progress smoothly, build it in two parts — desk first, then the cabinet.

Making the Desk

1

Plane, rip, and cut the desk parts to the sizes shown in the Bill of Materials, except the foot molding and small glue blocks. Plane and rip the molding and glue block stock to the proper thickness and width, but don't cut them to length or shape them yet.

2

Cut the joinery needed to assemble the desk:

- ³/₄"-wide, ³/₈"-deep dadoes in the front-to-back divider and right stiffener, as shown in *Section A*
- ³/₈"-wide, ³/₄"-long tenons on the ends of the aprons, as shown in the *Leg-to-Apron Joinery Detail*
- ³/₈"-wide, ³/₄"-deep, 4"-long mortises in the inside surfaces of the legs, as shown in *Section A*
- ³/₈"-wide, ³/₄"-deep, 1¹/₄"-long mortises in the outside edges of the breadboards, as shown in the *Breadboard Joinery Detail* and *Breadboard Layout/ Side View*

SIDE VIEW

FRONT VIEW

PLAN OF PROCEDURE

3

Notch the top and bottom edges of the apron tenons to fit in the leg mortises.

4

Drill screw pockets in the stiffeners and back aprons, as shown in *Section A*.

BREADBOARD LAYOUT/SIDE VIEW

SECTION A

5

Cut 2¹/₂° tapers in the *inside* surfaces of the legs, as shown in the *Leg Layout*.

6

Attach the breadboards to the lids with #12 x 1¹/₂" roundhead wood screws and flat washers, as shown in the *Breadboard Joinery Detail*. Glue breadboard caps in the breadboard mortises to hide the screw heads.

7

Finish sand the breadboard assemblies and the other parts of the desk. Assemble the legs and aprons with glue.

8

Round the bottom portion of the small pegs, as shown in the *Small Peg Detail*.

SECTION B

SECTION C

SECTION D

5/16" 5/16"

B   B

C   C

D   D

1"

SMALL PEG DETAIL

(Make from *very* hard wood.)

3/16" Wd × 1/2" Lg Slot

1¹/₄"

3/4"

1/2"

3/8"

3/8" Wd × 3/4" Dp × 1¹/₄" Lg Mortise

#12 × 1¹/₂" RHWS & Washer

1¹/₄"

BREADBOARD JOINERY DETAIL

1/2" 3/8"

1/2"

4"

5"

3/4"

7/8"

1³/₄

1³/₄

1/2"

LEG-TO-APRON JOINERY DETAIL

1³/₄"

3/8"

1/2"

4"

5"

1³/₄"

1/2"

28¹/₄"

23¹/₄"

2¹/₂°

1"

LEG LAYOUT

PLAN OF PROCEDURE

9

Drill two 5/16"-diameter, 1"-deep holes through each mortise-and-tenon joint that holds the legs to the aprons. Drive small pegs into each of the holes.

10

Attach the front-to-back divider to the front and back aprons with glue and square-cut nails. Make sure the dado is toward the front of the desk, and it faces right. Set the heads of the nails.

11

Glue the stiffeners to the side aprons. Make sure the screw pockets face up and toward the inside. Also make sure the stiffener with the dado is on the right, and that the dado is directly opposite the dado in the front-to-back divider.

12

Rip a 45° bevel in the small glue block stock, as shown in the *Small Glue Block Detail*, then cut the blocks to length.

13

Turn the desk upside down and position it over the desk top. Attach the desk top to the desk with #10 x 1¼" flathead wood screws, driving the screws through the screw pockets and into the underside of the top.

14

Cut a notch in each corner of the bottom, as shown in the *Desk Bottom Notch Detail,* to fit around the legs.

15

While the desk is still upside down, put the bottom in place. Attach small glue blocks to the aprons to secure the bottom. Tack the bottom to the front-to-back divider with finishing nails. Set the nails.

16

Turn the desk right side up and install the side-to-side divider. Set it in the dadoes in the right stiffener and front-to-back divider, but do *not* glue it in place. Leave it loose, so that you can remove it if you need to.

17

Cut hinge mortises in the lids and desk top. Mount the lids on the desk.

DESK BOTTOM NOTCH DETAIL

SMALL GLUE BLOCK DETAIL

SCREW POCKET DETAIL

18

Rip a bevel in one corner of the foot molding stock, as shown in the *Foot Molding Profile.* Then set the stock aside — *don't* attach it to the desk yet.

Making the Cabinet

Note: The pigeonholes and divider shown in the drawings are optional. If you wish, you can make a simpler cabinet with 2–3 adjustable shelves, as shown in the lead photograph.

19

Plane, rip, and cut the cabinet parts to the sizes shown in the Bill of Materials, except for the crown molding, large glue blocks, and pegs. Plane and rip the molding and glue block stock to the proper thickness and width, but don't cut them to length or shape them yet. Cut large and small pegs 1/4"– 1/2" longer than specified.

20

Cut the joinery needed to assemble the case:

■ 3/4"-wide, 3/8"-deep dadoes in the inside surfaces of the sides, as shown in the *Side Layout,* to hold the bottom, middle, and upper shelves

■ 3/4"-wide, 3/8"-deep dadoes in the inside surface of the top and the top surface of the upper shelf, to hold the center shelf divider, as shown in the *Cabinet/ Front View*

SIDE LAYOUT

FOOT MOLDING PROFILE

PLAN OF PROCEDURE

- 1/2"-wide, 3/8"-deep rabbets in the back edges of the sides, to hold the backboards
- 1/2"-wide, 1/4"-deep dadoes in the upper, middle, and bottom shelves to hold the pigeonhole dividers
- 3/8"-wide, 3/8"-deep dadoes in the inside surfaces of the sides to hold the top
- 3/8"-wide, 3/8"-deep rabbet in each end of the top
- 3/8"-wide, 1/4"-deep rabbets in the edges of the backboards, as shown in the *Top View*
- 1/4"-wide, 1"-long tenons in the ends of the face frame rails, as shown in the *Face Frame Joinery Detail*
- 1/4"-wide, 1"-deep, 2"-long mortises in the inside edges of the face frame stiles, near the bottom end, as shown in the *Face Frame Joinery Detail*
- 1/4"-wide, 1"-deep, 3"-long mortise in the inside edges of the face frame stiles near the top end

21

Notch the top and bottom edges of the face frame tenons to fit the mortises.

22

Drill 1/4"-diameter, 1/2"-deep holes in the inside surfaces of the sides, as shown in the *Side Layout*. Drill 1/4"-diameter holes following the same layout completely through the long divider. These holes will hold pegs to support the adjustable shelves.

23

Finish sand the parts of the cabinet you've made so far. Assemble the sides, shelves, top, center shelf support, and pigeonhole dividers with glue.

24

Attach the backboards to the case with finishing nails. Set the heads of the nails.

**FACE FRAME
JOINERY DETAIL**

25

Assemble the face frame rails and stiles with glue.

26

Round the bottom portion of the small pegs, as shown in the *Small Peg Detail.*

27

Drill a 5/16"-diameter hole through each mortise-and-tenon joint that holds the rails to the stiles. Drive small pegs into each of the holes. Cut the pegs off flush with the back surface of the face frame.

**CABINET/FRONT VIEW
(WITHOUT DOORS AND MOLDING)**

PLAN OF PROCEDURE

28

Attach the face frame to the case with glue and square-cut nails. Set the nails.

29

Bevel the edges of the crown molding and large glue block stock, as shown in the *Crown Molding Detail* and *Large Glue Block Detail*.

CROWN MOLDING DETAIL

TOP VIEW

LARGE GLUE BLOCK DETAIL

30

Compound-miter the crown molding to fit the top of the case. Attach the molding with glue, large glue blocks, and finishing nails. Set the nails.

31

Cut the joinery needed to assemble the door, as shown in the *Door Assembly Detail:*

- ³/8"-wide, ³/8"-deep rabbets in the outside edges of the inside door stiles, so the doors will overlap
- ¹/4"-wide, ³/8"-deep grooves in the inside edges of the rails and stiles
- ¹/4"-wide, 1"-deep, 2¹/4"-long mortises in the upper ends and the middle of the stiles
- ¹/4"-wide, 1"-deep, 3¹/4"-long mortises in the lower ends of the stiles
- ¹/4"-wide, 1"-long tenons in the ends of the rails

32

Notch the tenons, as shown in the *Door Assembly Detail,* to fit the mortises.

33

Bevel the edges of the panels at 15°, as shown in the *Door/Panel Section.*

DOOR ASSEMBLY DETAIL

PLAN OF PROCEDURE

34

Finish sand the parts of the door. Assemble the rails and stiles with glue. Insert the panels in the grooves, beveled side facing in, but do *not* glue the panels in place. Let them float in the grooves.

35

Round the bottom portion of the large pegs, as shown in the *Large Peg Detail.*

LARGE PEG DETAIL

(Make from *very* hard wood.)

36

Drill a 3/8"-diameter hole through each mortise-and-tenon joint in the doors, then drive the pegs through the holes from the outside. Cut the pegs off flush with the inside surface of the door frame.

37

Cut hinge mortises in the door frames and face frame, then mount the doors in the case.

38

Install the door catch on the inside of the cabinet, and the door latch and pull on the outside of the door frame.

Finishing Up

39

Place the completed cabinet on the desk. Miter the foot molding to fit around the base of the cabinet and attach it to the desk top with glue and finishing nails. Set the nails. Do *not* attach the molding to the cabinet itself.

40

Remove the cabinet from the desk. Disassemble the doors from the cabinet and the lids from the desk. Remove all hardware and set it aside.

DOOR/PANEL SECTION

41

Do any necessary touch-up sanding, then apply a finish to *all* sides — inside and outside, top and bottom — of the desk, cabinet, lids, and doors.

42

Reassemble the completed project. Do *not* attach the cabinet to the desk, just let it sit inside the moldings. This will allow you to disassemble the components easily when you need to move or repair the project.

DOOR LAYOUT

COUNTRY CRAFTSMAN'S KNOW-HOW: ATTACHING MOLDINGS

Country furniture is often decorated with *applied* moldings — narrow, molded strips of wood attached to the main assembly.

1 When the wood grain of the surface is parallel to the grain of the molding, you can simply glue the molding in place.

2 When the wood grain of the surface is perpendicular to that of the molding, attach the molding with wire brads or finishing nails. Brads and nails bend slightly as the wood expands and contracts beneath the molding. The molding remains in place, but it doesn't restrict the movement of the wood.

3 Set the heads of the finishing nails slightly below the surface of the molding, and cover the heads with wood putty, such as Durham's Water Putty. If you wish, mix the putty with stain or aniline dye to match the finish you will put on the project.

4 Never glue a molding to a surface so wood grains are perpendicular. The molding will buckle or the board to which it's applied will cup. Eventually, the glue bond will break and the molding will fall off.

5 Sometimes glue and finishing nails aren't enough. To help reinforce large moldings that angle out from the top of a piece, such as crown moldings and bed moldings, use glue blocks in addition to glue and nails.

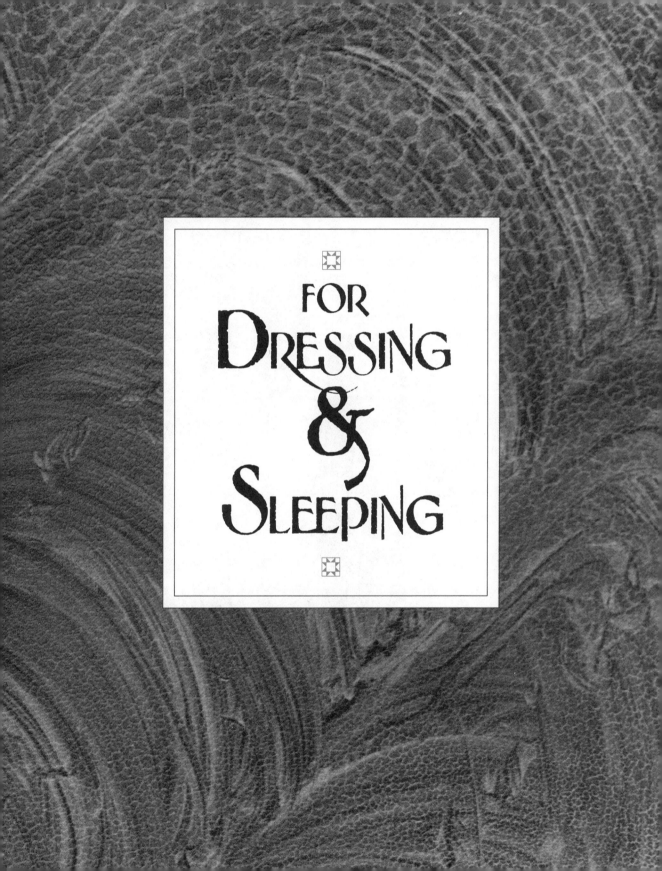

FOR DRESSING & SLEEPING

KEEPING BOX

Early American households used dozens of chests and boxes of all sizes and shapes for storage. Sometimes a family member would make a small or medium-size box to keep his or her personal treasures — documents, jewelry, keepsakes, and so on. These were called, appropriately enough, keeping boxes.

While most storage boxes were constructed simply, craftsmen usually put forth extra effort when building keeping boxes. Most of these boxes were very sturdy — the keeping box shown is made from thick boards (for its size), which are dovetailed together. They were secure — this one has a metal latch and lock. Many were very stylish and ornately decorated. Craftsmen painted, carved, inlaid, or laced the surfaces with veneers and moldings. The extra pains that they took when making the boxes attested to the value of the things stored in them.

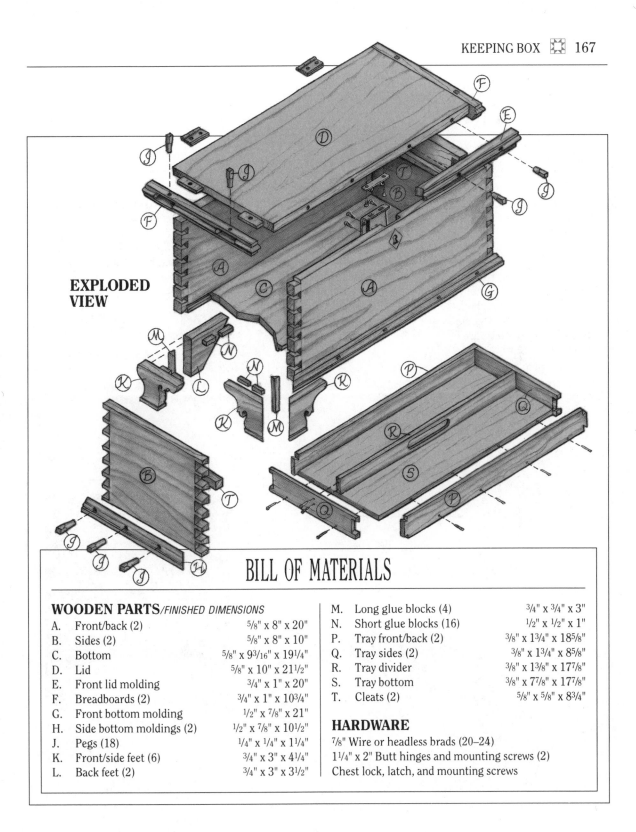

EXPLODED VIEW

BILL OF MATERIALS

WOODEN PARTS/*FINISHED DIMENSIONS*

A.	Front/back (2)	5/8" x 8" x 20"
B.	Sides (2)	5/8" x 8" x 10"
C.	Bottom	5/8" x 9³/₁₆" x 19¹/₄"
D.	Lid	5/8" x 10" x 21¹/₂"
E.	Front lid molding	3/4" x 1" x 20"
F.	Breadboards (2)	3/4" x 1" x 10³/₄"
G.	Front bottom molding	¹/₂" x ⁷/₈" x 21"
H.	Side bottom moldings (2)	¹/₂" x ⁷/₈" x 10¹/₂"
J.	Pegs (18)	¹/₄" x ¹/₄" x 1¹/₄"
K.	Front/side feet (6)	3/4" x 3" x 4¹/₄"
L.	Back feet (2)	3/4" x 3" x 3¹/₂"

M.	Long glue blocks (4)	3/4" x 3/4" x 3"
N.	Short glue blocks (16)	¹/₂" x ¹/₂" x 1"
P.	Tray front/back (2)	3/8" x 1³/₄" x 18⁵/₈"
Q.	Tray sides (2)	3/8" x 1³/₄" x 8⁵/₈"
R.	Tray divider	3/8" x 1³/₈" x 17⁷/₈"
S.	Tray bottom	3/8" x 7⁷/₈" x 17⁷/₈"
T.	Cleats (2)	5/8" x 5/8" x 8³/₄"

HARDWARE

⁷/₈" Wire or headless brads (20–24)
1¹/₄" x 2" Butt hinges and mounting screws (2)
Chest lock, latch, and mounting screws

PLAN OF PROCEDURE

1

Plane, rip, and cut the parts to the sizes shown in the Bill of Materials, except the moldings, breadboards, and feet. Plane and rip the top molding, breadboards, and feet to the proper thickness and width, but don't cut them to length yet. Plane stock to the proper thickness for the bottom moldings, but don't cut them to width or length.

2

Cut ¼"-wide, ¼"-deep double-blind grooves inside the front, back, and sides, near the bottom edge, as shown in the *Bottom Groove Layout*. Cut a ¼"-wide, ¼"-deep rabbet in the edges and ends of the bottom, as shown in the *Bottom-to-Box Joinery Detail*.

3

Lay out and cut the dovetails and pins in the front, back, and sides, as shown in the *Box Dovetail Detail*. Dry assemble the front, back, sides, and bottom.

4

Mark the lid and the back for the hinge mortises. Take the box apart and cut these mortises in both parts.

3/8"

1/4"

1/4"

¼" Wd × ¼" Dp
Double Blind Groove

BOTTOM GROOVE LAYOUT

Side or End
Gap (Sides Only)
Bottom

1/4"

5/8"

1/4"

**BOTTOM-TO-BOX
JOINERY DETAIL**

10 ¾"

10"

11 5/8"

10 7/16"

SIDE VIEW

TOP VIEW

1¼" × 2" Butt Hinges (Typ)

Hardwood Peg

1"
2"
4"
2"
1"
¾"
10"
10¾"
20"
21½"

FRONT VIEW

Hardwood Pegs

5/8"
1"
3/4"
3/8"
5/8"
8"
3"

Painted Escutcheon

½"
4¼"
21"
2½"
1"
¾"

Glue Block (Typ)

PLAN OF PROCEDURE

5

Cut a mortise in the inside surface of the front for the chest lock, as shown in the *Lock Mortise Detail*. Also, drill a keyhole. The size of the lock mortise and the location of the keyhole will depend on the make of the lock.

6

Finish sand the front, back, sides, and bottom. Assemble the front, back, and sides with glue. Put the bottom in the box, but don't glue it — let it float in the grooves. After the glue dries, sand the joints clean and flush.

7

Temporarily hinge the lid to the box. Mark the location of the latch, then remove the lid from the box. Cut the mortise for the latch.

8

Cut ¼"-wide, ¾"-long tenons in the ends of the lid. Cut the tenon so it runs the entire width of each end, then notch these tenons, as shown in the *Lid Tenon Detail*, to make two split tenons in each end of the lid. Each tenon should be 2" long.

LOCK MORTISE DETAIL

LID TENON DETAIL

BOX DOVETAIL DETAIL

9

Cut the front lid molding and the breadboards to fit the lid.

10

Cut ¼"-wide, 2"-long mortises in the breadboards to fit over the lid tenons.

PEG DETAIL
(Make from very hard wood.)

▨ **SECTION A**

◍ **SECTION B**

◍ **SECTION C**

11

Finish sand the lid. Glue the front lid molding and the breadboards to the lid. (Apply glue along the edge of the lid and to the tenons, but not to the ends.)

12

When the glue dries, sand molding and breadboard joints clean and flush. Shape the front lid molding and the breadboards as shown in the *Lid Molding Profile.*

BOTTOM MOLDING PROFILE

¼" Rad Bead
½" Ogee
⅞"
½"

LID MOLDING PROFILE

½" Rad Bead
⅛"
½"
1"
½" Ogee

13

Shape the edge of the bottom molding stock, as shown in the *Bottom Molding Profile.* Rip the bottom molding from the stock.

14

Finish sand the bottom molding and cut it to length, mitering the adjoining ends at 45°. Glue the molding to the box.

15

Round the bottom portion of the pegs, as shown in the *Peg Detail.*

BOTTOM DETAIL

¾" × ¾" × 3" Glue Block (Typ)
½" × ½" × 1" Glue Blocks (Typ)
¾"
3½"
¾"
4¼"
4¼"
4¼"
¾"

PLAN OF PROCEDURE

16

Drill a ¼"-diameter hole through each mortise-and-tenon joint in the breadboards, then drive pegs through the holes from the top. Cut the pegs flush with the bottom surface of the breadboards.

17

Drill ¼"-diameter, 1¼"-deep holes through the front lid molding and the bottom moldings, where shown in the *Front View* and *Side View*. Drive pegs in the holes.

18

Cut the back feet to length, then shape the remaining stock to the profile shown in the *Foot Pattern*.

19

Cut the front and side feet to length, mitering the adjoining ends.

20

Lay out the front and side bracket feet on the stock, as shown in the *Foot Pattern*, then cut the shapes of the feet. Sand the sawed edges.

21

Assemble the feet with glue, reinforcing the joints with the long glue blocks. When the glue dries, sand the joints clean and flush. Finish sand the outside surfaces of the feet.

22

Glue the feet to the box, and reinforce the joints with short glue blocks.

23

Cut the dovetails that join the front, back, and sides of the tray, as shown in the *Tray Dovetail Detail*.

1 Square = ¼"

FOOT PATTERN

TRAY DOVETAIL DETAIL

24

Make the handle cutout in the tray divider. Sand the sawed edges.

25

Finish sand the parts of the tray and assemble them with glue and wire brads. *Don't* glue the ends of the tray bottom to the tray sides — just attach the parts with brads. Set the heads of the brads.

26

Finish sand the cleats. Attach them to the inside surfaces of the box side with glue and brads. Set the brads.

27

Place the tray on the cleats to check the fit. Install the latch in the lid and mount the lid back on the box to check the fit and the action of the latch. If necessary, adjust the fit of the tray or the lid.

28

Disassemble the box, removing the tray, lid, and all the hardware. Set the hardware aside and apply a finish to the box. If you wish, paint an escutcheon around the keyhole, as shown in the *Front View*. When the finish dries, reassemble the box.

TRAY DETAIL

18⅝"

⅜" (Typ)

3¾"

8⅝"

7⅞"

17⅞"

TOP VIEW

18⅝"

7⅛"

3⅝"

⅜" Rad

1¾"

⅜"

FRONT VIEW

8⅝"

SIDE VIEW

PENCIL-POST BED

In winters gone by, bedrooms were cold places after the fire had died down. Folks hung heavy canopies over and around their beds, warding off drafts and creating tents that could be warmed by their own body heat. In warmer weather, lighter hangings protected them from insects. Winter or summer, the canopies provided privacy. Several people — sometimes whole families — slept in the same room.

At first, these canopies were suspended from the ceiling. Around 1550, English craftsmen began to extend the bedposts to support "testers," wooden frames over which the canopies were draped. The posts of these early "tent" beds were massive and often richly carved. As styles changed, the posts narrowed. By the early eighteenth century, both English and American craftsmen were making slender, graceful bedposts. Among country folks, octagonal "pencil posts" were particularly popular, because they could make these without using a large, expensive lathe.

The pencil-post bed is a versatile design. As shown, the bed supports a standard queen-size mattress and box springs. You can easily change its size to fit almost any mattress — just alter the length of the rails and canopy. If you eliminate the support brackets, you can build the frame to surround a water bed. Hang a dust ruffle from the bed rails to hide the supporting platform. The pencil posts will support either a straight or Queen Anne (arched) canopy. The plans show straight testers. These were the most common; country folks rarely made arched testers. However, if you wish to arch them, shorten the bedposts. You can also change the shape of the headboard, or add a footboard, to suit your taste.

EXPLODED VIEW

BILL OF MATERIALS

WOODEN PARTS/*FINISHED DIMENSIONS*

A.	Posts (4)	$2^1/2$" x $2^1/2$" x $81^1/8$"
B.	End bed rails (2)	$2^1/2$" x $3^1/2$" x $62^1/2$"
C.	Side bed rails (2)	$2^1/2$" x $3^1/2$" x $82^1/2$"
D.	Headboard	$3/4$" x 12" x $62^1/2$"
E.	End tester rails (2)	$7/8$" x 1" x $64^1/2$"
F.	Side tester rails (2)	$7/8$" x 1" x $84^1/2$"
G.	Tester stretchers (2)	$7/8$" x 1" x $64^1/2$"
H.	Nut caps (8)	$1/2$" x $3/4$" x $3/4$"

HARDWARE

$1/2$" x $4^1/2$" Bed bolts, flat washers, and nuts (8)

Box springs support brackets and mounting screws (6–8)

$1/4$"-dia. x 2" Metal pins (4)

PLAN OF PROCEDURE

1

Plane, rip, and cut the parts to the sizes shown in the Bill of Materials, except for the nut caps. Cut these about 1/16" thicker and wider than specified.

2

Cut the joinery needed to assemble the bed:

- 3/4"-wide, 3/4"-deep, 3 1/2"-long mortises in the inside surfaces of the bedposts, as shown in the *Bedpost Layout,* to hold the rails
- 3/4"-wide, 3/4"-long tenons on the ends of the rails, as shown in the *End Rail Layout* and *Side Rail Layout,* to fit the bedpost mortises
- 3/4"-wide, 3/4"-long, 1 5/8"-deep mortises in the inside surfaces of the rails, as shown in the *Rail and Headboard Joinery Detail,* to hold the nuts and washers that secure the rails to the posts
- 3/4"-wide, 3/4"-deep, 7"-long mortises in the inside surfaces of the head bedposts, as shown in the *Bedpost Layout/Inside Side View,* to hold the headboard

- 2"-wide, 3/8"-deep dadoes in all four rails, as shown in the *Side Rail Layout/Side View* and *End View,* to hold the box spring support brackets

- 1"-wide, 7/16"-deep rabbets in the ends of the tester rails, as shown in the *Tester Joinery Detail,* so the rails will overlap at the corners

RAIL AND HEADBOARD JOINERY DETAIL

TESTER JOINERY DETAIL

- ½"-wide, 1"-long mortises through the inside surface of the side tester rails to hold the tester stretchers

- ½"-wide, 1"-long tenons in the ends of the tester stretchers to fit the mortises

TOP VIEW

END VIEW   **SIDE VIEW**

END RAIL LAYOUT

TOP VIEW

SIDE VIEW   **END VIEW**

SIDE RAIL LAYOUT

INSIDE SIDE VIEW   **INSIDE END VIEW**

BEDPOST LAYOUTS

PLAN OF PROCEDURE

3

Drill the holes needed:

- 1/2"-diameter holes through the bedposts, as shown in the *Bedpost Bolt Hole Layout,* for the bed bolts
- 1/2"-diameter, 2³/4"-deep holes in the ends of the rails, as shown in the *End Rail Layout* and *Side Rail Layout,* for the bed bolts
- 1/4"-diameter, 1¹/8"-deep holes in the top ends of the bedposts, as shown in the *Bedpost Layout,* to hold the tester pins
- 1/4"-diameter holes through the tester rails, near the ends, as shown in the *Tester Joinery Detail,* to fit over the tester pins

4

Cut the octagonal tapers in the upper portions of the bedposts, as shown in the *Bedpost Layout* and explained in Making Pencil Posts on page 181.

BEDPOST BOLT HOLE LAYOUT
OUTSIDE ISOMETRIC VIEW

END VIEW

5

Cut the shape of the headboard, as shown in the *Headboard Layout*. Sand the sawed edges.

½"

¾"

¾"

NUT CAP DETAIL

84½"

½" Wd × 1" Lg
Mortise Thru

1" Wd × 7⁄16" Dp
Lap Joint

⅞"

¾"

1"

6" Rad

5"

7"

82"

HEADBOARD LAYOUT

82½"

3½"

2" Wd × ⅜" Dp Dado
for Mattress Support
Brackets

2" (Typ)

17½"

9"

28½"

28½"

9"

2½"

2½"

86"

SIDE VIEW

PLAN OF PROCEDURE

6

Finish sand all the parts of the bed and assemble them to test the fit of the joints. Using hot glue or epoxy, glue the nuts and washers in place, inside the bed rails. Be careful not to get any glue on the bolt threads. When you take the bed apart, the nuts and bolts should remain in their mortises.

7

Sand the nut caps, slightly tapering the ends and sides, so they fit the nut mortises like plugs. With the bed bolts, nuts, and washers in place, glue the caps in place. Sand them flush with the surface of the rails.

8

Attach the box spring support brackets to the rails.

9

Disassemble the bed and remove all the hardware (except for the nuts and washers inside the rails). Do any necessary touch-up sanding and apply a finish to the completed project.

Mattress Support Bracket

1"(Typ)

1"

2½"

25"

30½"

25"

2½"

1"

64½"

TOP VIEW

COUNTRY CRAFTSMAN'S
KNOW-HOW: MAKING PENCIL POSTS

Country craftsmen cut the octagonal tapers in long pencil posts with simple hand tools — a drawknife, a plane, chisels, and scrapers. These are still the best tools for the job, although you can save some time by roughing out the tapers with a band saw.

1 To shape each post, you must make *eight* tapers — four *face* tapers and four *corner* tapers. To begin, mark two tapers for *opposing* faces, using a long straightedge.

2 Rough-cut the first two tapers on a band saw, cutting a little wide of the lines.

3 Using a hand plane, smooth the tapers. Carefully cut down to the lines, but *no farther!*

4 Repeat Steps 1, 2, and 3 for the two remaining face tapers. When you're finished, the post should taper on all four sides.

(Continued)

COUNTRY CRAFTSMAN'S
KNOW-HOW: MAKING PENCIL POSTS — *CONT.*

5 Scribe all four of the corner tapers. The shoulders of these tapers (where the octagonal, tapered portion of the post ends and the square, straight portion begins) are rounded. Use a template to mark these so they're all precisely the same.

6 Clamp the post in two or more V-blocks so one of the corners faces up. Using a drawknife or spokeshave, remove stock down to the lines.

7 Cut the rounded shoulder with a chisel. Then repeat Steps 6 and 7 for each corner taper.

8 Smooth all the tapers with a hand scraper and sandpaper. Use a sanding block so you preserve the hard edges of the octagonal shape.

CHEST OF DRAWERS

Chests have been popular storage pieces since Egyptian times, but they have always presented the same problem: How do you retrieve an item on the bottom of the chest without disturbing everything piled on top of it? You couldn't, until the late sixteenth century when English Renaissance joiners introduced the *mule chest* — a chest with a single *drawing box* or *till* (as a drawer was then called) at the bottom. This finally solved the problem.

This chest with drawer grew increasingly popular in the seventeenth century. Gradually, English craftsmen added more drawers until the chest portion was just a shallow bin at the top of the piece. At first, the makers hid the drawers behind paneled doors so the piece retained the same appearance as a traditional chest. By the second half of the century, however, they began to omit these doors. Finally, about mid-century, the craftsmen completely filled the chest with drawers, made it much taller than previously, and fixed the lid in place. This was the beginning of the *chest of drawers* as we know it.

American craftsmen began to make chests of drawers about the same time and continued through the eighteenth and nineteenth centuries. They were fond of tall chests and made them long after they had gone out of style in England — perhaps to provide their clients

with more storage and make better use of the available space. This tall six-drawer chest is a copy of an early nineteenth-century piece made by a Shaker craftsman at the Union Village community near Lebanon, Ohio.

EXPLODED VIEW

BILL OF MATERIALS

WOODEN PARTS/*FINISHED DIMENSIONS*

A.	Sides (2)	3/4" x 18" x 62"
B.	Top	3/4" x 19" x 42"
C.	Web frame rails (14)	3/4" x 3" x 39 1/2"
D.	Web frame stiles (14)	3/4" x 1 1/4" x 12 1/4"
E.	Baseboard	3/4" x 5 3/4" x 40"
F.	Backboards (5–6)	1/2" x (variable) x 56 1/4"
G.	Drawer fronts (6)	3/4" x 8 7/16" x 38 3/8"
H.	Drawer sides (12)	3/4" x 8 7/16" x 17 1/8"
J.	Drawer backs (6)	3/4" x 7 15/16" x 37 5/8"
K.	Drawer bottoms (6)	1/2" x 17 1/8" x 37 9/16"
L.	Drawer pulls (12)	1 1/4" dia. x 1"

HARDWARE

6d Square-cut nails (40–48)
1 1/4" Wire or headless brads (36–40)
#10 x 1 1/4" Flathead wood screws (10)
#10 x 1 1/2" Flathead wood screws (12)

PLAN OF PROCEDURE

1

If necessary, glue up stock to make the sides and top. Plane, rip, and cut the parts to the sizes shown in the Bill of Materials, except the backboards and drawer parts. Rip the backboards so they will form a single panel 39¼" wide, with a 1/16" gap between each board. Make the drawer fronts, sides, backs, and bottoms about 1/16" wider and longer than specified. Cut two pieces 1½" x 1½" x 10" to make the turning stock for the pulls.

2

Cut the joinery needed to assemble the case:

- ½"-wide, ³/₄"-deep, 2¼"-long dovetail sockets in the top ends of the sides to hold the top web frame rails, as shown in the *Top Web Frame Joinery Detail*
- 2¼"-wide, ½"-long dovetails in the ends of the top web frame rails
- ½"-wide, ½"-deep, 3"-long dovetail grooves in the sides to hold the remaining web frame rails, as shown in the *Side Layout*
- ½"-thick, ½"-long dovetail tenons in the ends of the remaining web frame rails, as shown in the *Web Frame Joinery Detail*
- ½"-wide, ³/₈"-deep, 56¼"-long blind rabbets in the sides to hold the backboards

- ¼"-wide, ³/₈"-deep, 1³/₄"-long grooves in the inside edges of all web frame rails to hold the web frame stiles
- ¼"-thick, ³/₈"-long tenons in the ends of the web frame stiles

3

Drill and countersink ³/₁₆"-diameter pilot holes through the top web frame rails and stiles. Make the countersinks on the bottom faces of these parts. Make three to four pilot holes in each rail, and two pilot holes in each stile. The positions of these holes are not critical, but they should be centered in the boards and evenly spaced.

WEB FRAME LAYOUT

PLAN OF PROCEDURE

4

Drill 1/8" pilot holes (for nails) through the web frame stiles, from edge to edge. Make three holes in each stile. Once again, the positions aren't critical, but they should be evenly spaced.

5

Lay out and cut the shapes of the feet in the baseboard and sides, as shown in the *Front View* and *Side Layout*. Sand the sawed edges.

TOP WEB FRAME JOINERY DETAIL

3/16" Dia Thru with C'Sink

1/2"

10°

3"

2"

2¼"

1/2"   3/4"   1/4"

WEB FRAME JOINERY DETAIL

1/2"

3"

1/4"

1/2"

1/4"

Web Frame Rail

Web Frame Stile

1/4" Wd × 3/8" Dp × 1¾" Lg Groove

1/4" Wd × 3/8" Lg Tenon

1¼"

1/4"

SIDE LAYOUT

3"   11½"   3"

½" Wd × 3/8" Dp Rabbet

½" Wd × ½" Dp Dovetail Groove (Typ)

5/16"

3/4"

Nail Drawer Guides Here

9¼" O.C. (Typ)

6⅛" O.C.   5¾"

2" Rad

3/4"

2¾"   11"   3½"

18"

6

Lay out and cut the notches that hold the baseboard in the front edges of the sides.

7

Finish sand the parts of the case and assemble them in the following order:

- Set the sides on a flat surface with the bottom edge down. Glue the top web frame rails and the baseboard in place. Reinforce the baseboard with nails.
- Glue the remaining front web frame rails in the dovetail grooves in the sides.
- Turn the assembly over so the sides rest on their front edges. Glue the web frame stiles to the front web frame rails, inserting the tenons in the grooves.
- Apply glue to the back tenons on the web frame stiles. Slide the back web frame rails into their dovetails. As you do so, insert the stile tenons in the grooves.
- Nail the stiles to the sides, driving the nails through the 1/8"-diameter pilot holes. Do *not* glue the stiles to the sides.
- Place the case on its feet. Attach the top with #10 x 1¹/4" flathead wood screws,

driving the screws through the top web frame rails and stiles. Do *not* glue the top in place.
- Using wire or headless brads, attach the backboards to the sides and back web frame rail. Do *not* glue the backboards in place.

Sand all joints clean and flush as you work. After the case is assembled, set the heads of the nails slightly below the surface. If you wish cover the heads of the baseboard nails with putty.

DOVETAIL LAYOUT

1/4"
1¹/4"
1¹/4"
3/4"
20°
3/8"

8

Turn the drawer pulls on a lathe. Turn six pulls from each piece of turning stock, and finish sand them on the lathe. Cut them apart with a band saw and do any necessary touch up sanding to remove the saw marks.

9

Cut the joinery needed to assemble the drawers:

- 3/4"-wide, 3/8"-deep dadoes in the sides, to hold the backs, as shown in the *Drawer/Top View*
- 1/4"-wide, 3/8"-deep grooves in the front and the sides to hold the bottom
- Half-blind dovetails that fasten the sides to the fronts, as shown in the *Dovetail Layout*

For more information for cutting these dovetails, refer to Making Hand-Cut Dovetails on page 112.

1¹/4" Dia
5/8" Dia
3/4" Dia
1/8" Dia
x 3/4" Dp

¢

1/4" 5/8" 1/8"
1"

DRAWER PULL

PLAN OF PROCEDURE

10

Drill and countersink $3/16$"-diameter holes through the drawer fronts where you wish to mount the pulls.

11

Finish sand the drawer parts, then assemble them in the following order:

- Assemble fronts, sides, and backs with glue.
- Reinforce the side-to-back joints with nails and set the heads.

- Slide the drawer bottoms into their grooves. Drive one or two headless brads through the bottoms and into the backs. Do *not* glue the bottoms in place.
- Mount the drawer pulls to the drawer fronts with #10 x $1\frac{1}{2}$" flathead wood screws.

12

Fit the drawers to the case. If necessary, plane a little stock from the assemblies until they slide in and out of the case easily.

13

Remove the drawers from the case and do any necessary touch-up sanding. Apply a finish to the drawer fronts and *all* sides of the case — inside and outside. Do *not* finish the drawer sides, backs, or bottoms.

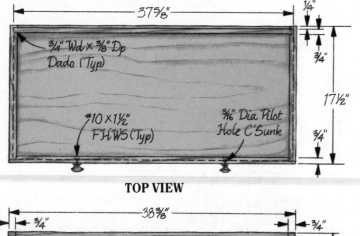

$37\frac{5}{8}$"
$3/4$" Wd x $3/8$" Dp Dado (Typ)
$\frac{1}{4}$"
$3/4$"
$17\frac{1}{2}$"
$3/4$"
#10 x $1\frac{1}{2}$" FHWS (Typ)
$3/16$" Dia Pilot Hole C'Sunk

TOP VIEW

Bevel Edge to Fit
$\frac{1}{4}$"
$\frac{1}{2}$"
$3/8$"
$3/4$"

DRAWER BOTTOM DETAIL

$3/4$"
$38\frac{3}{8}$"
$3/4$"
$8\frac{7}{16}$"
$\frac{1}{4}$"
$\frac{1}{4}$"

FRONT VIEW

DRAWER

$17\frac{1}{2}$"
$3/4$"
$3/4$"
$\frac{1}{4}$"
$7\frac{15}{16}$"
Blind Dovetails
$\frac{1}{4}$" Wd x $3/8$" Dp Groove (Typ)

SIDE VIEW

TOP JOINERY DETAIL

Top

Top Brace

#10 × 1¼" FHWS

3/16" Dia Pilot Hole C'Sink

42"

¾"

1"

¾"
¾"

A

1"

¾"

62¾"

¾" (Typ)

8½" (Typ)

56¼"

3" (Typ)

5¾"

19"

1"

3¾"

2" Rad

½"

3½"

33"

A

3½"

¾"

18"

40"

FRONT VIEW

SECTION A

SHAKER CRADLE

Although the Shakers practiced celibacy, they sometimes accepted whole families, including the children, into their communities. They also took in unwed mothers, foundlings, and orphans. Consequently, there were often infants — and cradles — in the Shaker nurseries. The cradle shown is a copy of one now on display in the Shaker Museum in Old Chatham, New York. It was made by Shaker craftsmen early in the nineteenth century, although its community of origin is not clear.

The design is typical of many country cradles made during this period. The headboard and the sides are raised to protect the uncovered head of the infant from drafts. The rockers are extended far beyond the sides not only for stability, but so the mother could rock the infant while she attended to other chores. She would sit next to the cradle with a pile of clothes to mend or beans to shell and place a foot on the knobbed end of one rocker. As she worked, she'd push gently on the knob, rocking the cradle.

EXPLODED VIEW

BILL OF MATERIALS

WOODEN PARTS/*FINISHED DIMENSIONS*

A. Sides (2) $3/4" \times 16" \times 391/4"$
B. Headboard $3/4" \times 17" \times 171/2"$
C. Footboard $3/4" \times 141/4" \times 151/2"$
D. Bottom $3/4" \times 97/8" \times 317/8"$
E. Rockers (2) $7/8" \times 45/8" \times 227/8"$
F. Stretcher $3/4" \times 11/4" \times 253/8"$
G. Wedges (2) $5/16" \times 7/16" \times 2"$

HARDWARE

#8 x 1 1/2" Flathead wood screws (4)
4d Square-cut nails

PLAN OF PROCEDURE

1

Glue up stock to make the wide boards needed for the headboard, footboard, sides, and bottom. Plane the parts to the thicknesses needed, then rip and cut the stretcher and wedges to the sizes shown in the Bill of Materials. Cut the other parts about 1/2" wider and longer than specified.

2

Compound-miter the ends of the headboard, footboard, and sides with the miter gauge angled at 79¼° and the saw blade tilted to 2°. When assembled, all four parts will slope at 11°.

3

Lay out and cut the dovetails. Lay out the baselines (bottoms) of the tails and pins parallel to the *ends* of the headboard, footboard, and sides. Then lay out the tails on the sides, as shown in the *Dovetail Layout/Side View.* Note that the centerline of these tails is parallel to the *bottom edge* of each board. Transfer the layout lines across the end grains so that they will be parallel to the bottom edge of the headboard or footboard, as shown in the *Dovetail Layout/End View.*

1 Square = ½"

11°

39¼"

17½"

¾"

31⅞"

⅜"

14¼"

¾"

Footboard

Headboard

45° Stopped Chamfer

4½"

25⅜"

22⅜"

⅞"

⅞"

4½"

¾"

33⅛"

SIDE VIEW

Cut the sides of the tails with a dovetail saw, then remove the waste with a chisel. Chisel along each baseline, cutting halfway through the board. Then flip the board over and chisel from the other side. Trim the bases (the spaces between each tail) so they're parallel to the end of the board.

Position the finished tails over the end grain of the adjoining headboard or footboard. Trace around the tails with an awl to lay out the ends of the pins. Connect the ends of the pins to the baselines. Remember, the pins must be parallel to the bottom edges of the boards. Cut and chisel out the pins. For further instructions, see Making Hand-Cut Dovetails on page 112.

END VIEW

END VIEW

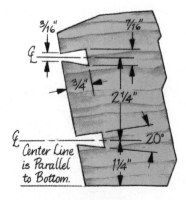

SIDE VIEW
DOVETAIL LAYOUT

PLAN OF PROCEDURE

4

Dry assemble the headboard, footboard, and sides. Fit the bottom to the assembly, beveling the edges and ends at 11°.

5

Cut the joinery needed to assemble the rockers and stretcher:

- 1/2"-wide, 1¼"-long mortise through the rocker stock, as shown in the *End View*
- 5/16"-wide, 5/16"-long mortises through the ends of the stretcher, as shown in the *Stretcher Joinery Detail*
- 1/2"-thick tenons on the ends of the stretcher, as shown in the *Stretcher Tenon Detail*

6

Cut tapers and bevels in the wedges, as shown in the *Stretcher Joinery Detail*.

7

Lay out and cut the shapes of the headboard, footboard, sides, and rockers. Sand the sawed edges.

STRETCHER JOINERY DETAIL

STRETCHER TENON DETAIL

8

Cut a stopped chamfer in all four corners of the stretcher, as shown in the *Side View* and *Section A.*

9

Round over the top edges of the headboard, footboard, and sides with a 3/8" quarter-round bit. Round over the bottom of the rockers with the same bit.

10

Finish sand all the parts of the cradle. Glue the headboard, footboard, and sides together. Then attach the bottom with nails, driving the nails through the headboard, footboard, and sides. Do *not* glue the bottom in place. Sand the joints clean and flush.

11

Set the nails and, if you wish, cover the heads with putty.

12

Assemble the rockers and stretchers with glue. Before the glue dries, press the wedges into the ends of the stretcher to pin the parts together.

13

Attach the rocker assembly to the cradle with flathead wood screws. Do *not* glue the rockers to the bottom. Countersink the heads of the screws.

14

Do any necessary touch-up sanding, then apply a finish to the cradle.

SECTION A

Six-Board Chest

The simple chest — a box with a lid — is probably the oldest form of furniture. Since prehistoric times, people have hollowed logs and fitted them with lids of rived wood or animal skins to store and transport their possessions. Dug-out chests or *trunks* were used in Western Europe through the Middle Ages.

In the thirteenth century, joiners began to nail boards together to form plank chests. These usually consisted of just six major parts — the four sides, the top, and the bottom. At first, these chests rested on short tables or stands to keep them off the damp earth. Then craftsmen lengthened the side boards, creating a built-in stand.

This simple six-board design proved so practical that it was used by country folks in Europe, and then in America, for hundreds of years. Depending on the prevailing fashion at the time, the planks might be gaily painted, covered with intricate ironwork, or decorated with moldings and chip carvings. The basic design, however, remained the same. The six-board chest shown is typical of many built by the early settlers in New England.

EXPLODED VIEW

BILL OF MATERIALS

WOODEN PARTS/*FINISHED DIMENSIONS*

A.	Front/back (2)	$3/4$" x $11^{1}/_2$" x $28^{3}/_4$"
B.	Sides (2)	$3/4$" x $14^{1}/_2$" x 19"
C.	Bottom	$3/4$" x 13" x 28"
D.	Lid	$3/4$" x $14^{9}/_{16}$" x $28^{7}/_8$"
E.	Side trim (2)	$3/4$" x 1" x $15^{5}/_{16}$"
F.	Front trim	$3/4$" x 1" x $30^{3}/_8$"

HARDWARE

6d Square-cut nails (16)
$1^{1}/_2$" x 3" Butt hinges and mounting screws (1 pair)
Chest lock, latch, and mounting screws

PLAN OF PROCEDURE

1

If necessary, glue up the stock to make the front, back, sides, bottom, and lid. Plane, rip, and cut the parts to the sizes shown in the Bill of Materials, except the side and front trim. Cut these ½"–1" longer than specified.

2

Rout or cut a ¾"-wide, ⅜"-deep dado in the inside surface of each side, as shown in the *Side Layout*.

3

Cut a ¾"-deep, 11½"-long notch in the front and back edges of each side, as shown in the *Side Layout*.

4

Lay out the shape of the feet on the sides, as shown in the *Side Layout*, and cut them with a band saw or saber saw. Sand the sawed edges.

5

Cut a mortise in the inside face of the front for the lock. With a drill and a file, create a hole for the key.

6

Finish sand the parts you have made, then join the bottom and sides, gluing the bottom into the dadoes. Reinforce the glue joints with square-cut nails.

30⅜"

1"

11½"

¾" Wd × ⅜" Dp
Dado

¾"

28¾"

FRONT VIEW

7

Join the front and back to the sides and bottom. Glue the front and back to the bottom, but *not* the sides. If you glue the front and back to the sides, the long, horizontal parts won't be able to expand and contract properly. The glue joints will eventually pop, and the wood may warp, cup, or split. Instead, nail the front and back to the sides and set the heads. The nails will give slightly when the wood moves.

8

Fit the trim to the lid, mitering the adjoining ends. Glue the front trim to the front edge of the lid and reinforce it with nails. Then nail (but do *not* glue) the side trim to the ends of the lid.

SIDE VIEW   **SIDE LAYOUT**

PLAN OF PROCEDURE

9

Using a handplane, cut a 45°
chamfer in the bottom outside
corner of the three trim parts,
as shown in the *Trim Profile*.

10

Set all the nails, and cover the
heads with putty.

11

Mortise the lid and the back for
hinges, then mount the lid on
the chest. The trim must fit
over the front and sides.

12

Install the lock in the front.
Mark the location of the latch
on the bottom face of the lid,
then remove the lid from the
chest and cut a mortise for
the latch.

13

Remove all the hardware from
the chest. Do any necessary
touch-up sanding, then apply
a finish to the *outside* wooden
surfaces. Leave the inside of
the chest unfinished. When the
finish dries, reassemble the lid
to the chest. Replace the lock
and the latch.

TRIM
PROFILE

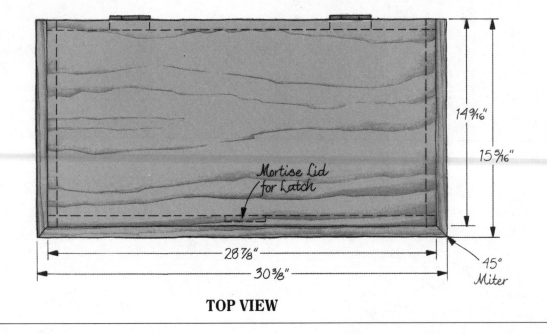

TOP VIEW

FRETWORK MIRROR

Country mirrors were framed in many ways, but one of the most popular was an ornate fretwork frame. The intricate shapes were copied in the mid-eighteenth century from Japanese "cloud forms." Cabinetmakers first saw these forms on furniture imported from the Orient. The English architect and designer, Thomas Chippendale, and others began to use them on their furniture, and soon fretwork was all the rage. As American craftsmen imitated their English counterparts, the style became popular on both sides of the Atlantic. Complex, veneered fretwork mirrors appeared in American cities. Country craftsmen copied these, making simpler, solid-wood versions.

Although the frame looks difficult, it's actually simple to make. The basic frame is made like any other, using ordinary miter joints reinforced with splines. The fretwork is cut from thin stock, then glued to the frame and backed up with glue blocks.

EXPLODED VIEW

BILL OF MATERIALS

WOODEN PARTS/*FINISHED DIMENSIONS*

A.	Side stretchers (2)	$7/8$" x $1^3/8$" x 19"
B.	Top/bottom stretchers (2)	$7/8$" x $1^3/8$" x $12^1/2$"
C.	Top fretwork	$1/4$" x 5" x $12^1/2$"
D.	Bottom fretwork	$1/4$" x $2^3/4$" x $12^1/2$"
E.	Top side fretwork (2)	$1/4$" x $1^1/2$" x 5"
F.	Bottom side fretwork (2)	$1/4$" x $1^3/4$" x $4^3/4$"
G.	Splines (4)	$1/8$" x 1" x $2^1/4$"

H.	Glue blocks (26)	$1/4$" x $1/4$" x 1"
J.	Mirror back	$1/4$" x $10^1/4$" x $16^3/4$"

HARDWARE

$10^3/16$" x $16^{11}/16$" Mirror
$7/8$" Wire or headless brads (6–8)
$1/4$" Eye screws (2)
Picture-hanging wire (16")

PLAN OF PROCEDURE

1

Plane the stock to the thicknesses specified in the Bill of Materials. Rip the stretcher and spline stock to the proper width, but don't cut them to length yet. Cut the fretwork stock into rectangles about 1/4" wider and longer than specified. Cut the glue blocks and mirror back to the sizes specified.

2

Cut or rout the shape of the stretchers, as shown in the *Stretcher Profile*. Make this shape in three separate passes, cutting a portion of the shape with each pass:

- Cut a 5/6"-diameter bead in the outside corner.
- Cut a 1"-radius cove in the inside corner. (You can create large coves on your table saw by making a *cove cut*.)
- Cut a 1/4"-radius cove inside the larger cove.

3

Cut or rout a 1/4"-wide, 3/8"-deep rabbet in the back inside edge of the stretcher stock.

4

Cut the stretcher stock to the proper length, mitering the ends at 45°.

5

Using a table saw blade that cuts a 1/8"-wide kerf, cut 1/8"-wide, 1/2"-deep spline grooves in the mitered ends of the stretchers.

6

Cut the splines to the proper length and shape them to look like small feathers, as shown in the *Spline Layout*. Pay careful attention to the grain direction of the splines. It must run side to side, across the *width* of the parts, not the length.

SPLINE LAYOUT

STRETCHER PROFILE

PLAN OF PROCEDURE

7

Dry assemble the stretchers and splines to check the fit of the joints. Finish sand the stretcher parts, then assemble the stretcher frame with glue. As you assemble the frame, fit the splines in the grooves, as shown in the *Stretcher Joinery Detail*.

8

When the glue dries, sand the joints clean and flush.

9

Lay out the fretwork patterns on the fretwork stock. Once again, pay careful attention to the grain direction, as indicated in the pattern drawings. Cut the shapes of the fretwork and sand the sawed edges.

10

Finish sand the fretwork, then glue it to the frame, reinforcing the joints with glue blocks, as shown in the *Side View*.

1 Square = ½"

TOP SIDE FRETWORK

1 Square = ½"

BOTTOM SIDE FRETWORK

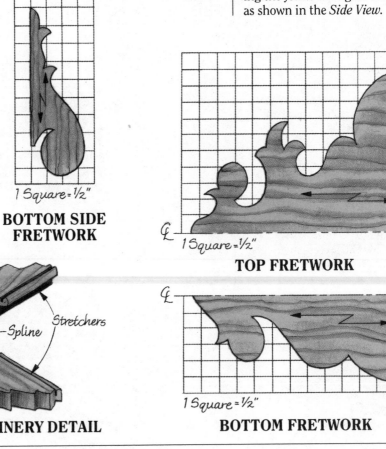

1 Square = ½"

TOP FRETWORK

1 Square = ½"

BOTTOM FRETWORK

⅛"
¼"
⅛"
⅛"

Spline

Stretchers

STRETCHER JOINERY DETAIL

11

Do any necessary touch-up
sanding, then paint or finish
the completed frame.

12

Install the mirror and mirror
back in the frame, securing
them with 1" wire brads.

13

Install eye screws in the back of
the frame, one on either side,
toward the top. Stretch picture-
hanging wire between them.

FRONT VIEW   **SIDE VIEW**

TURNED-POST BED

Beds were in short supply in the American wilderness. When families first arrived, they often slept huddled together on the floors of their hastily built cabins. Later, as they settled the land and had time to attend to their own comfort, they began to build simple beds, similar to the one shown. The posts were thick and heavy, usually turned, and often had large, round finials on the ends. Later, these were nicknamed "cannonball" beds.

These early bedsteads were short by our standards, and always had a wide headboard at one end. From the seventeenth until well into the nineteenth century, folks customarily slept sitting up, with their shoulders and head resting against the headboard. (They believed that if they slept lying down, their lungs would fill with fluid and they might suffocate.) The mattresses were supported by ropes woven between the stretchers.

Although the turned posts of this bed are copied from an early nineteenth-century antique, the remainder of the project has been updated in two important ways. First, it's been lengthened to accommodate a standard-size twin mattress — you can sleep lying down. Second, the traditional ropes have been eliminated. Instead, metal brackets support a contemporary box spring.

EXPLODED VIEW

BILL OF MATERIALS

WOODEN PARTS/*FINISHED DIMENSIONS*

A. Head bedposts (2) $3^1/4$" x $3^1/4$" x 34"
B. Foot bedposts (2) $3^1/4$" x $3^1/4$" x 26"
C. End rails (2) $2^1/2$" x $3^1/2$" x $41^1/2$"
D. Side rails (2) $2^1/2$" x $3^1/2$" x $77^1/2$"
E. Headboard $3/4$" x 12" x $41^1/2$"
F. Nut caps (8) $1/2$" x $3/4$" x $3/4$"

HARDWARE

$1/2$" x 5" Bed bolts, flat washers, and nuts (8)
Box springs support brackets and mounting
   screws (8)

PLAN OF PROCEDURE

1

Plane, rip, and cut the parts to the sizes shown in the Bill of Materials, except for the nut caps. Cut these to the thickness specified, but make them about 1/16" longer and wider than shown.

2

Cut the joinery needed to assemble the bed:

- 3/4"-wide, 3/4"-deep, 3 1/2"-long mortises in the inside surfaces of the bedposts, as shown in the *Head Bedpost Layout* and *Foot Bedpost Layout,* to hold the rails
- 3/4"-wide, 3/4"-long tenons on the ends of the rails, as shown in the *End Rail Layout* and *Side Rail Layout,* to fit the bedpost mortises
- 3/4"-wide, 3/4"-long, 1 5/8"-deep mortises in the inside surfaces of the rails to hold the nuts and washers that secure the rails to the posts

- 3/4"-wide, 3/4"-deep, 4 3/4"-long mortises in the inside surfaces of the head bed-posts, as shown in the *Head Bedpost Layout,* to hold the headboard

- 2"-wide, 3/8"-deep dadoes in all four rails, as shown in the *Top View,* to hold the box spring support brackets

HEADBOARD LAYOUT

END VIEW

TOP VIEW

77½"

41½"

¾" Wd × ¾" Dp
Mortise (Typ)

Box Spring
Support Brackets
(8 Req'd)

Post

¾"

2½"

Headboard

Rails

2" Wd × ⅜" Dp
Dado (Typ)

SIDE VIEW

82½"

76"

3¼"

3¼"

5¼"

4¾"

4½"

6½"

3½"

3½"

26"

16"

6"

2"

29¾"

2"

Box Spring
Support Brackets

2"

29¾"

2"

6"

16"

34"

PLAN OF PROCEDURE

3

Drill the holes needed:

- $1/2$"-diameter holes through the bedposts, as shown in the *Bedpost Bolt Hole Layout,* for the bed bolts
- $1/2$"-diameter, $2^3/4$"-deep holes in the ends of the rails, as shown in the *End Rail Layout* and *Side Rail Layout,* for the bed bolts

4

Turn the shapes of the bedposts, as shown in the *Head Bedpost Layout* and *Foot Bedpost Layout.*

5

Cut the shape of the headboard, as shown in the *Headboard Layout.* Sand the sawed edges.

BEDPOST BOLT HOLE LAYOUT

END RAIL LAYOUT

SIDE RAIL LAYOUT

TOP VIEW

SIDE VIEW

END VIEW

6

Finish sand all the parts of the bed and assemble them to test the fit of the joints. Put the bed bolts and nuts in place. Using hot glue or epoxy, glue the nuts and washers in place, inside the bed rails. Be careful not to get any glue on the bolts' threads. When you take the bed apart, the nuts and bolts should remain in their mortises.

7

Sand the nut caps, slightly tapering the ends and sides, so they fit the nut mortises like plugs. With the bed bolts, nuts, and washers in place, glue the caps in place. Sand them flush with the surface of the rails.

NUT CAP DETAIL

FOOT BEDPOST LAYOUT

HEAD BEDPOST LAYOUT

PLAN OF PROCEDURE

8

Attach the box spring support brackets to the rails.

9

Disassemble the bed and remove all the hardware (except for the nuts and washers inside the rails). Do any necessary touch-up sanding and apply a finish to the completed project. When the finish dries, reassemble the bed.

Headpost

3/4" Wd × 3/4" Dp × 4 3/4" Lg Mortise

Headboard

3/4"

1/2" Dia × 5" Lg Bolt

3/4" Wd × 3/4" Dp × 3 1/2" Lg Mortise

4 3/4"

Side Rail

2 1/2"

3/4" 7/8"

Head Rail

2 1/2"

7/8"

3 1/2"

3/4" Wd × 3/4" Lg × 1 5/8" Dp Mortise

Nut Cap

Nut and Washer

3 1/2"

**POST-TO-RAIL
JOINERY DETAIL**

FOR
SITTING
&
REFLECTING

LADDER-BACK CHAIR

The ladder-back chair was a popular furniture design throughout Europe long before America was discovered. In the American colonies, English immigrants began to make ladder-back chairs in the late seventeenth century, and the Germans, shortly after that. These early American ladder-backs were fairly heavy and intricately turned — not much different than their European predecessors. Then in the late eighteenth century, an obscure religious sect modified this chair to produce one of America's most-admired country furniture designs.

In 1789, the United Society of Believers in Christ's Second Appearing (better known as the Shakers) began making these chairs for use in their community dwellings. Because they believed in the virtues of utility and simplicity, Shaker craftsmen avoided unnecessary ornament in their furniture. They stripped the ladder-back design to its barest essentials, creating a light, austere chair that was surprisingly elegant and durable.

The Shakers also believed that their love of God was expressed in the integrity of their work and, therefore, quickly earned a reputation for excellent workmanship. By the early nineteenth century, outsiders were asking to buy Shaker furniture. At first, the Shakers simply sold their excess chairs to the "world's people." By the 1820s, they increased production and began to actively market ladder-back chairs and rockers. In

1852, they standardized their designs, and in 1873 built a chair factory at their community in New Lebanon, New York. This factory continued to produce the distinctive Shaker chairs until 1935.

This ladder-back armchair is copied from one made in the early nineteenth century, before Shaker chair designs were standardized. Although its community of origin is not certain, it was probably built at Union Village, Ohio.

EXPLODED VIEW

BILL OF MATERIALS

WOODEN PARTS/*FINISHED DIMENSIONS*

A.	Back legs (2)	$1^3/8$" dia. x $41^1/2$"
B.	Front legs (2)	$1^3/8$" dia. x $24^1/4$"
C.	Front rungs/stretchers (3)	1" dia. x 20"
D.	Side rungs/stretchers (6)	1" dia. x $15^7/8$"
E.	Back rungs/stretchers (2)	1" dia. x 16"
F.	Top/middle slats (2)	$1/4$" x 3" x $16^7/8$"
G.	Bottom slat	$1/4$" x $2^3/4$" x $16^7/8$"
H.	Arms (2)	$1^3/8$" dia. x $18^1/4$"
J.	Pegs (2)	$1/4$" dia. x $5/8$"

HARDWARE

Tape or rush (sufficient to weave the seat)
- A tape seat requires 30 yards of 1"-wide tape
- A rush seat requires 2–3 lbs. of $5/32$" fiber cord.

You may also need small tacks, cotton batting, or foam rubber, depending on the type of seat you weave.

PLAN OF PROCEDURE

1

Plane, rip, and cut the parts to the sizes shown in the Bill of Materials, except for the turned parts — legs, arms, stretchers, and rungs. Make these about 1"–2" longer than specified.

2

Turn the legs, arms, stretchers, and rungs to the shapes shown. Turn 5/8"-diameter, 3/4"-long tenons on both ends of the rungs and stretchers, on the top end of each front leg, and on the back end of each arm.

Lay out the mortises by scoring the pieces with a skew as they turn, as shown in the *Back Leg Layout* and *Front Leg Layout*. Finish sand the turnings on the lathe.

FRONT LEG TURNING DETAIL

FINIAL DETAIL

BOTTOM VIEW ARMREST LAYOUT

FRONT LEG LAYOUT

BACK LEG LAYOUT

14½"

¼"

100°

Bend Slat to
28⅞" Rad

80°

17½"

18½"

1⅜"

TOP VIEW

¾"   20"   18½"   ¾"

1" Dia

¾"Dia

⅝" Dia

FRONT RUNG DETAIL

¾"   16"   14½"   ¾"

1" Dia

¾"Dia

⅝"Dia

BACK RUNG DETAIL

¾"   15⅞"   14⅜"   ¾"

1" Dia

¾"Dia

⅝" Dia

SIDE RUNG DETAIL

¼" Dia × ⅝" Lg
Pegs

16⅞"
True Length

3"

3"

2¾"

6⅜"

5¹⁵⁄₁₆"

5¹⁵⁄₁₆"

5¼"

20"

FRONT VIEW

17½"   90°

41½"

Drill Holes for Side Rungs
and Stretcher at 2"

Stretchers
are
Straight

Rungs are
Tapered

23½"   15⅞"

92°

SIDE VIEW

PLAN OF PROCEDURE

3

Drill 5/8"-diameter, 13/16"-deep mortises in the legs to hold the rungs and stretchers. Note that the back leg mortises for the side rungs and stretcher must be drilled 2° off perpendicular, as shown in the *Side View*. Also drill mortises in the arms to fit the front leg tenons.

4

Rout 1/4"-wide, 3/4"-deep, 2"-long mortises in the back legs to hold the top and middle slats, and 1/4"-wide, 3/4"-deep, 13/4"-long mortises to hold the bottom slat.

5

Miter the bottom ends of the back legs at 92°, as shown in the *Side View*.

6

Cut the shapes of the slat, as shown in the *Slat Layout and Pattern*. Chamfer the top edge of each slat. Sand the sawed edges.

7

Using heat, hot water, or steam, bend the slats to a 287/8" radius, as shown in the *Top View*. If you use water or steam, make a bending form from a 3"-thick block of hardwood or glued up particleboard. The parts will spring back partially when you remove them from the bending form, losing about 20 percent of their curve. To compensate, make the bending form with a 22" radius. Steam or boil the slats for 45–60 minutes, then place them in the form. Clamp the two halves of the form together, bending the slats. Let them dry in the jig for at least two weeks.

8

Finish sand the slats. Dry assemble all the parts of the chair to be sure of the fit, then assemble the parts with glue.

9

From the front of the chair assembly, drill 1/4"-diameter, 11/16"-deep holes near the top end of each back leg, through the mortise that holds the top slat. Glue a peg in each hole, letting the ends protrude slightly. Round over the ends of the pins with sandpaper, but don't sand them completely flush.

10

Do any necessary touch-up sanding, and paint or finish the chair frame. Then weave a tape or rush seat onto the stretchers.

Back Rest

23°

100° Back Rung

Side Rung

80° Front Rung

MORTISE LAYOUT

1 Square = 1/2"

℄

Chamfer Edge at 45° (Typ)

2" 13/4"

Cut Here For Bottom Back Rest

8 7/16"

SLAT LAYOUT AND PATTERN

COUNTRY CRAFTSMAN'S KNOW-HOW: WEAVING A TAPE SEAT

Tape chair seats first appeared in the early nineteenth century. They were rare until the Shakers began to cover the seats of the chairs they sold to the "world's people" with cloth tape or "listing," as it was called then. As Shaker chairs became more popular, so did the tape seats. By the twentieth century, tape was as common as rush or reed.

Cloth tape comes in two common widths — 5/8" and 1". The wider tape is the most popular and the easiest to work with, especially if you're weaving a simple checkerboard pattern. More complex patterns are best woven from 5/8"-wide tape. The tape also comes in a variety of colors. Most seat weavers prefer to mix two colors, using one color for the warp (front-to-back tape) and another for the woof (side-to-side tape).

Tape normally comes in 5- and 10-yard rolls. A typical chair seat requires 30 yards of tape — 15 yards of each color, if you're weaving a two-color seat. In addition to the tape, you'll also need:

- 20–24 small upholstery tacks and a tack hammer to secure the tape to the chair frame
- A needle and thread to splice the tape
- A 1"-thick foam rubber pad to make a seat cushion
- Scissors, to cut and trim the tape
- A metal spoon, to help adjust the weave

You can purchase the tape and other supplies from:

The Connecticut Cane and Reed Company
P.O. Box 1276
Manchester, CT 06040

Shaker Workshops
P.O. Box 1028
Concord, MA 01742

1 Before you begin, decide what pattern you want to weave. The two most common are the *checkerboard* and *herringbone* patterns shown.

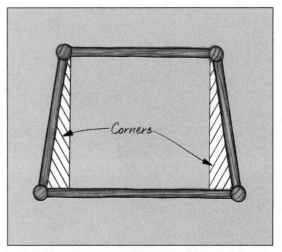

2 Chair seats are, more often than not, trapezoid-shaped when you look at them from the top. The warp and woof are square to each other — the weave forms a rectangle. When you impose a rectangle on top of a trapezoid, it leaves two "corners" on either side. Find these corners with a square and mark them on the front stretcher. Later on, you'll fill in these corners with short lengths of tape.

(Continued)

COUNTRY CRAFTSMAN'S
KNOW-HOW: WEAVING A TAPE SEAT — *CONT.*

3 Begin by weaving the warp. If you're using two colors of tape, use the *darker* color for the warp. Because the warp covers the front stretcher, the dirt will show less. Tack the end of a roll of cloth tape to the left side stretcher, near the back stretcher.

4 Stretch the warp tape under, then back over the back stretcher. Bring it forward, over, and under the front stretcher, then back under and over the back stretcher. Do *not* fill in the corners at this time; leave them open. Continue wrapping the tape onto the stretchers until you've covered the back stretcher. Tack the warp tape to the right side stretcher and cut it off.

5 The top and bottom warps will have a space between them. Cut a 1"-thick foam rubber pad to the trapezoid shape of the seat, and stuff it into this space.

6 Next, weave the woofs into the warps. Insert the end of a roll of tape into the space between the warps, near the back stretcher. Temporarily spread the warps on the back stretcher apart and tack the woof tape to the left stretcher near the back leg.

7 Stretch the woof tape under the left side stretcher, bring it over the stretcher, then begin weaving the tape over and under the warps as needed to achieve the pattern. Go over and under the right side stretcher, then continue weaving on the bottom of the seat. (The pattern of both the seat bottom and top should be identical.) Repeat, alternating the weave at the beginning of each new row as needed to create the pattern.

8 Every two or three rows, stop weaving and "comb" the woof tapes with your fingers, as shown. Even them out so the woofs and warps are square to one another.

9 If the roll of tape runs out in the middle of the warps or woofs, splice another roll onto the end of the first. Overlap the ends and sew them together. Make these splices on the *bottom* of the seat where they won't show.

10 As you finish up the woofs, the weaving will become tighter and more difficult. During the last few rows, you may not be able to weave with your fingers. Instead, use the handle of a spoon to push the woofs between the warps. You can also use the spoon to comb the tape.

(Continued)

COUNTRY CRAFTSMAN'S
KNOW-HOW: WEAVING A TAPE SEAT — *CONT.*

11 When you've covered the side stretchers with woofs, tack the tape to the underside of the front stretcher and cut it off.

12 Fill in the corners with short lengths of warp tape, completely covering the front stretcher. Weave these short warps over and under the woofs, following your pattern.

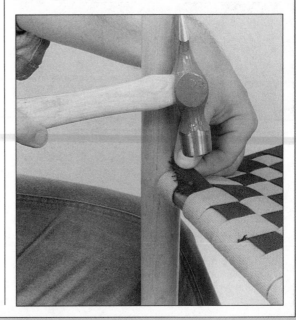

13 When you've completely covered the front stretcher, spread the woof tapes apart and tack the ends of the short warp tapes to the side stretchers. Put the woof back in place so you can't see where the warps are attached. Comb the weave so it's even, and trim any loose tape ends or threads that may be hanging out.

SPLAY-LEG SIDE TABLE

Small "side" tables first appeared in country homes in the seventeenth century. As the name suggests, they were used beside chairs, beds, and larger furniture to hold candles, needlework, serving bowls, and pitchers.

This particular side table is typical of the early nineteenth century. Like so many country designs, this one is a blend of styles. The slender, tapered legs echo the Hepplewhite style, while the fretwork aprons and heart cutouts show the influence of the German and Scandinavian immigrants. Practically speaking, the small size and simple, lightweight construction made the table easy to move. The splayed legs helped to steady the small surface, keeping it from becoming top-heavy.

EXPLODED VIEW

BILL OF MATERIALS

WOODEN PARTS/*FINISHED DIMENSIONS*

A. Tabletop $3/4$" x 15" x 15"
B. Aprons (4) $3/4$" x $5^1/2$" x $11^1/8$"
C. Legs (4) $1^1/4$" x $1^1/4$" x $27^3/16$"
D. Pegs (12) $3/8$" x $3/8$" x $1^1/4$"

HARDWARE

#8 x $1^1/4$" Flathead wood screws (8)

PLAN OF PROCEDURE

1

Plane, rip, and cut the parts to the sizes shown in the Bill of Materials. As you cut the parts to size, bevel the edges of the aprons at 86° and compound-miter the ends of the legs at 4°.

2

Cut two 1/4"-wide, 3/4"-deep, 1⁵/₈"-long mortises in each inside surface of each leg, as shown in the *Leg Mortise Layout*. These mortises meet in the center of each leg, as shown in the *Leg-to-Apron Joinery Detail*.

LEG MORTISE LAYOUT

TOP VIEW

SIDE VIEW

PLAN OF PROCEDURE

3

Cut a 2° taper in each inside surface of each leg, as shown in the *Leg Layout*.

4

Miter the ends of the aprons at 94°, then bevel them at 45°. The 45° bevel will allow the tenons to meet inside the leg mortises.

5

Cut 1/4"-wide, 3/4"-long tenons in both ends of each apron. Notch each tenon, as shown in the *Apron Layout*, to make two split tenons, each 1 5/8" long.

6

Drill two screw pockets in the top edge of each apron as shown in the *Top-to-Apron Joinery Detail*.

APRON LAYOUT

LEG-TO-APRON JOINERY DETAIL

Table Top

3/8" × 3/8" × 1 1/4"
Square Hardwood Peg

5/8" Dia × 1 1/4" Dp Hole

Leg

86°

TOP-TO-APRON JOINERY DETAIL

2° Taper (2 Sides Only)

4° Compound Miter

1 1/4"

4° Compound Miter

27 3/16"

1/2"

LEG LAYOUT

7

Lay out and cut the *Apron Pattern* in the bottom edge of each apron. Sand the sawed edges.

8

Dry assemble the legs and aprons to check the fit of the joints. Make any necessary adjustments. Finish sand all the parts of the table, then assemble the legs and aprons with glue.

9

Round the bottom portion of the pegs, as shown in the *Peg Detail*.

10

Drill a 3/8"-diameter, 1¼"-deep hole through the *bottom* mortise-and-tenon joints in each leg, then drive the pegs into the holes from the outside.

11

Put the top upside down on the workbench and attach the top to the aprons with #8 x 1¼" roundhead wood screws and flat washers. Drive the screws through the screw pockets and into the underside of the top, as shown in the *Top-to-Apron Joinery Detail*.

12

Turn the table right side up and drill a 3/8"-diameter, 1¼"-deep hole through the tabletop and into the end of each leg. Drive pegs into the holes, as shown in the *Top-to-Leg Joinery Detail*.

13

Do any necessary touch-up sanding on the table. Then apply a finish to the completed project.

1 Square = ¼"

APRON PATTERN

Table Top

86°

¾"

Apron

#8 x 1¼" FHWS

Screw Pocket

TOP-TO-LEG JOINERY DETAIL

3/8"

3/8"

1¼"

A — A

B — B

C — C

PEG DETAIL

SECTION A

SECTION B

SECTION C

(Make from *very* hard wood.)

STEP-DOWN WINDSOR CHAIR

It's not clear how the term "Windsor" came to describe these simple, graceful chairs. The basic design — a carved plank or "saddle" seat with spindle-turned legs and rungs — is centuries old, probably descended from the traditional four-legged stool. Sometime before the seventeenth century, English country chairmakers, called *bodgers,* began to produce these chairs throughout England — not just Windsor.

There is an interesting (although unfounded) folktale that could explain the association. The story goes that one day the duke of Windsor was out riding in his woods. He came upon an itinerant bodger who had set up his portable pole lathe near a grove of young trees. The duke inspected the bodger's work and found it much more delicate and well made than the ordinary country chair. He was also astonished to find that a chair so delicate could also be sturdy. He ordered a set of chairs from the bodger and proudly displayed them at the next ducal dinner. His guests admired the bodger's work, and soon they were ordering their own "Windsor" chairs.

Whatever the origin, American country craftsmen embraced the Windsor style in the early eighteenth century and made it their own. It was more comfortable than traditional straight-backed seating, such as the ladder-back chair and the settle, yet not much more difficult to make. It was also lightweight and easily moved. Americans made several distinct changes in the traditional English design — they raked the legs at a more pronounced angle and began to make the backs, as well as the legs, from spindles. Throughout New England and the Midwest, dozens of variations on the Windsor chair appeared.

The chair shown is one such variation. It's typical of American Windsors made in the Federal period, during the late eighteenth and early nineteenth centuries. The bamboo-turned legs are Sheraton-inspired designs, simplified for country tastes. The crest rail is another popular Sheraton pattern — it's wide in the middle, then "steps down" at the ends.

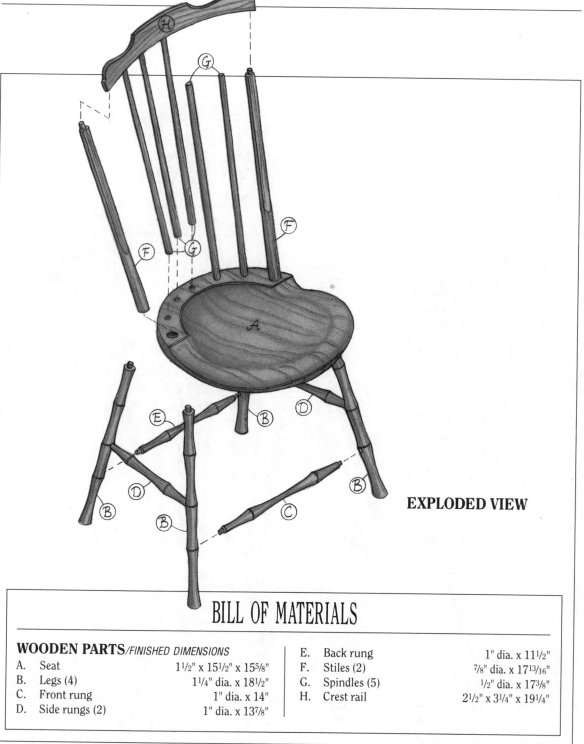

EXPLODED VIEW

BILL OF MATERIALS

WOODEN PARTS/*FINISHED DIMENSIONS*

A.	Seat	$1^1/_2$" x $15^1/_2$" x $15^5/_8$"
B.	Legs (4)	$1^1/_4$" dia. x $18^1/_2$"
C.	Front rung	1" dia. x 14"
D.	Side rungs (2)	1" dia. x $13^7/_8$"

E.	Back rung	1" dia. x $11^1/_2$"
F.	Stiles (2)	$7/_8$" dia. x $17^{13}/_{16}$"
G.	Spindles (5)	$1/_2$" dia. x $17^3/_8$"
H.	Crest rail	$2^1/_2$" x $3^1/_4$" x $19^1/_4$"

PLAN OF PROCEDURE

1

Plane, rip, and cut the seat and
the crest rail to the sizes shown
in the Bill of Materials. Make
the remaining parts — the
turned parts — slightly wider
and longer than specified.

Note: Traditionally, a
Windsor chair is made from
several different woods. To
make an accurate reproduction, use white pine or poplar
for the seat; chestnut, oak, or
hickory for the crest rail; and
oak, ash, hickory, maple, or
birch for the turned parts.

TOP VIEW

15½"   15⅝"

B   B

A   A

SIDE VIEW

Flatten This Portion Of The Stile   16⁵⁄₁₆"   12°

20°

B   B

10°

12⅜"

16½"

FRONT VIEW

19¼"   2½"

18⅛"

36⅝"

1½"

17"

12½"   10°

17¾"

A   A

2

Lay out the shape of the seat, as shown in the *Seat Layout/ Top View* and *Seat Layout/Bottom View*. Measure and mark the locations of the round mortises for the legs, stiles, and spindles.

3

Drill the mortises in the seat:

- $7/8$"-diameter, 1"-deep holes in the bottom of the seat
- $7/8$"-diameter, $3/4$"-deep holes in the top of the seat, on either side
- $1/2$"-diameter, $3/4$"-deep holes in the top of the seat, near the back edge

Each of these mortises must be drilled at an angle: Drill the $7/8$"-diameter leg mortises at a compound 10° angle, so the legs will *splay* outward, away from the corners. Drill the $7/8$"-diameter stile mortises at 20°, and the $1/2$"-diameter spindle mortises at 12°. Both the stile and the spindle mortises should tilt toward the back edge.

Note: Most country chairmakers eyeballed these angles; they don't have to be precise. As long as the angles are within 1°–2°, the parts will fit just fine.

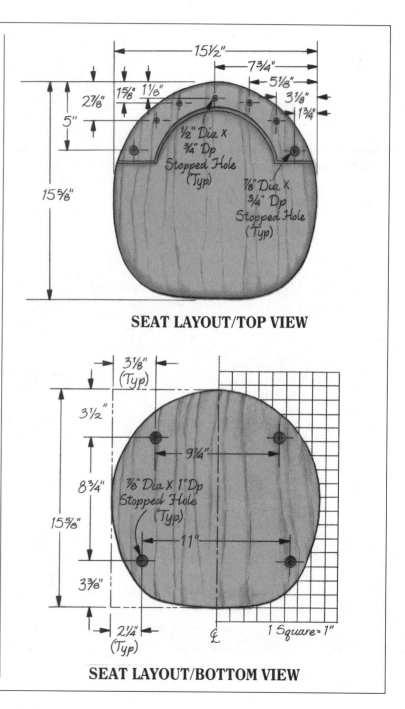

SEAT LAYOUT/TOP VIEW

SEAT LAYOUT/BOTTOM VIEW

Plan of Procedure

4

Turn the legs and rungs to simple cylinders, then shape the tenons on the ends. Score the leg cylinders where you want to drill round mortises for the rungs.

5

Drill the 1/2"-diameter, 3/4"-deep mortises in the legs. These must be angled at 10°, as shown in the *Leg Detail*.

6

Fit the legs, rungs, and seat stock together to be certain that the joints fit. When you're satisfied that they do, disassemble the parts.

7

Carve or "scoop" the shape of the saddle in the top surface of the seat. Bevel the front and side edges and round the back edges, on the bottom, as shown in *Section A/Side View* and *Section B/Front View*. Finish sand the seat.

8

Finish turning the shapes of the legs and rungs, as shown in the *Leg Detail, Front Rung Detail, Side Rung Detail,* and *Back Rung Detail.* Finish sand the parts on the lathe.

9

Lay out the shape of the crest rail and mark the location of the stile and spindle mortises, as shown in the *Crest Rail Pattern* and *Crest Rail Mortise Layout.* Drill the 3/8"-diameter, 3/4"-deep mortises. The holes for the stiles must be drilled at 20°, and those for the spindles at 12°. All the holes must slant toward the front face of the rail.

SECTION A/SIDE VIEW

15⅝"   5½"   1½"

SECTION B/FRONT VIEW

15½"   1½"

1 square = ½"

TOP VIEW

1 square = ½"

FRONT VIEW

CREST RAIL PATTERN

LEG DETAIL

FRONT RUNG DETAIL

SIDE RUNG DETAIL

BACK RUNG DETAIL

CREST RAIL MORTISE LAYOUT

PLAN OF PROCEDURE

10

Turn the spindles and the stiles and finish sand them on the lathe.

11

Fit the stiles, spindles, seat assembly, and crest rail stock together to check the fit of the joints. When you're satisfied, disassemble the parts.

12

Using a band saw, cut the shape of the crest rail. Tilt the saw table to 12° and cut the inside and outside curves. Tape the waste back on the stock, tilt the table back to 0°, and cut the front profile. Remove all the waste and sand the sawed surfaces.

13

Assemble the parts with glue, then let the glue cure for at least 24 hours.

14

Using a block plane, flatten the fronts of the stiles as shown in the *Side View.* (A chair stile that has been flattened in the front is sometimes called a "mule ear" stile.) The flat portion of the stile should be flush with the front surface of the crest rail.

15

Do any necessary touch-up sanding and apply a finish to the completed chair.

SPINDLE DETAIL

STILE DETAIL

COUNTRY CRAFTSMAN'S
KNOW-HOW: TURNING SLENDER SPINDLES

The most striking feature of American Windsor furniture is its long, slender turnings. These are not difficult to make, but they do require finesse and precision.

First, choose an appropriate stock. Soft woods (such as poplar or pine) may split or splinter. Instead, use a hard, dense wood. Old-time Windsor chairmakers preferred maple, birch, chestnut, hickory, and oak. After you've selected the stock, cut it approximately ⅛" thicker and wider than the final diameter and ½"–1" longer than the final length. (The extra length is necessary to turn the spindle smaller than the diameter of the lathe centers. Cut the spindle to length *after* you've finished turning it.)

1 Mount the stock solidly between the lathe centers, but not too tightly. If you squeeze the stock between the centers, it may bow as you turn it. If the spindle wants to bow, vibrate, or "whip," brace it with a steadyrest.

2 Make very light cuts, feeding the chisels very gently — especially as you approach the final diameter. Shearing cuts work best; scraping puts too much pressure on the wood.

¼" Wd × 4½" Lg Slot on Center

2×2

2×4

Non-Swiveling Ball-Bearing Casters

Variable

1"

¼" × 3½" Carriage Bolt, Washer & Wing Nut

¼" × 4" Carriage Bolt, Washer & Wing Nut

1"

¾"

Variable

10"

12"

2×4

Base Clamps to Lathe Bed. Modify to Suit.

3 Many tool manufacturers offer steadyrests as accessories for their lathes. You can also make your own from scrap wood and casters, as shown.

POUTING CHAIR

Although this looks like a child's chair, it wasn't originally. The German immigrants who settled in Pennsylvania in the eighteenth and nineteenth centuries often made stepstools with high backs. The back served as a handle, letting them move the stool around easily, without having to bend over and pick it up. These high-back stools proved indispensable in country kitchens, helping the cooks reach the high shelves in the pantry and cupboards.

When not in use, the stool was often kept in an out-of-the-way corner — probably the same corner where naughty children were banished from time to time. The children would sit on the stool while they contemplated their misdeeds. Consequently, the high-back stool acquired a whimsical nickname — the "pouting chair."

Today, the pouting chair remains as useful as it ever was — for *both* its applications. The chair shown is built from planks, in the same manner as a settle. The sides have been extended to add a bit of decoration and make the stool look like a miniature wing-and-arm chair.

EXPLODED VIEW

BILL OF MATERIALS

WOODEN PARTS/*FINISHED DIMENSIONS*

A. Back $5/8" \times 9" \times 23\,3/4"$
B. Sides (2) $5/8" \times 10\,3/8" \times 21\,3/4"$
C. Seat $5/8" \times 8\,7/8" \times 12"$

HARDWARE

4d Square-cut nails

PLAN OF PROCEDURE

1

Plane, rip, and cut the parts to the sizes shown in the Bill of Materials, except the seat. Cut this 1/4"–1/2" longer than specified. When you rip the parts, cut the following bevels:

- Both edges of the back at 10°
- The back edges of the sides at 10°
- Both edges of the seat at 3½°
- The bottom end of the back at 3½°

2

Rout a 5/8"-wide, 5/16"-deep dado in each side, on the inside face, as shown in the *Side Pattern*.

3

Enlarge the *Side Pattern* and *Back Pattern* and trace them on the stock. Cut the shapes of the back and sides, then sand the sawed edges.

4

Miter the ends of the seat at 10° and fit it to the back and sides. Leave the seat a little long when you first miter it, then shave it down a little bit at a time until it fits properly.

5

Finish sand all the parts, then assemble them with glue and nails. Sand all the joints clean and flush.

5/8" Wd × 5/16" Dp Dado

1 Square = ½"

SIDE PATTERN

1 Square = ½"

BACK PATTERN

6

Set the heads of the nails and cover them with putty.

7

Do any necessary touch-up sanding, then apply a finish to the completed pouting chair.

TOP VIEW

SIDE
VIEW

FRONT
VIEW

SOFA TABLE

The invention of the sofa table is usually credited to the English draftsman and teacher, Thomas Sheraton. In his collection of patterns, *The Cabinet-Maker and Upholsterer's Drawing Book,* published between 1791 and 1794, he included a design for a table "to take a useful place before the sofa." The idea appealed to folks on both sides of the Atlantic, and both English and American cabinetmakers built sofa tables well into the nineteenth century.

True sofa tables were rare in the country, since country folks rarely had sofas. While sofas and sofa tables were more common among the stylish upper class, country folks did have tables that resembled sofa tables. However, these had an entirely different purpose. They were long, narrow, waist-high sideboards, used for cooking, serving, and (occasionally) eating. The sofa table shown is copied from these simple sideboards.

EXPLODED VIEW

BILL OF MATERIALS

WOODEN PARTS/*FINISHED DIMENSIONS*

A.	Top	3/4" x 15" x 50"
B.	Breadboards (2)	3/4" x 1 1/4" x 15"
C.	Plugs (6)	3/8" x 1/2" x 1 1/4"
D.	Legs (4)	1 1/2" x 1 1/2" x 28 1/4"
E.	Front/back aprons (2)	3/4" x 5" x 41 1/2"
F.	Side aprons (2)	3/4" x 5" x 11 1/2"
G.	Pegs (16)	3/8" x 3/8" x 1"

HARDWARE

#12 x 1 1/2" Roundhead wood screws (6)
#12 Flat washers (6)
#8 x 1 1/4" Flathead wood screws (10)
#8 Flat washers (10)

PLAN OF PROCEDURE

1

If necessary, glue up stock for the 15"-wide top. Then plane, rip, and cut the parts to the sizes shown in the Bill of Materials.

2

Cut three 3/8"-wide, 3/4"-deep, 1 1/4" long mortises in the outside edge of each breadboard. Then drill a 3/16"-wide, 1/2"-long slot, centered in each mortise, as shown in the *Breadboard Joinery Detail.*

3

Fasten the breadboards to the tabletop, driving #12 x 1 1/2" roundhead wood screws (with washers) through the slots and into the pilot holes in the ends of the top. Do *not* glue the breadboard to the top.

4

Glue plugs in the breadboard mortises, covering the heads of the screws. The *end grain* of each plug must face out, so it appears to be a tenon. Sand the plugs flush with the outside edges of the breadboards.

**BREADBOARD
JOINERY DETAIL**

SIDE VIEW

3½"　　　　　　　　　　　3½"

1"

15"

1"

47½"

50"

1¼"　　　　　　　　　　　　　1¼"

TOP VIEW

1½"　　　　40"　　　　1½"

5"

¾"

28¼"

2°
Taper

1"

FRONT VIEW

PLAN OF PROCEDURE

5

Cut two 3/8"-wide, 3/4"-deep, 1½"-long mortises in the inside surfaces of each leg, as shown in the *Leg Layout*.

6

Cut a 2° taper in the inside surfaces of each leg, as shown in the *Front View* and *Side View*.

7

Cut 3/8"-wide, 3/4"-long tenons in the ends of each apron. Notch each tenon, as shown in the *Front/Back Apron Layout*, to make two "split tenons," each 1½" wide.

8

Drill two screw pockets in the top edge of each side apron, as shown in the *Top-to-Apron Joinery Detail*. Drill three screw pockets in the top edges of the front and back aprons.

9

Lay out and cut the shapes in the bottom edges of the front and back aprons, as shown in the *Front/Back Apron Layout*. Sand the sawed edges.

LEG-TO-APRON JOINERY DETAIL

FRONT VIEW
FRONT/BACK APRON LAYOUT

1 Square = 1"

END VIEW

10

Dry assemble the legs and aprons to check the fit of the joints. Finish sand all the parts of the table, then assemble the legs and aprons with glue.

11

Round the bottom portion of the pegs, as shown in the *Peg Detail.*

12

Drill a 3/8"-diameter, 1 1/4"-deep hole through the mortise-and-tenon joints in each leg, then drive the pegs into the holes from the outside. Leave about 1/16" of the peg protruding.

PEG DETAIL
**(Make from
very hard wood.)**

13

Turn the table upside down on the top and attach the top to the aprons with #8 x 1 1/4" flathead wood screws. Drive the screws through the screw pockets and into the top, as shown in the *Top-to-Apron Joinery Detail.*

14

Do any necessary touch-up sanding on the table. Then apply a finish to the completed project.

**SECTION
A**   **SECTION
B**   **SECTION
C**

LEG LAYOUT

#8 x 1 1/4" FHWS

1/4" Dia
Oversized
Pilot Hole

Top

15°

Apron

3/4" Dia
C'Bore

**TOP-TO-APRON
JOINERY DETAIL**

QUEEN ANNE YORK CHAIR

By the mid-eighteenth century, the Queen Anne style, with its delicate S-curved shapes, became popular in America. Craftsmen in large cities, such as Philadelphia and New York, began to produce furniture with cabriole legs, ogee moldings, bonnet tops, and other curved, flowing lines. Rural cabinetmakers copied this style, but not to the extent of their city counterparts. They still retained some of the familiar turnings and rectilinear forms of the earlier Pilgrim and William and Mary design traditions — these were much easier to make with their limited tools and skills. They began to build furniture that combined both old and new styles.

The chair shown is one such piece. Chairs like this were first produced in the farmlands and towns surrounding New York and became known as *York* or Hudson Valley chairs. The vase-shaped back splat and rounded crest rail shows the influence of the Queen Anne style. The legs and rungs are more slender than was common in earlier furniture — another concession to the newer fashion. These parts, however, are still turned in the same manner as seventeenth-century carver's chairs and early eighteenth-century William and Mary furniture.

The design for this chair is similar to the Dominy chairs now preserved in the Winterthur Museum near Baltimore, Maryland. Nathanial Dominy IV and his son, Nathanial V, produced furniture in their shop in rural Long Island from 1768 to 1840.

EXPLODED VIEW

BILL OF MATERIALS

WOODEN PARTS/*FINISHED DIMENSIONS*

A.	Back legs (2)	$1\frac{1}{2}$" dia. x $39\frac{1}{8}$"
B.	Front legs (2)	$1\frac{1}{2}$" dia. x $18\frac{1}{4}$"
C.	Back stretchers/rungs (3)	$3/4$" dia. x 13"
D.	Side stretchers/rungs (6)	$3/4$" dia. x $14\frac{1}{2}$"
E.	Front seat stretcher	$3/4$" dia. x 18"
F.	Front rung	$1\frac{3}{4}$" dia. x 18"
G.	Crest rail	$3/4$" x 2" x $14\frac{5}{8}$"
H.	Back splat	$3/8$" x 5" x $17\frac{3}{4}$"
J.	Bottom rail	$3/4$" x $1\frac{3}{4}$" x 13"

HARDWARE

Tape or rush (sufficient to weave the seat)
- A tape seat requires 30 yards of 1"-wide tape
- A rush seat requires 2–3 lbs. of $5/32$" fiber cord

Plan of Procedure

1

Plane, rip, and cut the parts to the sizes shown in the Bill of Materials, except for the turned parts — legs, stretchers, and rungs. Make these about 1"–2" longer than specified.

2

Turn the legs, stretchers, and rungs to the shapes shown. Turn tenons on both ends of the rungs and stretchers and on the top ends of the back legs. Finish sand the turnings on the lathe.

3

Drill 5/8"-diameter, 3/4"-deep round mortises in the legs to hold the rungs and stretchers.

4

Drill 1/2"-diameter, 3/4"-deep round mortises in the crest rail stock to fit over the tenons on the tops of the back legs.

5

Rout 3/8"-wide, 3/4"-deep, 1 1/2"-long grooves in the back legs to hold the bottom rail.

6

Rout a 3/8"-wide, 1/2"-deep, 4"-long groove in the crest rail stock and a 3/8"-wide, 3/4"-deep, 4 1/2"-long groove in the bottom rail stock.

ROUND TENON DETAIL

45° Chamfer
45° Shoulder
3/4"
5/8"
3/4"
1/16"

FRONT LEG LAYOUT

1 3/8" Dia
1 1/2" Dia
1 1/4" Dia
1 1/2" Dia
1" Dia
1 1/2" Dia
1 1/4" Dia
1 1/2" Dia
7/8" Dia
1 1/8" Dia
1 1/2" Dia
5/8" Dia X 3/4" Dp Holes (Typ)
1 1/4" Dia
1 1/2" Dia
1" Dia
1 1/2" Dia

1/8"
3 3/4" 1/4"
1 1/2" 1/8"
1/2" 1/8" 1/8"
3 1/2"
1/2"
1/4" 1 3/4"
1/8" 1/8"
3 1/2"
1/4" 1 3/4"
18 1/4"

TOP VIEW

FRONT VIEW
BOTTOM RAIL

BACK
LEG
LAYOUT

FRONT RUNG
LAYOUT

PLAN OF PROCEDURE

7

Cut the shapes of the crest rail, back splat, and bottom rail and cut the tenons on the bottom rail.

8

Chamfer the edges of the back splat, as shown in the *Back Splat Pattern.*

9

Finish sand the crest rail, back splat, and bottom rail. Dry assemble all the parts of the chair to be sure of the fit.

10

Assemble all the parts of the chair with glue, *except* for the back splat. Let the splat float in its grooves.

11

Do any necessary touch-up sanding, then paint or finish the chair frame.

12

Weave a tape or rush seat onto the stretchers.

3/8" Wd × 1/2" Dp Groove

1 Square = 1"

1/2" Dia × 3/4" Dp Hole

CREST RAIL PATTERN

45° Chamfer

1 Square = 1"

BACK SPLAT PATTERN

5/8" Dia × 3/4" Dp Hole (Typ)

100°

BACK LEG

80°

5/8" Dia × 3/4" Dp Hole (Typ)

FRONT LEG

1½" 11½" 1½"

3/8" 3/16"

13"

1½" 16½" 1½"

TOP VIEW

TAPE SEAT PATTERN

RUSH SEAT PATTERN

14⅝"

4"

2"

½" Dia × ¾" Dp Hole (Typ)

⅜" Wd × ½" Dp Groove

16½"

45° Chamfer

⅜" Wd × ¾" Dp Groove

⅜" Wd × ¾" Dp × 1½" Lg Groove

1¾"

4½"   ¼"

5"

1⅝"

6½"

6½"

1¾"

3⅝"

18¼"

19½"

FRONT VIEW

¾"

¾"

16⅝"

40⅜"

1½"

4½"

Scribe Lines

6½"

¾" (Typ)

6½"

2¾"

16"

SIDE VIEW

COUNTRY CRAFTSMAN'S KNOW-HOW: WEAVING A RUSH SEAT

Rush grew in great abundance in the American colonies, consequently many country seats had woven rush seats. Today, rush has been replaced by fiber cord — stiff, twisted strands of paper. Fiber cord looks almost exactly like rush on a finished chair seat, but it's much easier to work with. You can purchase fiber cord in several different diameters and colors from:

The Connecticut Cane and Reed Co.
P.O. Box 762
Manchester, CT 06040

To weave a rush/fiber cord seat, you'll need:
- 2–3 lbs. of $5/32''$ fiber cord (more if the cord is smaller and less if it's larger)
- 30–40 small upholstery tacks and a tack hammer, to attach the cord to the chair frame
- Masking tape, to splice lengths of cord together
- Cotton batting, to "pad" the chair seat as you weave it
- A pail of water, to wet the cord before you work with it
- A combination square to check your work
- Scissors, needle-nose pliers, a spring clamp, a pencil, and a short length of scrap wood

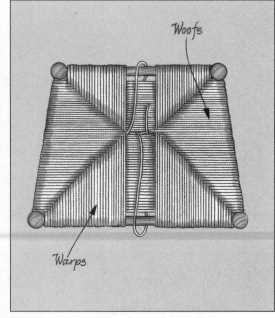

1 As you weave the seat, you'll wind *warps* and *woofs* of fiber cord onto the chair frame. Warps are the front-to-back strands of rush, and the woofs are the side-to-side strands.

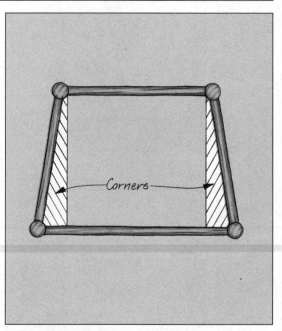

2 Begin the seat by "filling in the corners." Turned chair frames are, more often than not, trapezoid shaped when you look at them from the top. However, the warp and the woof form squares. When you impose a square on a trapezoid, it leaves two triangular "corners" on either side of the chair. These must be filled in with short lengths of cord.

3 Find the corners on your chair frame with a combination square, as shown. Hold the square against the front seat stretcher and mark the beginning of each corner with a pencil.

4 Cut a short length of cord from the coil, a little longer than the front rail. Wet it in water for a few minutes — wet fiber cord is easier to work with. Tack one end to the left seat stretcher, near the front rail. Bring the cord forward, *over and around* the front rail, back *over* itself, then *over and around* the side rail. This is the basic technique for weaving rush. Every time you come to a corner, go over, over, and over.

5 Bring the cord sideways, over and around the right seat stretcher, back over the cord itself, then over and around the front rail. Tack the cord to the right stretcher, near the front rail, and cut off any excess. Repeat this process until you fill in the corners. Each time you repeat, cut the cord a little longer and tack it to the side rails a little further from the front rail.

6 Every third or fourth cord, check your work with the combination square. *This is very important!* The warps must be perpendicular to the front rail, and the woofs must be parallel to it. If they aren't, there will be holes or gaps in your pattern when you finish the seat. Note: The secret to keeping the warps and woofs square is knowing when to pull the cord taut. Put lots of tension on the cord during the first "over" in each corner, but not as much during the last two "overs."

(Continued)

COUNTRY CRAFTSMAN'S
KNOW-HOW: WEAVING A RUSH SEAT — *CONT.*

7 If the warps and woofs are out of square, there are several ways to bring them back into the proper alignment. If the warp takes up too much space on the front rail, place the wooden block against the last warp and tap it back toward the corner. If the warp takes up too little space, place the scrap on top of all the warps and tap it with the hammer. This will mash the cord, spreading the warps out along the rail. If the hammer doesn't work, untwist the cord with needle-nose pliers where it loops over the rail — this will spread out the fibers.

8 As you work, stuff cotton batting between the rush to pad the seat. The weave creates small pockets between the cords at the corners. Every third or fourth "warp and woof," fill these pockets with batting. Be careful not to stuff the pockets too full — put in just enough cotton to hold the cords taut.

9 After you fill the corners, begin a continuous post-to-post weave. Cut a length of cord 10–20 feet long off the coil — not too long, or it will be difficult to work with. Wet the cord, tack one end to the left seat stretcher, as near the back stretcher as possible. Weave the front left corner, front right corner, back right corner, and back left corner, proceeding around the chair in a clockwise direction. Repeat.

10 Continue weaving corner after corner. Check your work occasionally and keep the cord damp. When you come to the end of a length of cord, splice another length to it. Untwist the tail end of the old length and the leading end of the new one, then twist the ends together. Wrap the splice with masking tape. Be careful to make these splices where they won't show — *between* the warps and woofs that are building out from the corners. This way, they won't show on the completed chair.

11 On most chairs, the weave will cover the side stretchers before the front and back stretchers. When you get to this point, begin weaving *warps only*, front to back. Cut an extra-long length of cord before you start this portion of the weave — enough to finish the chair. There will be no place to hide a splice. Weave the cord *over* the front rail, up through the center of the woofs, *over* the back rail, and up through the center again.

12 Cover the front and back rails completely, filling in the weave. Then tack the end of the cord to the bottom side of the back rail, where it won't show. Some rush weavers prefer to tie the cord to an adjacent warp on the bottom side of the chair, using string or twine.

13 Wait for the fiber cord to dry completely before using the chair. If you wish, you can apply a stain or a finish. Traditionally, rush is finished with either a thin shellac or a mixture of linseed oil and turpentine.

WING-AND-ARM CHAIR

Country chairs evolved from two different medieval woodworking traditions. Most familiar to us is the "turner's" chair, which was assembled of parts "thrown" on a lathe. The Shaker ladder-back chair and Sheraton step-down chair are examples of the turner's tradition.

"Joiner's" chairs are less familiar. The parts were ordinary planks and boards, assembled in the same manner as a chest or a cabinet. The five-board bench, the table/chair, and similar kinds of country seating descended from the joiner's tradition. This tradition survives today in upholstered armchairs and sofas. Springs, webbing, and batting have replaced the broad wooden planks, but many of the furniture forms remain the same.

The chair shown is typical of the joiner's tradition. This form first appeared in the seventeenth century as a shortened version of the settle and was sometimes called a settle chair. Later, joiners replaced the side planks with shaped wings and arms, calling it a "wing-and-arm" chair. This was the forerunner of the upholstered wing chair.

While the wings are strictly decorative today, they once added to the warmth and comfort of the folks who sat in these chairs. When facing the fire, the broad surfaces reflect heat onto the person sitting in the chair. The wings also protect them from cold drafts.

A wing-and-arm chair, like any chair built of flat planks, is hard. Their owners often padded them with rugs, cushions, or small pillows. You can make your own cushions and stuff them with down, horsehair, or shredded foam. With a little padding, the chair will be surprisingly comfortable.

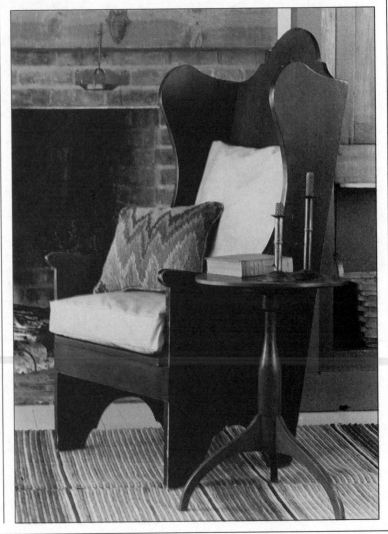

EXPLODED VIEW

BILL OF MATERIALS

WOODEN PARTS/*FINISHED DIMENSIONS*

A.	Back	3/4" x 20" x 53 3/4"
B.	Sides (2)	3/4" x 30" x 48 3/4"
C.	Seat	3/4" x 22 1/2" x 23 1/2"
D.	Apron	3/4" x 4" x 25"
E.	Back seat support*	3/4" x 3 1/4" x 18 1/2"
F.	Side seat supports*	3/4" x 3" x 21"

HARDWARE

8d Square-cut nails (1/4 lb.)

#10 x 1 1/4" Roundhead wood screws (9)

#10 Flat washers (9)

4d Finishing nails (4–6)

These parts must be hand-fitted. The lengths are approximate.

PLAN OF PROCEDURE

1

Plane, rip, and cut the parts to the sizes shown in the Bill of Materials, except the supports — cut these slightly longer than specified. While you're cutting the parts to size, bevel the following ends and edges:

- Both edges of the back at 5°
- Back edges of the sides at 5°
- Both ends of the apron at 5°
- Bottom end of the back at 10°
- Top edge of the back seat support at 10°
- Back edge of the seat at 10°

2

Lay out the *Side Pattern* and *Back Patterns* on the stock, then cut the shapes. Sand the sawed edges.

3

Finish sand the sides, back, and apron, then assemble them with glue and square-cut nails. Set the heads of the nails.

1 Square = 1"

BACK PATTERN

1 Square = 1"

SIDE PATTERN

4

Cut the side seat supports to fit in the chair assembly. Bevel the front ends of the supports at 5°. Compound-miter the back ends, setting the blade at 5° and the miter gauge at 10°. Tack the supports in place with finishing nails, but don't drive them all the way home.

5

Fit the back seat support in the same manner as the side support, beveling the ends at 5°.

SIDE VIEW

FRONT VIEW

PLAN OF PROCEDURE

6

Pull the finishing nails out of the side seat supports and discard them. Remove the supports from the chair. Drill a series of holes to make $3/16$"-wide, $1/2$"-long slots in both the side and back supports, as shown in the *Support Slot Detail*.

7

Attach the supports to the sides and back with #10 x $1\frac{1}{4}$" roundhead wood screws and flat washers, driving the screws through the slots. *Don't* glue these parts in place. The screws and slots in the supports will allow the sides and back to expand and contract.

8

Cut the shape of the seat as shown in the *Top View,* mitering the sides at 85°. Chamfer the front corners at 45°. Fit the seat to the chair.

9

Finish sand the seat. Attach it to the sides, back, back support, and apron with glue and square-cut nails. To secure the edges of the seat, drive the nails down through them into the apron and back seat support. To secure the ends, drive nails horizontally through the sides and into the seat. Set the heads of the nails. *Don't* glue or nail the seat to the side seat supports — just let it rest on them.

10

Do any necessary touch-up sanding and apply a finish to the project.

#10 x 1¼"
RHWS & Flat
Washer

1½"

½"

3/16"

SUPPORT SLOT DETAIL

21½"

20"

5°

31¼"

22½"

45°

¾"

23½"

TOP VIEW

FIVE-BOARD BENCH

Benches are among the oldest and most versatile furniture designs. Originally, common folks used them for working as well as sitting. The surface was long and flat to hold a craftsman's tools and materials while he straddled the bench. (This is the origin of the word *workbench*.) Over thousands of years, various cultures have adapted the bench to make seats, beds, and low tables.

The traditional American five-board bench is descended from the medieval *form,* a backless stool that was used throughout Europe in the Middle Ages. A form was made much like a trestle table — the plank seat was supported by two vertical slabs and stabilized by one or more horizontal rails. To minimize ground contact — and help prevent rot — the bottom end of each supporting slab was shaped, creating two "feet." The rails were often scalloped or pierced with designs to add decoration to the otherwise utilitarian form.

This simple design proved so serviceable that it has been used up through the present day, without modification. The five-board bench shown is typical of many built in colonial America for sitting and working. You can build it almost any length, depending on the available space and how you want to use it. You shouldn't make it any longer than 78", however, without adding additional legs or brace work or the bench may start to sag.

EXPLODED VIEW

BILL OF MATERIALS

WOODEN PARTS/*FINISHED DIMENSIONS*

A. Top $7/8"$ x $11^1/2"$ x (variable)
B. Legs (2) $7/8"$ x $10^1/2"$ x $17^1/8"$
C. Rails (2) $7/8"$ x $4"$ x (variable)

HARDWARE

6d Square-cut nails (14–16)

PLAN OF PROCEDURE

1

If necessary, glue up stock for the legs and seat. Plane, rip, and cut the parts to the sizes shown in the Bill of Materials.

2

Lay out and cut the shape of the legs, creating the feet, as shown in the *End View*. Sand the sawed edges. Notch the edges of the legs, near the top ends, to hold the rails.

3

Rout or cut beads in the front face of the rails, near the bottom edges, as shown in the *Rail Profile*.

4

Lay out and cut the shapes of the rails, as shown in the *Front View*. Sand the sawed edges.

5

Finish sand the parts of the bench and dry assemble them to check the fit. Reassemble the parts with glue and square-cut nails. Set the nails and cover the heads with putty.

6

Do any necessary touch-up sanding and apply a finish to the completed project.

END VIEW

RAIL PROFILE

FRONT VIEW

OCCASIONAL TABLES

Because floor space was at a premium, country folks often designed their furniture to fill a particular space. These occasional tables are tailored for two common household spaces. The triangular table fits in a corner, and the half-round table sits against a wall.

Like so much country furniture, the designs are strictly utilitarian — although they have been influenced by other styles, both classic and traditional. The half-round table echoes the lines of bow-front side tables and sideboards that were popular during the Federal period. The corner table is reminiscent of three-legged "cricket" tables that were used in English taverns during the seventeenth and eighteenth centuries. In both cases, however, their beauty derives mainly from their simplicity.

Both tables are built in exactly the same manner, except the shapes of the tops. Each top rests on three tapered legs, joined by a T-shaped apron.

EXPLODED VIEW

BILL OF MATERIALS

WOODEN PARTS/*FINISHED DIMENSIONS*

A.	Corner tabletop	$3/4$" x $17^1/4$" x $31^{11}/_{16}$"
	Half-round tabletop	$3/4$" x 16" x 32"
B.	Legs (3)	$1^1/2$" x $1^1/2$" x 27"
C.	Long apron	$3/4$" x 4" x $26^1/2$"
D.	Short apron	$3/4$" x 4" x $12^1/2$"
E.	Pegs (6)	$3/8$" x $3/8$" x $1^1/4$"

HARDWARE

8d Square-cut nails (6–8)

PLAN OF PROCEDURE

1

If necessary, glue up the stock to make the tabletop. Then plane, rip, and cut the parts to the sizes shown in the Bill of Materials.

2

Cut a 1/4"-wide, 3/4"-deep, 3"-long mortise in the inside surface of each leg, as shown in the *Leg Mortise Layouts*. Note that the position of the mortise in each back leg is different from that in the front leg.

3

Cut a 1° taper in all four surfaces of each leg, as shown in the *Front View*.

4

Cut 1/4"-wide, 3/4"-long tenons in *both* ends of the long apron and in one end of the short apron. Notch the tenons, as shown in the *Tenon Layout,* so they are 3" from edge to edge.

TOP VIEW

SIDE VIEW

TENON LAYOUT

FRONT VIEW

SIDE VIEW

5

Cut a 3/4"-wide, 3/8"-deep dado, centered in the inside face of the long apron, as shown in the *Base Layout/Top View.*

6

Lay out and cut the shape of the top, as shown in the *Half-Round Table/Top View* or *Corner Table/Top View.* Sand the sawed edges.

7

Dry assemble the legs and aprons to check the fit of the joints. Finish sand all the parts of the table, then assemble the legs and aprons with glue.

8

Reinforce the dado joint connecting the long and short aprons with square-cut nails.

9

Round the bottom portion of the pegs, as shown in the *Peg Detail.*

10

Drill two 3/8"-diameter, 11/4"-deep holes through the mortise-and-tenon joint in each leg, then drive the pegs into the holes from the outside. Leave about 1/16" of each peg protruding.

LEG MORTISE LAYOUTS

MIDDLE LEG

END LEG

BASE LAYOUT
TOP VIEW

PLAN OF PROCEDURE

11

Attach the top to the aprons with square-cut nails. When the top expands and contracts, the nails will give slightly. Do *not* glue the top to the aprons or legs; this would restrict the wood movement.

12

Set all nails, then cover the heads with putty.

13

Do any necessary touch-up sanding on the table. Then apply a finish to the completed project.

HALF-ROUND TABLE/TOP VIEW

CORNER TABLE/TOP VIEW

PEG DETAIL
(Make from *very* hard wood.)

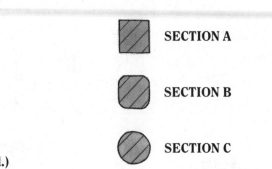

SECTION A

SECTION B

SECTION C

FOR
COOKING
&
BAKING

BUCKET BENCH

When America was first settled, every cabin had a "bucket bench" just outside the back door. This bench held two or three buckets of water ready for drinking, cooking, and washing. As a bucket emptied, it was quickly refilled so the cook always had fresh water.

The settlers built bucket benches in all shapes and sizes. Some had several shelves to help organize buckets and other materials. On the bench shown, the drinking water was probably kept on the bottom shelf. The middle shelf prevented debris from falling into the drinking water buckets. The middle shelf also held wash water, supporting the buckets at a comfortable height to wash dishes, clothes, or your hands and face. The small top shelf held soap, washrags, dippers, and cups.

These simple (but indispensable) pieces quickly developed into more convenient forms. Craftsmen added work surfaces and splashboards, making pieces like the Water Bench. Later, they enclosed the shelves, brought the unit inside, and called it a *dry sink*. The old bucket benches began to serve other purposes. Today, they are useful shelving and display units.

The design shown is a copy of a late eighteenth-century bucket bench, possibly built by a pioneer in the Northwest Territory (now Ohio, Michigan, Indiana, and Illinois).

EXPLODED VIEW

BILL OF MATERIALS

WOODEN PARTS/*FINISHED DIMENSIONS*

A. Sides (2) $3/4$" x 12" x 44"
B. Top shelf $3/4$" x 8" x 36"
C. Lower shelves (2) $3/4$" x 12" x $35 1/4$"

HARDWARE

6d Square-cut nails (16)

PLAN OF PROCEDURE

1

Plane, rip, and cut the parts to the sizes shown in the Bill of Materials.

2

Cut 3/4"-wide, 3/8"-deep dadoes in the sides, as shown in the *Side View.*

3

Lay out and cut the shape of the sides, as shown in the *Side View.*

4

Cut a 3/4"-wide, 6"-long dovetail notch in the top ends of the sides, and cut matching dove-tail tenons on both ends of the top shelf, as shown in the *Top Shelf Layout.*

5

Finish sand the parts of the bucket bench and dry assemble them to check the fit of the joints. Reassemble the parts with glue and square-cut nails. Set the heads of the nails.

6

Do any necessary touch-up sanding and apply a finish to the completed project.

TOP SHELF LAYOUT

3/4" Wd x 3/8" Dp
Dado (Typ)

FRONT VIEW   **SIDE VIEW**

PIE SAFE

ate in medieval times, joiners began to enclose the shelves on which cooks stored food. They found that they needed to ventilate these enclosures, or the food in them quickly developed molds. Throughout the centuries that followed, these ventilated cupboards were known by many names — aumbries, hutches, livery cupboards, and food presses, to list a few.

There were also many different ways to ventilate these cupboards. Some had woven reed or lattice panels; others used frame doors with close-set slats or spindle turnings. One of the most popular ventilation methods was to pierce a wooden panel with many small holes. These holes usually formed a design.

In the early nineteenth century, advances in metallurgy made thin sheets of metal cheaper and more abundant. American craftsmen began to use pierced metal panels to ventilate food cupboards. Perhaps because these cupboards were partially made of metal, they reminded folks of a bank safe. Their makers gave them a whimsical nickname that has stuck to this day: *pie safe.*

**CABINET
EXPLODED VIEW**

**DOOR
EXPLODED VIEW**

BILL OF MATERIALS

WOODEN PARTS/*FINISHED DIMENSIONS*

A.	Legs (4)	2" x 2" x 68³/₄"
B.	Top front rail	³/₄" x 6" x 40"
C.	Bottom front rail	³/₄" x 4" x 40"
D.	Top side rails (2)	³/₄" x 9" x 15¹/₄"
E.	Middle side rails (4)	³/₄" x 3" x 15¹/₄"
F.	Bottom side rails (2)	³/₄" x 7" x 15¹/₄"
G.	Top/middle back rails (2)	³/₄" x 3" x 40"
H.	Bottom back rail	³/₄" x 7" x 40"
J.	Back panels (2)	¹/₂" x 18⁷/₈" x 38⁵/₈"
K.	Shelves (3)	³/₄" x 15³/₄" x 41¹/₄"
L.	Top	¹/₂" x 21" x 49¹/₂"
M.	Front cove molding	³/₄" x 4⁵/₈" x 48¹/₂"
N.	Side cove moldings (2)	³/₄" x 4⁵/₈" x 20¹/₂"
P.	Front bead molding	³/₄" x 1" x 44"
Q.	Side bead moldings (2)	³/₄" x 1" x 18¹/₄"

R.	Door stiles (3)	³/₄" x 3" x 39³/₈"
S.	Left inside door stile	³/₄" x 3¹/₂" x 39³/₈"
T.	Door rails (8)	³/₄" x 3" x 14¹⁵/₁₆"
U.	Door pull	1¹/₄" dia. x 2⁵/₈"
V.	Door latch	⁵/₈" x 1" x 2¹/₈"
W.	Pin	¹/₄" dia. x 1"
X.	Pegs (46)	¹/₄" x ¹/₄" x 1¹/₄"*
Y.	Three-bead molding (total)	⁵/₁₆" x ³/₄" x 640"

**Make the pegs at least this long, then — if necessary —
cut them to length after installing them.*

HARDWARE

1¹/₂" x 2" Butt hinges and mounting screws (2 pairs)
10" x 14¹/₄" Tin panels, 24 gauge (12)
1" Wire or headless brads (160–180)
6d Square-cut nails (16–24)

PLAN OF PROCEDURE

If necessary, glue up stock to make the wide parts — the shelves and back panels. Plane, rip, and cut the parts to the sizes shown in the Bill of Materials, except the moldings and door parts. Don't cut the door parts or the three-bead moldings yet; wait until you've built the case. Cut the cove moldings 1"–2" longer than specified.

2

Cut 1/4"-wide, 3/8"-deep grooves in the inside edges of the back rails and the back legs, as shown in the *Back Layout Detail* and *Left Back Leg Layout.* These grooves will hold the back panels.

3

Cut the 1/4"-wide, 1"-deep mortises in the inside faces of the legs, as shown in the *Left Front Leg Layout* and *Left Back Leg Layout.*

BACK LAYOUT DETAIL

SECTION B

4

Cut ¼"-wide, 1"-long tenons on the ends of the case rails. Notch the shoulders of these tenons to fit the leg mortises, as shown in the *Top Front Rail Layout, Bottom Front Rail Layout, Top Side Rail Layout, Middle Side Rail Layout, Bottom Side Rail Layout,* and *Back Layout Detail.*

5

Cut ¾"-wide, ⅜"-deep dadoes in the inside faces of the middle and bottom side rails, as shown in the *Middle Side Rail Layout* and *Bottom Side Rail Layout.*

6

Lay out and cut the shapes of the shelves, as shown in the *Shelf Layout.* Also bevel the back panels as shown in *Section B.*

7

Cut a ⅜"-wide, ⅜"-deep, 1¾"-long mortise in the top shelf, as shown in the *Shelf Layout.* This mortise will hold the door catch.

LEFT FRONT LEG LAYOUT

LEFT BACK LEG LAYOUT

PLAN OF PROCEDURE

FRONT VIEW

TOP FRONT RAIL LAYOUT

BOTTOM FRONT RAIL LAYOUT

TOP SIDE RAIL LAYOUT

MIDDLE SIDE RAIL LAYOUT

BOTTOM SIDE RAIL LAYOUT

SIDE VIEW

PLAN OF PROCEDURE

8

Finish sand the legs, rails, panels, and shelves. Assemble the parts of the case as follows:

- Glue the legs and side rails together, inserting the tenons in the mortises, and let the glue dry. This will make two side assemblies.
- Glue the front and back rails in the left side assembly.
- Before the glue dries, slide the back panels into the grooves in the back rails, but do *not* glue them in place. They must float in the grooves.
- Place the shelves in the dadoes in the left middle and bottom side rails. Again, this must be done before the glue on the rails dries, but do *not* glue the shelves in place.
- Glue the right side assembly to the front and back rails. Once again, do *not* glue the panels or shelves; let them float. Clamp the assembly together; make sure it's square, and let the glue dry.

9

Round the bottom portion of the pegs, as shown in the *Peg Detail*.

10

Drill a ¼"-diameter, 1¼"-deep hole through each mortise-and-tenon joint in the case. Drive a peg into each hole to secure the tenon in the mortise, letting the peg protrude slightly.

**PEG
DETAIL**

**(Make from *very*
hard wood.)**

11

Finish sand the top. Attach the top to the legs and top rails with nails. Don't drive these nails all the way in, in case you have to shift the position of the top when you attach the moldings.

12

Cut the coves in the cove moldings, then miter the edges at 45°, as shown in the *Top Molding Profile.*

 SECTION C

SECTION D

SECTION E

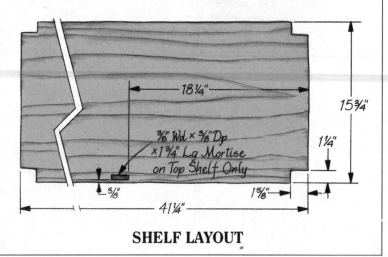

³⁄₈" Wd × ³⁄₈"Dp
×1³⁄₄" Lg Mortise
on Top Shelf Only

18¼"

15¾"

1¼"

³⁄₈"

1⁵⁄₈"

41¼"

SHELF LAYOUT

13

Round over the front edges of the bead moldings.

14

Fit the top moldings to the case, compound-mitering the adjoining ends at 45°.

15

Finish sand the cove moldings and attach them to the case with glue and nails. If necessary, shift the position of the top to center it over the moldings. Nail the top to the moldings, but do *not* glue it in place.

16

Fit the bead moldings, mitering the adjoining ends. Attach them to the case just below the cove moldings, using glue and nails.

17

Set the nails and cover the heads with putty.

18

Measure the door opening and make any necessary changes in the dimensions of the door parts. Cut the door parts to size, then cut the joinery needed to assemble the doors:

- 1/2"-wide, 3/8"-deep rabbets in the adjoining edges of the inside door stiles
- 1/4"-wide, 1"-deep, 2 1/4"-long mortises in the inside edges of the door stiles, as shown in the *Door Joinery Detail*
- 1/4"-thick, 1"-long tenons on the ends of the door rails

DOOR JOINERY DETAIL

TOP MOLDING PROFILE

PLAN OF PROCEDURE

19

Notch the tenons in the rails as shown in the *Door Joinery Detail,* fitting each tenon to its mortise.

20

Drill a 9/16"-diameter hole through the right inside door stile, as shown in the *Door Layout.* This hole will hold the door pull.

21

Finish sand the door parts and assemble the rails and stiles with glue.

22

Reinforce the mortise-and-tenon joints in the door frames with pegs, as you did on the face frame. Cut the pegs off flush with the back surfaces of the frames.

3/8"
2¼"
9⅞"
2¼"
9⅞"
3/8"
2¼"
3/8"
9⅞"
2¼"
3/8"

3"
9⅛"
3"
3/8" Wd × ½" Dp Rabbet
9⅛"
39⅞"
3"
9⅛"
3"

14¹⁵⁄₁₆"
12¹⁵⁄₁₆"
3"
3½"
½"
19⅞⁄₁₆"

LEFT DOOR LAYOUT

3½"
3/8" Wd × ½" Dp Rabbet
Door Rail
Door Stile
3"
3"

SECTION A

23

Mortise the door stiles and case for hinges, then mount the doors to the case.

24

Turn the shape of the door pull, as shown in the *Door Pull Layout.*

25

Cut the 60° taper in the door catch, as shown in the *Door Latch Detail,* and drill a 1/2"-diameter hole near one end.

26

Insert the door pull through the hole in the right door stile. Press the catch on the pull shaft to check the locking action. The door pull and the catch should turn together. When the catch is vertical, the tapered end must rest in the mortise in the top shelf.

27

Remove the doors and the hardware from the case. Also, disassemble the door pull and catch. Do any necessary touch-up sanding, then apply a finish to the pie safe. Finish *all* sides of the project — inside and out, top and bottom.

**DOOR PULL
LAYOUT**

DOOR LATCH DETAIL

PLAN OF PROCEDURE

28

Lay out the design on the tin panels, as shown in the *Tin Panel Pattern*. Punch the design with a nail set or large nail, then finish the panels. For more detailed information, see Making Tin Panels on page 285.

29

Cut the beads in the bead molding stock, as shown in the *Bead Molding Profile*.

30

Tack the tin panels over the openings in the case and door frames with the dimples facing *out*. (Country cabinetmakers believed this made it harder for insects to find their way into the pie safe.) Fit bead moldings around the perimeter of each panel, mitering the adjoining corners of the molding.

31

Finish sand the moldings and apply a finish to them. Nail (but do *not* glue) the moldings to the case and door frames. Set the heads of the nails.

32

Touch up the finish on the panels and three-bead moldings wherever necessary. Then replace the doors on the cabinet.

33

Replace the door pull in the right door and glue the catch onto the door pull shaft. Don't press the catch too tightly on the shaft — the pull and catch must turn freely. Drill a 1/4"-diameter hole through the catch and pull shaft; glue the pin in the hole.

TIN PANEL PATTERN

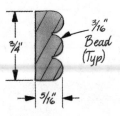

BEAD MOLDING PROFILE

COUNTRY CRAFTSMAN'S KNOW-HOW: MAKING TIN PANELS

Each tin panel on the Pie Safe is decorated with a six-pointed star or *rosette*. This is an ancient symbol, dating back to the Dark Ages. In the eighth and ninth centuries, the Germanic peoples of the Rhine Valley in Europe developed a system of religious and superstitious symbols, combining designs from the newly adopted Christian faith and their pagan heritage. They painted these symbols on their furniture, doors, fireplaces, houses, and barns. When the Germans began to settle in America, they still used many of these symbols to decorate their homes and furnishings.

Over the centuries, however, the symbols had lost their significance. By the time the German immigrants arrived in America, these symbols were more traditional than meaningful. It's now difficult to establish the original purpose of any one symbol, but the rosette may have once prevented bad fortune. It's thought that medieval Germans used it to keep the devil out of a building or cupboard on which it was displayed. If this is so, it makes good sense to decorate a pie safe with rosettes.

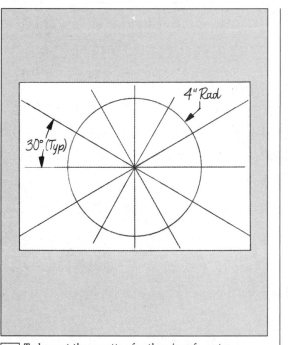

1 To lay out the rosettes for the pie safe, cut a piece of paper the same size as the tin panels — 10" x 14¼". Divide the paper into equal quadrants by drawing two perpendicular lines. Scribe a 4"-radius circle, using the point where the two lines intersect as the center. Then draw four more lines through the center, every 30°, dividing the circle into 12 wedge-shaped sections.

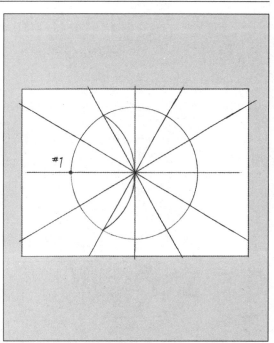

2 Without changing the setting of the compass, place the pivot on a point where the line through the long dimension of the paper intersects the circle. Draw a 4" radius arc from one side of the circle to the other. This arc should intersect the circle at the center and two points where other radial lines intersect it.

(Continued)

COUNTRY CRAFTSMAN'S
KNOW-HOW: MAKING TIN PANELS — CONT.

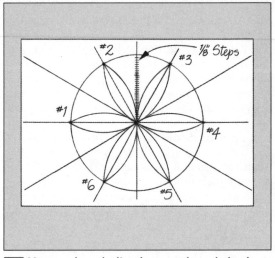

3 Move the pivot to a point where the last arc intersected the circle and draw another arc. Repeat until you've scribed six arcs — one every 60°. These arcs should meet at the center and the circumference of the circle, forming a rosette.

4 Measure along the line that runs through the short dimension of the paper, and mark every 1/8" out from the center.

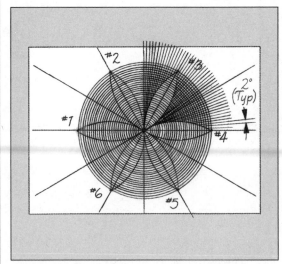

5 Place the compass pivot at the center of the circle and scribe concentric circles through the marks on the short line. The radius of each successive circle should be 1/8" larger or smaller than the one preceding.

6 Measure the circumference of the largest circle with a protractor, marking it every 2°. Draw radial lines from these marks to the center of the circle. Do *not* draw these radial lines inside the "leaves" of the rosette.

7 Make 12 photocopies of the pattern. Using spray adhesive, adhere a copy to each tin panel.

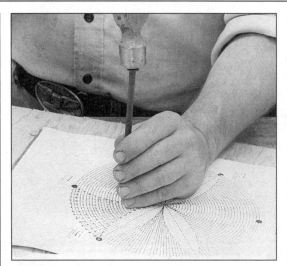

8 Temporarily tack each panel to a scrap of plywood with the pattern facing up. Grind a nail set or a 40d nail to a sharp, tapered point. Using a hammer to drive the tool through the tin, make a hole about $1/32"$–$1/16"$ in diameter.

9 Use the grid as a *guide* to help space the holes evenly, every $1/4"$ or so. (Don't try to punch holes everywhere the radial lines intersect the circles — the holes will be too close together, especially toward the center of the pattern.) Also, punch holes about every $1/4"$ from the circumference of the largest circle to the edge of the panel along the three longest lines shown.

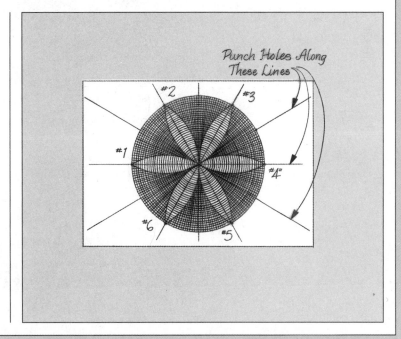

WATER BENCH

The water bench was an important step in the evolution of the kitchen sink. Before country homes had indoor plumbing, most folks fetched their water from a well outside. They brought the water up to the house in buckets and set the buckets on the back porch until they needed the water. They often built a special *bucket bench* to hold the buckets and added a top shelf at waist level to hold a basin and a pitcher for washing up.

Soon, the bucket bench moved inside — it was more convenient to have the water *inside* the house, especially on cold days. Craftsmen put splashguards around the top shelf to prevent the water from sloshing on the floor, and the bucket bench became a *water bench*.

The water bench shown is a simple, traditional design, with a high splashguard in back, and a lower one in front. A single, narrow shelf, running along the back splashguard, once held soap and other small wash-day items.

EXPLODED VIEW

BILL OF MATERIALS

WOODEN PARTS/*FINISHED DIMENSIONS*

A.	Sides (2)	$5/8$" x $16^1/4$" x 43"
B.	Bottom shelf	$5/8$" x $16^1/4$" x $29^1/2$"
C.	Top shelf	$5/8$" x 15" x $29^1/2$"
D.	Front splashguard	$5/8$" x $5^3/4$" x 30"
E.	Back splashguard	$5/8$" x $13^3/4$" x 30"
F.	Soap shelf	$5/8$" x $3^1/2$" x $28^3/4$"
G.	Cleats (2)	$5/8$" x $5/8$" x $3^1/2$"

HARDWARE

6d Square-cut nails ($1/4$ lb.)
4d Square-cut nails (6–8)

PLAN OF PROCEDURE

1

Plane, rip, and cut the parts to the sizes shown in the Bill of Materials.

2

Miter the ends of the cleats at 45°, as shown in the *Cleat Layout*.

3

Cut the joinery in the sides:

- 5/8"-wide, 3/8"-deep dadoes in the side stock, as shown in the *Side Layout*
- 5/8"-wide, 11 1/4"-long notches in both edges of the side stock, near the top*

When you cut the shape of the side, the front notch will be shortened to 5 3/4".

4

Lay out and cut the shape of the back splashguard and sides, as shown in the *Front View* and *Side View*.

5

Rout or cut a 5/16"-diameter bead in the bottom edge of the front splashguard, as shown in the *Front Splashguard Profile*.

SIDE VIEW

SIDE LAYOUT

TOP VIEW

30"

5/8"

3 1/2"

16 1/4"

5/8"

5/8"

28 3/4"

29 1/2"

30"

42" Rad

43"

5/8" Wd × 3/8" Dp
Dado

5/8" (Typ)

FRONT VIEW

5/8"

5 3/4"

**FRONT
SPLASHGUARD
PROFILE**

5/16"
Bead

6

Finish sand the parts of the water bench and dry assemble them to check the fit of the joints. Reassemble the parts — except the cleats and soap shelf — with glue and 6d square-cut nails. Set the heads of the nails.

7

Attach the cleats to the sides with glue and 4d square-cut nails. Once again, set the heads. Then lay the soap shelf across the cleats — do *not* attach it with glue or nails. The soap shelf on water benches and dry sinks was often left loose. Oftentimes, it was removed to make room for a large tub of water.

8

Do any necessary touch-up sanding and apply a finish to the completed project.

3 1/2"

5/8"

45°

CLEAT LAYOUT

HERB CUPBOARD

Although the United Society of Believers in Christ's Second Appearing — the Shakers — are best remembered for their simple, elegant furniture designs, they also excelled in many other industries. Among them was growing and curing herbs and spices. In fact, the Shakers of Sabbathday Lake, Maine (the last functional Shaker community), still sell their spices and teas worldwide.

This "herb cupboard" was designed to assist in the spice trade at the Pleasant Hill Shaker community in Kentucky. It was adapted from a common washstand design. The counter of the old washstand originally held buckets of water; the pegs (or *hangers*), towels and washcloths; the cupboard, soap and fresh linen. For this new application, the craftsman added more pegs and enlarged the counter. This provided a bigger work surface on which to process and package the spices. The pegs probably held bundles of cured herbs, waiting to be cut and cleaned. The cupboard may have held tins, boxes, and tools.

Today, it makes a useful addition to a kitchen, particularly if you spend a lot of time there. The top is well below normal counter height, and provides a comfortable sit-down work area.

EXPLODED VIEW

BILL OF MATERIALS

WOODEN PARTS/*FINISHED DIMENSIONS*

A. Top $3/4$" x $19^{1}/_{2}$" x 41"
B. Sides (2) $3/4$" x $16^{1}/_{4}$" x $27^{1}/_{4}$"
C. Front stiles (2) $3/4$" x 6" x $27^{1}/_{4}$"
D. Right/left backboards (2) $1/2$" x $7^{7}/_{8}$" x $27^{1}/_{4}$"
E. Middle backboards (2) $1/2$" x $7^{7}/_{8}$" x $23^{1}/_{2}$"
F. Shelves (2) $3/4$" x $15^{3}/_{4}$" x 30"
G. Front/back cleats (2) $3/4$" x $3/4$" x $29^{1}/_{2}$"
H. Side cleats (2) $3/4$" x $3/4$" x $14^{1}/_{4}$"
J. Door stiles (2) $3/4$" x 3" x $23^{7}/_{16}$"
K. Top door rail $3/4$" x 3" x $14^{7}/_{8}$"
L. Bottom door rail $3/4$" x 4" x $14^{7}/_{8}$"
M. Door panel $1/2$" x $13^{3}/_{8}$" x $17^{1}/_{8}$"

N. Pegs (4) $5/16$" x $5/16$" x $1^{1}/_{4}$"*
P. Door pull $1^{1}/_{4}$" dia. x $2^{7}/_{16}$"
Q. Door latch $1/2$" x $7/8$" x $2^{1}/_{4}$"
R. Wedge $1/4$" x $1^{1}/_{4}$" x $1^{1}/_{4}$"
S. Hangers (6)   1" dia. x $3^{3}/_{8}$"

Make the pegs at least this long, then cut them to length after you install them.

HARDWARE

$1^{1}/_{2}$" x 2" Butt hinges and mounting screws (1 pair)
4d Square-cut nails (24–30)
#8 x $1^{1}/_{4}$" Flathead wood screws (32)
#8 x 1" Flathead wood screws (4)

PLAN OF PROCEDURE

1

Glue up stock for the sides, top, shelves, and door panel. Plane, rip, and cut the parts to the sizes shown in the Bill of Materials, except the door parts and hangers. Wait to cut the door parts until after you've assembled the case. Cut the stock for the hangers 1/8"–1/4" thicker and wider than the specified diameter and 1/2"–1" longer.

Note: You can substitute commercially made Shaker pegs for the hangers, if you wish.

2

Cut the joinery needed to assemble the case:

- 3/4"-wide, 1/4"-deep dadoes in the sides to hold the shelves, as shown in the *Front View*
- 1/2"-wide, 1/4"-deep rabbets in the back edges of the sides to hold the backboards, as shown in the *Top View*
- 1/2"-wide, 1/4"-deep rabbets in the *adjoining* edges of the backboards, to overlap them

3

Drill the holes needed to assemble the case:

- 1/2"-diameter, 5/8"-deep holes in the sides to hold the hangers, as shown in the *Top View* and *Side View*
- 3/16"-diameter pilot holes in the cleats for the screws, as shown in the *Top Joinery Detail*

Drill the pilot holes in the cleats both side to side and top to bottom, so you can attach the top to the case. Countersink the holes on the *inside* surfaces for the heads of the screws. These pilot holes are slightly larger than the shafts of the screws. This will allow the wood to which the cleats are attached to expand and contract.

4 1/4"   3/4"

1/4" Wd x 1/2" Dp Blind Rabbet

4 1/4"   4 1/4"   4 1/4"

1/2"

B

SIDE VIEW   3 3/4"

3/4"   1"   10"   1"   2 1/2"

B

2 1/2"   17"

TOP VIEW

¼" Wd × ½" Dp Rabbet (Typ)

½" Wd × ¼" Dp Rabbet (Typ)

7⅞" (Typ)

Cleat

½" Dia × ⅝" Dp Hole (Typ)

17"

19½"

¾"

¾"

2½"

FRONT VIEW

41"

5"

6"

19" Opening

6"

5"

¾"   ¾"

¾" Wd × ¼" Dp Dado (Typ)

28"

A   A

¾" (Typ)

12"

4"

3¾"

1"

24"

1"

2½"

2½"

31"

PLAN OF PROCEDURE

4

Lay out the feet on the front stiles, sides, right backboard, and left backboard. Cut the shapes of the feet and sand the sawed edges.

5

If you're making the hangers (rather than buying commercially made pegs), turn them to the shape shown in the *Hanger Layout*. Finish sand the hanger on the lathe.

6

Finish sand the parts you've made so far. Assemble them in the following order:

- Fasten the sides to the shelves with glue and nails.
- Fasten the front stiles to the sides with glue and nails. Also, nail the stiles to the shelves, but do *not* glue these parts together.
- Nail the backboards to the assembly — do *not* glue them.

- Fasten the cleats to the front stiles and sides with 1¼"-long flathead wood screws. Fasten a cleat to the backboards with 1"-long screws — do *not* glue the cleats to the assembly.
- Fasten the top to the cleats with 1¼"-long screws — do *not* glue the top to the assembly.
- Glue the hangers in the holes in the sides. Sand all the joints clean and flush.

HANGER LAYOUT

TOP JOINERY DETAIL

SECTION A

7

Set all the heads of the nails and cover them with putty.

8

Measure the door opening, and — if necessary — adjust the dimensions of the door parts. Cut the door parts to size, except the door pull. Cut the stock for the pull $1/8$"–$1/4$" thicker and wider than the specified diameter and $1/2$"–1" longer.

3"

$2^1/8$"

1"

$5/8$"

Top Rail

$1/4$"

$1/2$"

$1/4$" Wd x
$3/8$" Dp Groove (Typ)

$3^1/8$"

$2^1/8$" $2^5/8$"

$1/4$"

1"

Bottom Rail

$3^1/8$"

$3^5/8$"

$1/4$" $1/2$"

**DOOR
ASSEMBLY
DETAIL**

Note: You can make the door pull out of a wooden knob and a short length of $1/2$"-diameter dowel, if you wish.

9

Cut the joinery needed to assemble the door, as shown in the *Door Assembly Detail:*

- $1/4$"-wide, $3/8$"-deep grooves centered in the inside edges of the rails and stiles
- $1/4$"-wide, 1"-deep, $2^1/8$"-long mortises in the upper ends of the stiles
- $1/4$"-wide, 1"-deep, $3^1/8$"-long mortises in the lower ends of the stiles
- 1"-long, $1/4$"-thick tenons in the ends of both rails; cut a $3/8$"-wide, $5/8$"-long notch or *haunch* in the tenons to fit the tenons to the mortises

10

Raise the door panel as shown in *Section A.*

PLAN OF PROCEDURE

11

Drill the holes needed to assemble the door:

- 9/16"-diameter hole through the left door stile, as shown in the *Door Layout,* for the door pull
- 1/2"-diameter hole through the door latch, as shown in the *Door Latch Detail,* to attach the pull

12

If you're making the door pull, turn it to the shape shown in the *Door Pull Layout.* Finish sand the pull on the lathe.

13

Cut tapers in the wedge and door latch, as shown in the *Wedge Detail* and *Door Latch Detail.*

14

Finish sand the door parts. Assemble the door stiles and rails with glue. Slide the panel in place, raised face toward the inside. Do *not* glue it to the rails or stiles. Let the panel float in the grooves.

WEDGE DETAIL

DOOR LATCH DETAIL

DOOR LAYOUT

DOOR PULL LAYOUT

Round the bottom portion of the pegs, as shown in the *Peg Detail.*

16

Drill a 5/16"-diameter hole through each mortise-and-tenon joint, then drive the pegs through the holes from the out-side. Cut the pegs off flush with the inside surface of the door frame.

17

Cut hinge mortises in the door frame and right front stile, then mount the door in the case.

18

Insert the door pull through the hole in the door frame, and glue the latch to it. Be careful not to press the pull too far into the hole in the latch or get any glue on the door frame. The pull and latch must rotate easily in the door frame.

19

Glue the wedge inside the left front stile, opposite the door pull and about 1/4" below it. The wedge should be flush with the inside edge of the stile, as shown in *Section A.*

SECTION C   SECTION D   SECTION E

20

Remove the door from the case and the hinges from the door. Do any necessary touch-up sanding, then apply a finish to the completed cupboard. When the finish dries, replace the hinges and the door.

(Make from *very hard* wood.)

PEG DETAIL

SECTION B

DRY SINK

This distinctive cupboard was once as much a fixture in American country kitchens as the kitchen sink is now. Over the span of the eighteenth and nineteenth centuries, the dry sink became a country institution.

It evolved from a simple bench that once sat outside the back door of a cabin and held buckets of water. As the land became more settled, craftsmen found the time to refine this bench. First, they added a shelf above the first to hold the water while they washed. Then they enclosed this upper shelf with splashguards to keep the water from dripping on the floor, creating a "sink." They extended the side to hold a third, smaller shelf above the sink. This held soap, dippers, brushes, and similar items. Finally, they enclosed the bottom shelf with doors to keep dirt from settling in the buckets of water.

In a few lucky cases, folks built their kitchens directly over wells. They installed cabinets similar to these over the well and mounted a pump on them. These were "wet sinks" — using the pump, the cook could draw water directly into the sink. Most people, however, weren't that fortunate. They had "dry sinks" and continued to haul water from an outside well and store it inside the cupboard.

EXPLODED VIEW

BILL OF MATERIALS

WOODEN PARTS/*FINISHED DIMENSIONS*

A.	Sides (2)	3/4" x 17 1/4" x 45 1/8"
B.	Top	7/8" x 7" x 50"
C.	Shelves (2)	3/4" x 16 3/4" x 47 1/4"
D.	Backboards (7)	1/2" x 7 5/32" x 41 1/2"
E.	Face frame rail	3/4" x 4" x 48"
F.	Face frame stiles (2)	3/4" x 4" x 31"
G.	Top door rails (2)	3/4" x 4" x 13 7/8"
H.	Bottom door rails (2)	3/4" x 5" x 13 7/8"
J.	Outside door stiles (2)	3/4" x 4" x 25 15/16"
K.	Inside door stiles (2)	3/4" x 4 1/2" x 25 15/16"
L.	Door panels (2)	1/2" x 12 3/8" x 17 5/8"
M.	Pegs (8)	5/16" x 5/16" x 1 1/4"*

N.	Door pull	1 1/4" dia. x 2 5/8"
P.	Door latch	5/8" x 1" x 2 5/8"
Q.	Wedge	1/4" x 1" x 1 1/2"
R.	Pin	1/4" dia. x 1"

Make the pegs at least this long, then cut them to length after you install them.

HARDWARE

1 1/2" x 2" Butt hinges and mounting screws (2 pairs)
Small door catch and mounting screws
6d Square-cut nails (24–30)
1 1/4" Wire or headless brads (30–36)

PLAN OF PROCEDURE

1

If necessary, glue up stock to make the wide parts — sides, shelves, and door panels. Plane, rip, and cut the parts to the sizes shown in the Bill of Materials, except for the pegs. Cut the pegs about 1/4" longer than specified.

2

Cut the joinery needed to assemble the case:

- 3/4"-wide, 3/8"-deep dadoes in the sides to hold the shelves, as shown in the *Side Layout*
- 1/2"-wide, 3/8"-deep, 41 1/8"-long blind rabbets in the back edges of the sides
- 1/2"-wide, 3/8"-deep, 47 1/4"-long double-blind rabbet in the back edge of the top, as shown in the *Top Layout/ Bottom View*
- 1/2"-wide, 1/4"-deep rabbets in *both* edges of the middle backboards and *one* edge of the right and left back-boards, as shown in the *Top View*
- 1/4"-wide, 1"-deep, 3 1/4"-long mortises in the bottom edge of the face frame rail, as shown in the *Face Frame Assembly Detail*
- 1/4"-thick, 1"-long, 3 1/4"-wide tenons on the top ends of the face frame stiles

**BOTTOM VIEW
TOP LAYOUT**

SIDE LAYOUT

SIDE VIEW

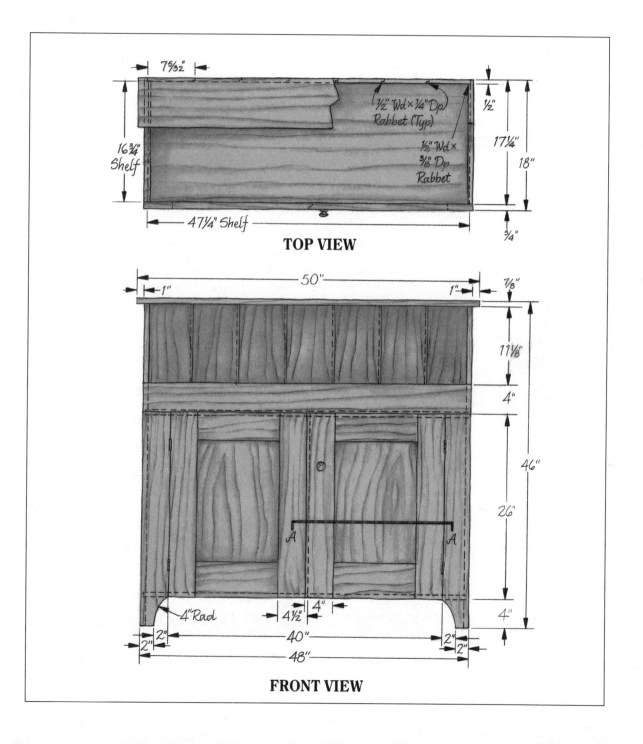

TOP VIEW

FRONT VIEW

7⅝₃₂"

½" Wd × ¼" Dp
Rabbet (Typ)

½" Wd ×
⅜" Dp
Rabbet

½"

17¼"

18"

16¾"
Shelf

47¼" Shelf

¾"

50"

1"

1"

⅛"

11⅛"

4"

46"

26"

A

A

4" Rad

4½"

4"

4"

2"

2"

40"

2"

2"

2"

48"

PLAN OF PROCEDURE

3

Lay out and cut the shapes of the sides and face frame stiles, as shown in the *Side Layout* and *Front View*. Sand the sawed edges.

4

Stain the rabbets in the backboards a dark brown or black.

FACE FRAME ASSEMBLY DETAIL

5

Finish sand the parts of the case and assemble them in the following order:

- Glue the shelves to the sides and reinforce the joints with square-cut nails.
- Glue the face frame stiles to the face frame rail, inserting the tenons in the mortises.
- Glue the assembled face frame to the case and reinforce it with nails.
- Attach the top to the sides with nails.
- Nail the backboards to the sides, top, and shelves with brads. Do *not* glue the backboards in place.

As you work, sand all joints clean and flush. Set the heads of the nails. If you wish, cover the heads of the nails in the sides and front with putty.

6

Cut the joinery needed to assemble the doors:

- 1/2"-wide, 3/8"-deep rabbets in the adjoining edges of the inside door stiles, as shown in *Section A*
- 1/4"-wide, 3/8"-deep grooves in the inside edges of all door rails and stiles, as shown in the *Door Assembly Detail*
- 1/4"-wide, 1"-deep, 3 1/4"-long mortises in the inside edges of the door stiles, 3/8" from the top ends
- 1/4"-wide, 1"-deep, 4 1/4"-long mortises in the inside edges of the door stiles, 3/8" from the bottom ends
- 1/4"-wide, 1"-long tenons on the ends of the door rails

SECTION A

8

Drill a 9/16"-diameter hole in the right inside door stile for the door latch assembly, as shown in the *Front View*.

7

Notch the tenons in the rails as shown in the *Door Assembly Detail,* creating a haunch in each tenon and fitting it to its mortise.

Raise the door panels, beveling the edges and ends to fit the grooves in the rails and stiles, as shown in *Section A*.

9

Finish sand the door parts and assemble the rails and stiles with glue. Put the panels in place as you glue up the door frames, but do not apply glue to them. The panels must float in the grooves.

10

Round the bottom portion of the pegs, as shown in the *Peg Detail*.

11

Drill a 5/16"-diameter hole through each mortise and tenon in the door frames. Drive a peg into each hole to secure the tenon in the mortise, then cut off the peg flush with the inside surface of the door frame.

DOOR ASSEMBLY DETAIL

TOP VIEW

**FRONT VIEW
LEFT DOOR LAYOUT**

PLAN OF PROCEDURE

12

Mortise the door stiles and face frame stiles for hinges, then mount the doors to the case.

13

Turn the door pull as shown in the *Door Pull Layout*. Finish sand the pull on the lathe.

PEG DETAIL
(Make from *very* hard wood.)

 SECTION A

SECTION B

SECTION C

14

Drill a ½"-diameter hole through the door latch, ½" from one end, as shown in the *Door Latch Assembly Detail*.

15

Bevel the end of the latch opposite the hole you just drilled. Also, cut a taper in the wedge.

16

Insert the door pull through the hole in the right inside stile. Glue the latch on the pull shaft. Don't press the latch too tightly on the shaft — the pull must turn freely. Drill a ¼"-diameter hole through the latch and pull; glue the pin in the hole.

17

Experiment with the position of the wedge on the left inside door stile. When you turn the pull counterclockwise, the beveled edge of the latch should contact the wedge, holding the right door snug against the left. When you find the proper position, glue the wedge to the inside surface of the stile.

18

Mount the door catch on the bottom side of the top shelf, just behind the left inside stile. The catch should hold the left door closed.

19

Remove the doors and the hardware from the case. Do any necessary touch-up sanding, then apply a finish to the completed dry sink. Finish *all* sides of the project — inside and out, top and bottom. Then reassemble the doors to the case.

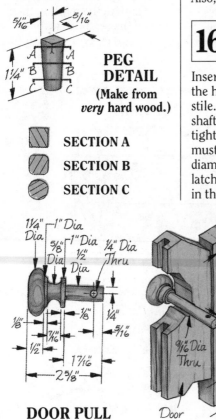

DOOR PULL LAYOUT

DOOR LATCH ASSEMBLY DETAIL

COUNTRY CRAFTSMAN'S
KNOW-HOW: MAKING BACKBOARDS

Country craftsmen often assembled wide panels at the backs of cupboards and cabinets from several boards. For strength and aesthetics, they rabbeted the edges of these boards, then lapped the rabbets. They did *not* glue the boards together, but left each backboard free to expand and contract independently of the others. This prevented the boards from cracking or splitting.

The boards did, however, show their seams. When the backboards contracted, the lapped rabbets opened up. This was especially distracting if the boards were stained or painted a dark color. Wherever the rabbets pulled apart, they would reveal raw, light-colored wood. To make these gaps less noticeable, cabinetmakers stained the rabbeted edges a dark brown or black.

1 Rabbet the adjoining edges of backboards so you can lap them when you assemble the case. This prevents light from showing through the back, and adds strength to the assembly.

2 Apply a dark stain to the rabbets *before* you attach the backboards to the cabinet.

3 Scrape the faces of the backboards to remove any stain that bleeds over onto the surfaces from the edges.

4 After staining the edges and scraping the faces, nail the backboards in place. Do *not* glue them to the case. The nails allow the backboards to move freely, flexing slightly as the wood expands and contracts.

SALT BOX

Salt was a precious commodity in colonial America. The colonists needed it not only for cooking, but to preserve food. In the days before refrigeration, salting meat and canning vegetables in brine (a salt solution) was the only way to keep the food from going bad.

Cooks kept their salt in a "salt box." There were no salt shakers — kitchen salt came in clumps or large crystals. For convenience, this small box usually hung near the stove. A lid kept soot and grease from settling in the salt.

Although salt was precious, craftsmen rarely wasted much effort or materials in making salt boxes. Owing to constant use and the chemical action of the salt, these boxes wore out quickly. So they were usually made simply, using inexpensive wood and as little hardware as possible. The hinges on this salt box are fashioned from linked cotter pins and were known as "snipe" hinges. This was a popular method of making inexpensive hinges for small, utilitarian projects during the eighteenth and early nineteenth centuries.

EXPLODED VIEW

BILL OF MATERIALS

WOODEN PARTS/*FINISHED DIMENSIONS*

A.	Back	$3/8$" x $5 1/4$" x $6 1/2$"
B.	Front	$3/8$" x $1 7/8$" x $5 1/4$"
C.	Sides (2)	$3/8$" x $2 1/2$" x 3"
D.	Bottom	$3/8$" x $2 1/2$" x $4 1/2$"
E.	Lid	$3/8$" x $3 3/4$" x $5 3/4$"

HARDWARE

$1 1/4$" Headless brads (12–16)
1" Cotter pins (4)

PLAN OF PROCEDURE

1

Plane, rip, and cut the parts to the sizes shown in the Bill of Materials. Bevel both edges of the lid and the top edge of the front at 25°. Miter the top ends of the sides at 65°, as shown in the *Side View*.

2

Lay out and cut the shape of the back, as shown in the *Back Pattern*. Sand the sawed edges.

3

Dry assemble the parts and mark where the lid touches the back. Then drill the necessary holes:

- ¼"-diameter hole through the back, as shown in the *Front View*
- ⅛"-diameter holes through the lid and the back, as shown in the *Side View* and *Hinge Detail*

Note: The holes in the lid are angled slightly. These holes and those in the back hold the cotter pin hinges. The location and spacing of these holes are not critical, but they should be equidistant from each side.

FRONT VIEW

SIDE VIEW

4

Finish sand the parts of the salt box and dry assemble them to check the fit. Reassemble the parts with glue and square-cut headless brads. Set the heads of the brads and cover them with putty.

5

Do any necessary touch-up sanding and apply a finish to the completed project.

6

Link two pairs of cotter pins as shown in the *Hinge Detail*. Insert one pin from each pair through the 1/8"-diameter holes in the lid, and bend over the ends. Insert the other pins through the 1/8"-diameter holes in the back. Once again, bend over the ends.

7

If you wish, hang the salt box from a nail. If you want to secure the project to the wall, drive a screw or Molly anchor through the 1/4"-diameter hole in the back.

1 Square = 1/2"

BACK PATTERN

1" Cotter Pins

1/4" Approx

HINGE DETAIL

SPICE CUPBOARD

Spices and herbs were precious commodities in centuries past. Country folk didn't have the variety of foods that we do today, and without a store of spices, their meals would have been bland and monotonous. They didn't have over-the-counter medicines, either. Instead, they collected and stored many different herbs to treat a wide assortment of ailments. For this reason, the cupboard where these commodities were stored was an important fixture in the early American home. It was a spice rack, a first-aid center, and a medicine cabinet all rolled into one.

Country folks often made these small, hanging cupboards with just the simplest tools. The parts were butt jointed and nailed together. The paneled doors were flat and plain; there were few decorations. The hinges were usually homemade, and the latch was a simple brass hook. Some craftsmen even used strips of leather for hinges and latches.

This reproduction preserves this simplicity. It has just a little decoration — an arched back and a double-paneled door. The construction is authentic; even the shelves are spaced to hold old-time spice boxes. The one contemporary addition is that the shelves sit loosely in dadoes. Only the middle and bottom shelves are fixed; the others can be moved — or removed completely. This allows you to rearrange the space inside the cupboard.

Variations: You can alter the height of the cupboard, if you wish, simply by changing the length of the vertical parts. (Don't make it too much longer than shown, or it will be too heavy to hang on the wall.) You may also turn the panels around in the door frame so the raised area faces out. This will give the piece a more formal appearance.

EXPLODED VIEW

BILL OF MATERIALS

WOODEN PARTS/*FINISHED DIMENSIONS*

A.	Backboard	⅝" x 14" x 40"
B.	Sides (2)	⅝" x 5¾" x 31½"
C.	Top	⅝" x 7" x 15"
D.	Bottom/middle shelves (2)	½" x 5¾" x 13½"
E.	Adjustable shelves (2–4)	½" x 5¾" x 13⅜"
F.	Door stiles (2)	¾" x 3" x 31½"
G.	Upper door rails (2)	¾" x 3" x 10"
H.	Lower door rail	¾" x 4" x 10"
J.	Door panels (2)	⅝" x 8⅝" x 11⅜"
K.	Pegs (6)	5/16" x 5/16" x 1"*

HARDWARE

Brass hook and eye
1" Door pull
4d Square-cut nails (24–30)
1½" x 2" Butt hinges and mounting screws (3)

*Make the pegs at least this long, then cut them to length
after you install them.*

PLAN OF PROCEDURE

1

Plane, rip, and cut the parts to the sizes shown in the Bill of Materials, except for the pegs. Cut these about ¼" longer than specified.

2

Cut ½"-wide, ¼"-deep dadoes and rabbets in the sides, as shown in the *Side Panel Layout*.

3

Cut the shape of the backboard as shown in the *Front View*, and drill a hole in the center of the arch so you can hang the cupboard on a peg or a nail.

FRONT VIEW

SIDE VIEW

**SIDE PANEL
LAYOUT**

4

Finish sand the parts of the case, then assemble the backboard, top, sides, middle shelf, and bottom shelf with glue and square-cut nails. Set the heads of the nails.

5

Cut ¼"-wide, ⅜"-deep grooves in the *inside* edges of all the door parts. Cut grooves in *both* edges of the middle rail.

6

Drill holes to rough out ¼"-wide, 1"-deep mortises in the door stiles, as shown in the *Door Frame Joinery Detail*. Square the sides and corners of the mortises with a chisel.

7

Cut ¼"-wide, 1"-long tongues on the ends of the door rails to fit the mortises in the stiles. Cut haunches on the upper and lower rails as shown in the *Door Frame Joinery Detail*.

8

Raise the door panels, as shown in the *Door Panel Detail*.

2½"

3/16" ⅝"

**DOOR FRAME
JOINERY DETAIL**

**DOOR PANEL
DETAIL**

PLAN OF PROCEDURE

9

Finish sand the parts of the door and assemble the rails and stiles with glue. Put the panels in place as you glue up the door frame, but do not apply glue to them. The panels must float in the grooves.

10

Round the bottom portion of the pegs, as shown in the *Peg Detail*.

11

Drill a 5/16"-diameter hole through each mortise and tenon in the door frame. Drive a peg into the hole to secure the tenon in the mortise, then cut off the peg flush with the inside surface of the door frame.

12

Mortise the door and the side of the cupboard for hinges, then mount the door to the cupboard.

13

Fit the adjustable shelves in the dadoes, shaving and rounding the shelf ends so the shelves will slide smoothly in and out of the case.

14

Remove the door from the case and all hardware from the cupboard. Do any necessary touch-up sanding and apply a finish to complete the cupboard.

15

Reassemble the cupboard and, if desired, mount it on a wall or hang it on a peg rail.

1/4"

3/4"

5/16" Sq. Peg Thru (Typ)

SECTION A

14"

3" 8" 3"

A

A 3"

1/4" Wd × 3/8" Dp Groove (Typ)

10 3/4"

3"

10 3/4"

4"

DOOR DETAIL

5/16" 5/16"

B B

C C

D D

1"

SECTION B

SECTION C

SECTION D

(Make pegs from *very* hard wood.)

PEG DETAIL

COUNTRY CRAFTSMAN'S
KNOW-HOW: DRIVING SQUARE PEGS IN ROUND HOLES

The country craftsman often pinned his door frames and other furniture assemblies together by driving square pegs into round holes. This method works much better than using round pegs or dowels. The corners of the square pegs wedge themselves in the holes and can't work loose.

1 Make the pegs from a wood much harder than the one you used to make the frame. Rock maple and hickory are the materials most country craftsmen used.

2 Cut each peg to a length you can comfortably grip. Whittle about three-quarters of its length, making it more and more round toward one end. When you're finished, one end should be round and the other square. The square portion should be just 1/4"–1/2" long.

3 Assemble the joint. Drill a hole, as big around as the peg is square, through the parts that are to be pegged together.

4 Coat the peg with glue, and drive it into the hole, rounded end first, with a mallet. Tap it in so the top is *almost* (but not quite) flush with the surface of the wood. (About 1/16" should protrude.) Make sure the square portion is wedged in the hole. Be careful, however, not to hit the peg so hard that it splinters.

(Continued)

COUNTRY CRAFTSMAN'S KNOW-HOW: DRIVING SQUARE PEGS IN ROUND HOLES — *CONT.*

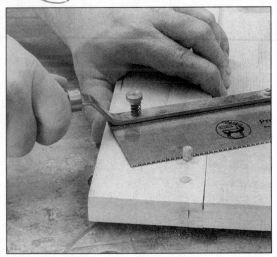

5 If the rounded portion protrudes from the back of the assembly, cut it flush with the surface of the wood. Leave the square end alone — don't sand it or cut it flush.

6 Lightly sand the front surface, rounding over the peg slightly. Do *not* sand it flush. If you inspect the pegs on old country pieces, you'll see that most of the pegs protrude. As the wood frame expands and contracts for a century or more, it begins to push the pegs out of the holes.

Feathers

7 To help hold the pegs in their holes, some craftsmen "feathered" them, as shown, with a pocketknife. These feathers always faced toward the "head" of the peg.

Chamfer

8 If the peg is to be driven through several parts, chamfer the round end. This will prevent it from catching on the edge of a board and possibly splitting the joint.

FOR STORING & KEEPING

HANGING CORNER CABINET

While cupboards were popular in the country, cabinets were less common. The reason has to do with the traditional difference between cupboards and cabinets, and how they were used: Solid-door cupboards were for storage whereas glass-door cabinets were for display. Cupboards are utilitarian; cabinets are special and tend to be more finely crafted. This distinction is why fine furnituremakers of the seventeenth century began to use the title *cabinetmaker*.

Early country life was a great deal like a cupboard — plain and practical. Country folks had lots to store, but little to display. The decorative knickknacks and collectibles that we take for granted would seem rare treasures to our great-great grand-parents. Consequently, cabinets were few and far between. If a country family had a cabinet, it was likely to be a small one, such as the cabinet shown. It has just three shelves, one of them open — probably more than enough for the treasures of simple country folks.

EXPLODED VIEW

BILL OF MATERIALS

WOODEN PARTS/*FINISHED DIMENSIONS*

A. Top/middle shelves (3) $1/2" \times 12" \times 20^3/4"$
B. Side stiles (2) $3/4" \times 3" \times 19^3/4"$
C. Front stiles (2) $3/4" \times 2^1/4" \times 19^3/4"$
D. Front backboards (2) $3/8" \times 5^3/4" \times 21^1/4"$
E. Middle backboards (2) $3/8" \times 5^3/4" \times 30"$
F. Right rear backboard $3/8" \times 4^3/4" \times 30"$
G. Left rear backboard $3/8" \times 4^3/8" \times 30"$
H. Bottom shelf $1/2" \times 5" \times 7^1/16"$
J. Side top moldings (2) $3/4" \times 2^1/4" \times 3^1/4"$
K. Front top molding $3/4" \times 2^1/4" \times 20^1/8"$
L. Door stiles (2) $3/4" \times 2" \times 19^{11}/16"$
M. Top door rail $3/4" \times 2" \times 11^5/8"$
N. Bottom door rail $3/4" \times 2^3/4" \times 11^5/8"$
P. Mullion $1/4" \times 3/4" \times 14^{15}/16"$
Q. Sashes (2) $1/4" \times 3/4" \times 4^7/16"$

R. Vertical glazing bars (2) $1/4" \times 1/2" \times 7^{23}/32"$
S. Horizontal glazing bar $1/4" \times 1/2" \times 10^3/8"$
T. Pegs (4) $5/16" \times 5/16" \times 1"*$
U. Door latch $1/4" \times 1/2" \times 1^1/4"$

*Make the pegs at least this long, then cut them to length after you install them.

HARDWARE

$1/2"$ Door pull
$1^1/2" \times 2"$ Butt hinges and mounting screws (2)
4d Square-cut nails (18)
4d Finishing nails ($1/4$ lb.)
$5" \times 7^5/8"$ Glass panes (4)
Glazing points (24)
#8 x 1" Flathead wood screw
Leather thong (12")

PLAN OF PROCEDURE

1

Plane, rip, and cut the parts to the sizes shown in the Bill of Materials, except for the moldings, mullion, sashes, glazing bars, and pegs. Plane and rip the moldings, mullion, sashes, and glazing bars to the proper thickness and width, but don't cut them to length yet. Make the pegs about 1/4" longer than specified.

TOP VIEW

3/8"

15½"

1/4" Dia Thru

3/8" Wd x 3/16" Dp Rabbet

2¼"

5/8"

67½°

3¼"

20⅛"

BACK VIEW

5/8"

15⅛"

15⅛"

8¾"

9½" 1/2" (Typ)

10" Rad

5"

5⅜"

FRONT VIEW

3/4"

A

A

19¾"

30¾"

10¼"

1/2"

2

Bevel the adjoining edges of the front and side stiles at 67½°, as shown in the *Bottom View.*

3

Cut the shapes of the top and middle shelves, as shown in the *Middle Shelf Layout.*

4

Cut the shape of the bottom shelf.

5

If you wish, cut or rout dovetail notches to hold spoons in the front edges of the middle shelves, as shown in the *Spoon Holder Layout.* These notches are optional.

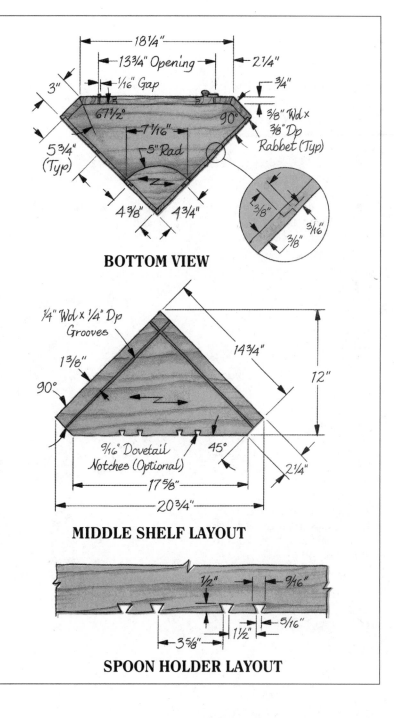

BOTTOM VIEW

MIDDLE SHELF LAYOUT

SECTION A

SPOON HOLDER LAYOUT

PLAN OF PROCEDURE

6

Cut the grooves and rabbets needed to assemble the case:

- 3/8"-wide, 3/8"-deep rabbets in the back edges of the side stiles
- 3/8"-wide, 3/8"-deep rabbets in the adjoining edges of the backboards
- 1/4"-wide, 1/4"-deep grooves in the middle shelves, 1 3/8" from the back edges

7

Drill a 1/4"-diameter hole for the thong in the top, as shown in the *Top View*.

8

Finish sand the parts of the case, then assemble them with glue, finishing nails, and square-cut nails. Drive the finishing nails in the back of the case, where they won't be seen, and the square-cut nails in the sides and front. Set the nails. Don't attach the bottom shelf yet.

9

Cut a 10"-radius curve in the lower portion of the backboards, as shown in the *Back View*. Sand the cut edges.

10

Attach the lower shelf with glue and finishing nails. Set the nails.

11

Round the edge of the top molding, as shown in the *Molding Detail*.

12

Cut the molding to length, mitering the adjoining ends at 67 1/2°.

DOOR LAYOUT

13

Finish sand the molding, then attach it to the case with glue and finishing nails. Set the nails.

14

Cut the joinery needed to assemble the door, as shown in the *Door Assembly Detail*:

- 1"-long, 1/4"-thick tenons the full width of the rails
- 3/8"-wide, 1/2"-deep rabbets in the inside edges of the rails
- 1/4"-wide, 3/8"-deep grooves centered in the inside edges of the stiles
- 1/4"-wide, 1"-deep, 1 1/4"-long mortises in the upper ends of the stiles
- 1/4"-wide, 1"-deep, 2"-long mortises in the lower ends of the stiles

MOLDING DETAIL

**DOOR ASSEMBLY
DETAIL
BACK VIEW**

Haunch

PLAN OF PROCEDURE

15

Cut a haunch in the tenons, as shown in the *Door Assembly Detail*.

16

Cut away the inside edge of the stiles to make double-blind rabbets for the glass, as shown in the *Door Assembly Detail*.

17

Finish sand the door frame parts, then assemble the door frame with glue.

18

Round the bottom portion of the pegs, as shown in the *Peg Detail*.

19

Drill a 5/16"-diameter hole through each mortise-and-tenon joint, then drive the pegs through the holes from the outside. Cut the pegs off flush with the inside surface of the door frame.

20

Cut the mullion, sashes, and glazing bars to the proper length, finish sand them, and glue them in the door frame. (They are attached with simple butt joints.)

21

Cut hinge mortises in the door frame and left front stile, then mount the door in the case.

 SECTION B

 SECTION C

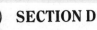 **SECTION D**

(Make pegs from *very* hard wood.)

PEG DETAIL

THONG DETAIL

22

Chamfer the outside corners of the latch, as shown in the *Latch Detail*.

23

Drill a pilot hole and a counter-sink in the latch, then attach the latch to the right front stile with a flathead wood screw, as shown in the *Front View*.

24

Remove the door and the latch from the case, and remove all hardware.

25

Do any necessary touch-up sanding, then apply a finish to the case, door, and latch.

26

Mount panes of glass in the door with glazing points and glazing compound. After the compound dries, paint it or stain it to match the cabinet.

27

Remount the door and the latch on the case.

28

Insert a leather thong through the hole in the top, and knot it as shown in the *Thong Detail*.

29

Reassemble the cabinet. Drive a nail into the corner where you want to mount the cabinet, and hang it by the thong. Fasten the cabinet securely to the wall with screws or Molly anchors. (**Note:** The thong is an *aid* to help mount the cabinet on the wall. It shouldn't be used as the sole support for the cabinet.)

1¼"   ¼"   ¼"

⅛" Hole Thru C'Sink   5/8"

½"   ¼"   ⅛"   ¼"

SIDE VIEW   **END VIEW**

LATCH DETAIL

COUNTRY CRAFTSMAN'S
KNOW-HOW: USING SQUARE-CUT NAILS

Much country furniture was assembled with nails. Craftsmen didn't often have the time, tools, or expertise to make fancy joinery, and metal screws were expensive. So they used common nails. These nails, however, were very different from modern common nails. They were hand forged, with square shanks and heads. You can still purchase hand-forged nails from:

Tremont Nail Co.
8 Elm Street
P.O. Box 111
Wareham, MA 02571

Tremont offers several sizes and styles of hand-forged nails, including a fine finishing nail. They cost a little more than regular hardware-store variety nails, but they have a more aesthetic look to them. And they will make your reproductions more authentic.

If you don't want to purchase special hand-forged nails, the closest type that's commonly available in most hardware stores is the *square-cut nail* (or, simply, cut nails). These are stamped from a sheet of thick steel, so they have square, tapered shanks and square heads. They are made to be used in cement and concrete, but will also work well in wood.

1 Whether you use a hand-forged nail or square-cut nail, you can't simply drive it into a board (particularly a hardwood board) because it acts like a small wedge and splits the wood. Instead, you must first drill a pilot hole. This hole should be slightly smaller than the width of the nail, measured about halfway along the shank.

2 Hammer the nail into the pilot hole until it protrudes just $^1/_{16}"$–$^1/_8"$ from the surface. If the nail is rectangular, rather than truly square, make sure the widest part of the shank is parallel to the wood grain.

3 Drive the nail the rest of the way into the wood with a nail set, so the head rests $^1/_{16}"$–$^1/_8"$ below the surface.

4 Cover the exposed head of the nail with wood putty, such as Durham's Water Putty. You can also make your own putty by mixing sawdust with clear epoxy glue. When the putty hardens, sand it flush with the surface. *Tip:* If you use a commercial putty, mix it with a stain or aniline dye to match the final finish on your project.

5 After you paint or finish the project, the nail holes will only be visible on close inspection. They will look as if you assembled the piece with old-time hand-forged nails.

PEWTER BENCH

In medieval Europe, it was the custom for a nobleman to display his "plate" or dinnerware on open shelves. These shelves were perhaps the most important piece of furniture in his inventory — the number of "steps" in the shelving unit showed his rank, and the quality of his plate indicated his success.

These shelves were designed to be light and transportable — European nobles and their courts often traveled to administer far-flung territories. As time went on, Europe became more politically integrated and nobles did less traveling. The plate shelves stayed put. Craftsmen began to elaborate on this form for their well-to-do clients, making it larger and heavier. By the seventeenth century, it had evolved into an ornate floor-to-ceiling cabinet with glass doors.

Country folks, however, continued to use the simpler, open shelves to store their dinnerware. These were called by many names — *open dresser, delft rack,* and *pewter bench,* to list a few — but they all referred to the same basic design.

They were particularly popular in early colonial America, where lack of tools and time prevented the colonists from building more stylish pieces. This pewter bench is patterned after a New England plate rack built in the first half of the eighteenth century.

EXPLODED VIEW

BILL OF MATERIALS

WOODEN PARTS/*FINISHED DIMENSIONS*

A.	Sides (2)	3/4" x 13" x 63 1/4"
B.	Top	3/4" x 6 3/4" x 51 1/2"
C.	Valance	3/4" x 1 1/2" x 50"
D.	Top shelf	3/4" x 6" x 49 1/4"
E.	Bottom shelves (3)	3/4" x 13" x 49 1/4"
F.	Plate rests (4)	3/4" x 3/4" x 50"

HARDWARE

6d Square-cut nails (36–40)

PLAN OF PROCEDURE

1

Plane, rip, and cut the parts to the sizes shown in the Bill of Materials.

2

Cut 3/4"-wide, 3/8"-deep dadoes in the sides, as shown in the *Side Layout*.

3

Lay out and cut the shape of the sides, as shown in the *Side Layout*. Also cut the 3/4" x 3/4" notches for the plate rests.

SIDE LAYOUT   **SIDE VIEW**

FRONT VIEW

PLAN OF PROCEDURE

4

Shape the front edge and both ends of the top shelf, as shown in the *Top Shelf Profile*.

5

Cut a 3/16" bead in the front face of the valance, near the bottom edge, as shown in the *Valance Profile*.

6

Cut 3/8"-wide, 3/8"-deep grooves in the top and all bottom shelves, 1 1/8" from the back edges as shown in the *Plate Groove Detail*. These grooves hold the edges of the plates.

7

Finish sand the parts of the pewter bench and dry assemble them to check the fit of the joints. Reassemble the parts with glue and square-cut nails.

8

Set the heads of the nails. If you wish, cover them with putty.

9

Do any necessary touch-up sanding and apply a finish to the completed project.

VALANCE PROFILE

3/4"

1 1/2"

3/16" Bead

3/4"

1/4"

1/2" Ogee

TOP SHELF PROFILE

3/8" Wd × 3/8" Dp Groove

1 1/8"

Back of Shelf

3/4"

PLATE GROOVE DETAIL

OHIO CORNER CABINET

During the eighteenth century, collecting fine ceramics — particularly Oriental porcelain or "china" — became the vogue among the upper class in colonial America. Cabinet-makers began to build *cabinets* — large case pieces with shelves and glass doors — to display these collections. The fad spread to the middle class, and displaying one's "good china" became a tradition. By the early nineteenth century, the china cabinet was a common sight in American homes, both city and country.

This cabinet is patterned after one built in Cincinnati, Ohio, between 1810 and 1820. It had the same basic form as a corner cupboard, a design that evolved in England several centuries earlier. And, in typical country fashion, it displayed a mix of styles. For example, the tapered Hepplewhite legs were characteristic of Federal period craftsmanship, but the fretwork skirt showed the lingering influence of Queen Anne and Chippendale design. Yet all the elements blended well.

The original cabinet was atypical in one respect — it was smaller than most. Country corner cabinets and cupboards tended to be monstrous affairs. This small size is better suited for modern homes.

**BASE DOOR
EXPLODED VIEW**

**BOTTOM CUPBOARD
EXPLODED VIEW**

**DRAWER
EXPLODED VIEW**

BILL OF MATERIALS

WOODEN PARTS/*FINISHED DIMENSIONS*

Base

A.	Front/corner stiles (4)	$3/4$" x $4^1/8$" x 40"
B.	Top rail	$3/4$" x 5" x $26^1/2$"
C.	Bottom rail	$3/4$" x 4" x $26^1/2$"
D.	Side/back panels (8)	$1/2$" x $6^1/2$" x 40"
E.	Shelves (4)	$3/4$" x 15" x $36^3/8$"
F.	Cleat	$3/4$" x $3/4$" x $33^5/8$"
G.	Drawer guides (2)	$1/2$" x $7/8$" x 14"
H.	Front middle molding	$1/4$" x $5/8$" x $32^7/8$"
J.	Corner middle moldings (2)	$1/4$" x $5/8$" x $4^1/4$"
K.	Pegs (6)	$5/16$" x $5/16$" x $1^1/4$"*

Base Door and Drawer

K.	Pegs (8)	$5/16$" x $5/16$" x $1^1/4$"*
L.	Drawer front	$7/8$" x $2^{15}/16$" x $9^{11}/16$"
M.	Drawer sides (2)	$1/2$" x $2^{15}/16$" x $13^1/2$"

N.	Drawer back	$1/2$" x $2^5/16$" x $9^{11}/16$"
P.	Drawer bottom	$1/2$" x $9^1/16$" x $15^1/8$"
Q.	Top/bottom cock beading (2)	$1/8$" x $1/2$" x $9^{11}/16$"
R.	Side cock beading (2)	$1/8$" x $1/2$" x $2^{15}/16$"
S.	Outside base door stiles (2)	$3/4$" x $2^{15}/16$" x $28^7/8$"
T.	Middle base door stile	$3/4$" x 3" x $23^7/8$"
U.	Top door rail	$3/4$" x 3" x $20^1/2$"
V.	Bottom door rail	$3/4$" x 4" x $20^1/2$"
W.	Base door panels	$1/2$" x $8^3/8$" x $22^1/2$"

Cabinet Top

A.	Front/corner stiles (4)	$3/4$" x $4^1/8$" x 40"
C.	Top rail	$3/4$" x 5" x $26^1/2$"
D.	Side/back panels (8)	$1/2$" x $6^1/2$" x 40"
E.	Shelves (4)	$3/4$" x 15" x $36^3/8$"
K.	Pegs (6)	$5/16$" x $5/16$" x $1^1/4$"*
X.	Bottom rail	$3/4$" x $1^1/2$" x $26^1/2$"

TOP CUPBOARD EXPLODED VIEW

TOP DOOR EXPLODED VIEW

Y.	Front top molding	3/4" x 31/2" x 35"
Z.	Corner top moldings (2)	3/4" x 31/2" x 5"
AA.	Glue blocks (6)	17/16" x 17/16" x 31/2"

Top Door

K.	Pegs (8)	5/16" x 5/16" x 11/4"*
U.	Top door rail	3/4" x 3" x 201/2"
V.	Bottom door rail	3/4" x 4" x 201/2"
BB.	Top door stiles (2)	3/4" x 215/16" x 333/8"
CC.	Sash stiles (2)	3/8" x 5/8" x 263/8"
DD.	Sash rails (6)	3/8" x 5/8" x 53/4"
EE.	Long vertical glazing bars (4)	1/8" x 3/8" x 9"
FF.	Short vertical glazing bars (2)	1/8" x 3/8" x 87/8"
GG.	Horizontal glazing bars (2)	1/8" x 3/8" x 191/4"

Make the pegs at least this long, then cut them to length after you install them.

HARDWARE

1" Door/drawer pulls (3)
13/4" x 2" Butt hinges and mounting screws (2 pairs)
Door latches (2)
65/16" x 91/8" Glass panes (4 — for corners)
65/16" x 815/16" Glass panes (2 — for right/left middle)
61/8" x 91/8" Glass panes (2 — for top/bottom middle)
61/8" x 815/16" Glass pane (1 — for middle)
Glazing compound
6d Square-cut nails (1 lb.)
7/8" Wire or headless brads (12–16)

PLAN OF PROCEDURE

To help this project progress smoothly, build it in two parts. First, build the cases — base and top. Then build the doors and drawer to fit the cases.

Making the Top and Base Cases

1

Glue up stock for the shelves. Then plane, rip, and cut the parts for the base and top to the sizes shown in the Bill of Materials, except the moldings. Cut the top molding stock to the proper thickness and width, but don't cut it to length yet. *Plane* the middle molding stock to the proper width (5/8"), but don't cut it to thickness or length. Bevel the adjoining edges of the front and corner stiles at 22½°, as shown in the *Top View.*

2

Cut the drawer opening in the top base rail, as shown in the *Front View.* Sand the sawed edges.

3

Cut the joinery necessary to assemble the cases:

- ■ 1/2"-wide, 3/8"-deep rabbets in the square edges of the corner stiles, as shown in the *Top Back Panel Detail* and *Base Back Panel Detail,* to hold the back panels
- ■ 3/8"-wide, 1/4"-deep rabbets in the adjoining square edges of the side and back panels, so the panels will overlap
- ■ 1/4"-wide, 1"-deep, 4¼"-long mortises in the inside edges of all four front stiles, 3/8" from the top ends

- ■ 1/4"-wide, 1"-deep, 3/4"-long mortises in the inside edges of the top front stiles, 3/8" from the bottom ends
- ■ 1/4"-wide, 1"-deep, 1¼"-long mortises in the inside edges of the base front stiles, 4³/8" from the bottom ends
- ■ 1/4"-thick, 1"-long tenons in the ends of all the rails; notch the tenons to fit the mortises

GLUE BLOCK

TOP VIEW

5"

40"

33½" Opening

1½"

5"

7⅜"

9¾" Opening

29" Opening

40"

6"

15 square = 1"

4⅛"

24½" Opening

32¾"

4⅛"

3" Opening

1"

FRONT VIEW

15⁹⁄₁₆"

8¼"

40"

12¹⁄₁₆"

3¼"

1"

15¼"

40"

12⅞"

5⅝"

¾" (Typ)

¾" (Typ)

½"

1¾"

1¾"

SECTION A

PLAN OF PROCEDURE

Note: You must cut 3/8"-wide notches in *most* of the tenons to fit them to their mortises, as shown in the *Case Joinery Detail*. When the stiles and rails are assembled, the outside edges of *most* of the rails should be flush with the ends of the stiles. The exception is the *bottom base rail*. Cut a 3/8"-wide notch in the top cheeks of the tenons, and 1 3/8"-wide notches in the bottom. When assembled, the outside (or bottom) edge of this rail should be 3" above the bottom ends of the stiles.

Lay out the shapes of the shelves, as shown on the *Top Shelf Layout* and *Base Shelf Layout*. Cut the shapes and sand the sawed edges.

5

If you wish, rout or cut dovetail notches on the front edges of the top middle shelves, as shown in the *Top Shelf Layout*. You can use the notches to hold spoons.

6

Rout 1/4"-wide, 1/4"-deep plate grooves near the back edges of the top middle shelves.

7

Rout or cut 3/16" beads near the adjoining edges of the top side and back panels, as shown in the *Top Back Panel Detail*.

CASE JOINERY DETAIL

TOP BACK PANEL DETAIL

BASE BACK PANEL DETAIL

8

Finish sand the parts of the cases. Assemble the front stiles and rails with glue.

9

Round the bottom portion of 12 pegs, as shown in the *Peg Detail.*

10

Drill 5/16"-diameter holes through the mortise-and-tenon joints in the face frames, as shown in the *Front View.* Note that the wider joints get two holes each, while the narrower joints get one. Drive the pegs through the holes from the outside. Cut the pegs off flush with the inside surfaces of the face frames.

11

Enlarge the foot pattern shown in the *Front View* and trace it on the base face frame. Cut the pattern, then sand the sawed edges.

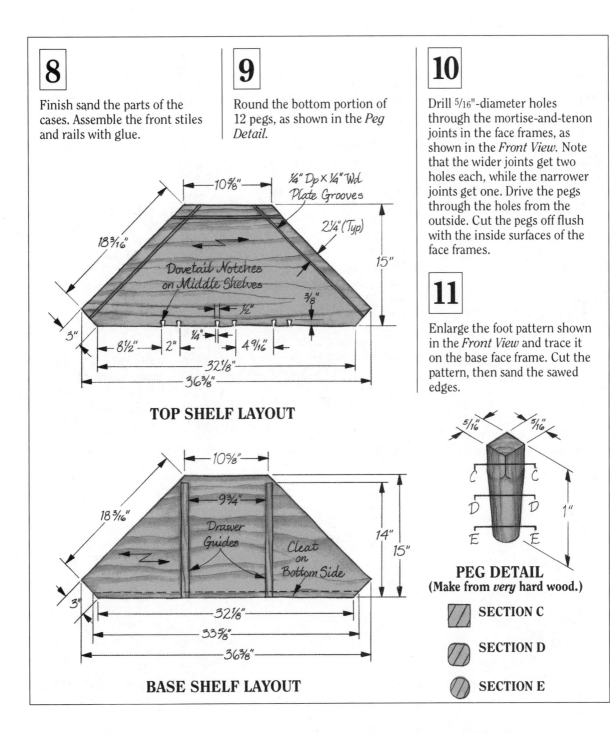

TOP SHELF LAYOUT

1/4" Dp × 1/4" Wd Plate Grooves

10 5/8"

2 1/4" (Typ)

15"

18 3/16"

Dovetail Notches on Middle Shelves

3/8"

1/2"

3"

8 1/2"   2"   1/4"   4 9/16"

32 1/8"

36 3/8"

BASE SHELF LAYOUT

10 5/8"

9 3/4"

18 3/16"

Drawer Guides

Cleat on Bottom Side

14"

15"

3"

32 1/8"

33 5/8"

36 3/8"

5/16"   5/16"

C   C

D   D

E   E

1"

PEG DETAIL
(Make from *very* hard wood.)

▨ **SECTION C**

◓ **SECTION D**

◯ **SECTION E**

PLAN OF PROCEDURE

Miter the ends of the cleat at 45°, then glue it to the inside surface of the base face frame.

Nail the drawer guides to the upper middle base shelf (the shelf that supports the drawer), as shown in the *Base Shelf Layout*.

Measure the positions of the shelves in the inside surfaces of the face frames. Remember, you must position the top middle shelves so they will be even with the horizontal sashes when the top door is installed. Attach the frames to the shelves with glue and nails. Temporarily, nail strips of wood to the back edges of the shelves to hold them parallel during the next few steps.

TOP MOLDING PROFILE

Apply a dark stain or black paint to the rabbeted edges of the panels. If the panels should shrink, the stain will make the gaps between them less noticeable. Otherwise, you would see strips of light-colored, raw wood in the gaps.

Attach the corner stiles and side panels to the shelves with nails and glue. When installing the two rearmost side panels, fit them to the cases. Mark the back edges and rip these panels to the proper width. Bevel the back edges at 45°, as shown in the *Top View,* then nail and glue them in place.

Remove the wooden strips that temporarily held the shelves parallel. Fit the back panels to the cases, mark the edges, and rip them to width. Once again, bevel the edges at 45°, then nail and glue them to the back edges of the shelves.

Sand all joints clean and flush, then rest the top assembly on the base.

19

Rout or cut the shape of the middle molding in the edges of the stock, as shown in the *Middle Molding Profile*. Rip the middle molding from the stock. Finish sand the molding.

20

Fit the middle molding to the base assembly, mitering the adjoining ends at 22½°. Using brads and glue, attach the molding to the base so it straddles the joint between the base and top. Do *not* attach the molding to the top. You should be able to remove the top from the base easily, when necessary.

MIDDLE MOLDING PROFILE

21

Bevel the edges of the top molding stock at 45°, as shown in the *Top Molding Profile.* Finish sand the molding.

22

Fit the top molding to the top assembly, mitering the adjoining ends at 22½°. Using nails and glue, attach the molding to the top. The top edge of the molding must be flush with the top of the case. Reinforce the molding with glue blocks, as shown in the *Top View.*

23

Set the heads of all the nails and brads. Cover them with putty.

Making the Drawer and Doors

24

Measure the openings for the drawer and doors — the dimensions may have changed slightly. If so, adjust the dimensions of the door and drawer parts. Plane, rip, and cut them to size, except the drawer bottom, cock beading, sash rails, sash stiles, and glazing bars. Cut the drawer bottom about ½" longer than specified in the Bill of Materials. Cut the remaining parts to the proper thicknesses and widths, but don't cut them to length yet.

BOTTOM VIEW

SIDE VIEW   **END VIEW**

DRAWER

PLAN OF PROCEDURE

25

Cut the joinery needed to assemble the drawer:

- Half-blind dovetails to join the front to the sides, and through dovetails to join the sides to the back. (See *Making Hand-Cut Dovetails* on page 112.)
- 3/8"-wide, 1/8"-deep rabbets all around the drawer front, as shown in the *Cock Beading Detail,* to hold the cock beading
- 1/4"-wide, 1/4"-deep grooves in the inside faces of the drawer front and sides, as shown in the *Drawer/End View,* to hold the drawer bottom

26

Finish sand the drawer front, sides, and back, then assemble them with glue. Sand the joints clean and flush.

27

Round one edge of the cock beading stock, then fit the beading to the drawer front. Miter the adjoining ends at 45°. Glue the beading in the top and bottom drawer front rabbets. Secure it with brads in the side rabbets.

28

Bevel the front end and both edges of the drawer bottom, so they taper to 1/4", as shown in the *Drawer/End View.* Finish sand the bottom and slide it in place in the grooves. Secure it to the drawer by driving several brads through the bottom and into the drawer back.

29

Install a pull in the drawer front, then test fit the drawer in the base. If it binds, sand or plane away small amounts of stock until it slides smoothly. Cut the drawer bottom to length so when it butts against the back panels, the drawer front will be flush with the face frame. (The cock beading should protrude 1/8".)

COCK BEADING DETAIL

30

Cut the joinery needed to assemble the doors:

- 1/4"-wide, 3/8"-deep grooves in the inside edges of the base door rails and stiles; cut grooves in *both* edges of the base door middle stile
- 1/4"-wide, 3/8"-deep *blind* grooves in the inside edges of the top door stiles — each groove should be 1"–2" long, open to the end of the board; make two grooves in each stile, cutting in from each end
- 1/4"-wide, 1"-deep, 2 1/4"-long mortises in the inside edges of all outside stiles, 3/8" from the top ends
- 1/4"-wide, 1"-deep, 3 1/4"-long mortises in the inside edges of all outside stiles, 3/8" from the bottom ends
- 1/4"-wide, 1"-deep, 2 1/4"-long mortises in the inside edges of the base door rails, equally distant from either end
- 1/4"-thick, 1"-long tenons in the ends of the rails and base door middle stile, where necessary; notch the tenons to fit the mortises, as shown in the *Top Door Frame Joinery Detail* and *Base Door Frame Joinery Detail*

31

Raise the base door panels, as shown in the *Base Door Panel Profile*.

32

Finish sand the door stiles, rails, and panels. Assemble them with glue. Slide the panels in place in the base door, but do *not* glue them to the door frames. The panels must float in the grooves.

33

Round the bottom portion of the remaining pegs, as shown in the *Peg Detail*.

34

Drill 5/16"-diameter holes through the mortise-and-tenon joints in the door frames, as shown in the *Top Door Layout* and *Base Door Layout*. Drive the pegs through the holes from the outside. Cut the pegs off flush with the inside surfaces of the frames.

**BASE DOOR
PANEL PROFILE**

35

Rout a 3/8"-wide, 3/8"-deep rabbet around the inside edges of the top door frame, on the back surface. Square the corners of the rabbet with a chisel.

36

Cut and install the sash rails, sash stiles, and glazing bars, following the procedure in Installing Glass in Cabinet Doors on page 393. Sand all the joints clean and flush.

**BASE
DOOR FRAME
JOINERY DETAIL**

**TOP
DOOR FRAME
JOINERY DETAIL**

**SASH RAIL/
SASH STILE/
GLAZING BAR
ASSEMBLY
DETAIL**

PLAN OF PROCEDURE

37

Mortise the left front stiles and left door stiles for hinges, then hang the doors in the cabinet. Install pulls and catches for both doors.

Glazing Compound

Glass

3/8"

1/8"

5/8"

3/8"

SECTION B

38

Remove the doors and drawer from the cabinet, and remove all the hardware from the doors and drawer. Take the top case off the base. Do any necessary touch-up sanding, then apply a finish to the cabinet. Coat all wooden surfaces — inside and out, front and back.

39

Put the top back on the base. Replace the hardware, then hang the doors and slide the drawer back in the cabinet.

40

Install glass panes in the top door, holding the glass in place with glazing compound. Mix paint or stain with the compound to match the finish.

24 3/8"

2 15/16"   7 3/4"   3"   7 3/4"   2 15/16"

3"

22 1/2"   23 7/8"

8 3/8"

21 7/8"

28 7/8"

4"

20 1/2"

BASE DOOR LAYOUT

24 3/8"

2 15/16"   18 1/2"   2 15/16"

3"

8 3/8"

B

B

3/8" Wd x 3/8" Dp Rabbet

5/8

33 3/8"

26 3/8"

5 3/4"

5/8"

Square Pegs (Typ)

4"

20 1/2"

TOP DOOR LAYOUT

CHIMNEY CUPBOARD

Cabinetmakers sometimes custom made cupboards for their clients to fit the available space. One oft-heard request was for a tall, narrow storage piece to fill the otherwise unusable area between two large objects. To satisfy this request, cabinetmakers sometimes made a "chimney cupboard" — so-called because its shape reminded folks of a chimney.

This cupboard is a copy of a Shaker piece built in the New Lebanon, New York, community. The original, which now resides at the Metropolitan Museum of Art in New York City, was made in the early nineteenth century to hold tinware.

The cupboard design shows the simplicity and utility characteristic of Shaker furniture, but the construction is puzzling. Why is the top door so much larger and why does it have more panels than the bottom one? Why not three doors? This, too, may have been due to customizing. In addition to simplicity and utility, Shaker craftsmen also believed in the virtue of economy. By building just two doors, even though three would seem the logical choice, the builder eliminated the need for a third pair of hinges.

EXPLODED VIEW

PLAN OF PROCEDURE

1

If necessary, glue up stock to make the wide parts — sides, top, and shelves. Plane, rip, and cut the parts to the sizes shown in the Bill of Materials.

2

Cut the joinery needed to assemble the case:

- $3/4$"-wide, $3/8$"-deep dadoes in the sides to hold the shelves, as shown in the *Side Layout*
- $1/2$"-wide, $3/8$"-deep rabbets in the back edges of the sides

- $1/2$"-wide, $3/8$"-deep, $17^{1/4}$"-long double-blind rabbet in the back edge of the top, as shown in the *Top Layout*
- $3/8$"-wide, $1/4$"-deep rabbets in *both* edges of the middle backboard and one edge of the right and left backboards, as shown in the *Backboard Joinery Detail/Top View*
- $1/4$"-wide, 1"-deep, $1^{1/4}$"-long mortises in the inside edge of each face frame stile, as shown in the *Face Frame Joinery Detail*
- $1/4$"-wide, 1"-long tenons in the ends of the face frame rails

3

Notch the tenons on the top and bottom face frame rails to fit the mortises. Do *not* notch the tenons on the middle rail.

4

Round the front edge and both ends of the top, as shown in the *Top Edge Detail*. Sand the shaped edges.

TOP EDGE DETAIL

BILL OF MATERIALS

WOODEN PARTS/*FINISHED DIMENSIONS*

A.	Sides (2)	$3/4$" x $11^{1/4}$" x $74^{1/8}$"
B.	Top	$7/8$" x $12^{3/4}$" x $19^{1/2}$"
C.	Backboards (3)	$1/2$" x 6" x 73"
D.	Shelves (7)	$3/4$" x $10^{3/4}$" x $17^{1/4}$"
E.	Face frame stiles (2)	$3/4$" x 2" x $74^{1/8}$"
F.	Top/bottom face frame rails (2)	$3/4$" x 2" x 16"
G.	Middle face frame rail	$3/4$" x $1^{1/4}$" x 16"
H.	Top door stiles (2)	$3/4$" x 3" x $37^{3/4}$"
J.	Bottom door stiles (2)	$3/4$" x 3" x $29^{7/8}$"
K.	Door rails (5)	$3/4$" x 3" x $9^{7/8}$"
L.	Top door panels (2)	$1/2$" x $8^{1/2}$" x $15^{1/16}$"
M.	Bottom door panel	$1/2$" x $8^{1/2}$" x $24^{9/16}$"

N.	Pegs (16)	$1/4$" x $1/4$" x $1^{1/4}$"*
P.	Door pulls (2)	$1^{1/4}$" dia. x $2^{5/8}$"
Q.	Door latches (2)	$5/8$" x 1" x $2^{5/8}$"
R.	Wedges (2)	$1/4$" x 1" x $1^{1/2}$"
S.	Pins (2)	$1/4$" dia. x 1"

Make the pegs at least this long, then cut them to length after you install them.

HARDWARE

$1^{1/2}$" x 2" Butt hinges and mounting screws (2 pairs)
6d Square-cut nails (36–40)
4d Square-cut nails (12–18)

PLAN OF PROCEDURE

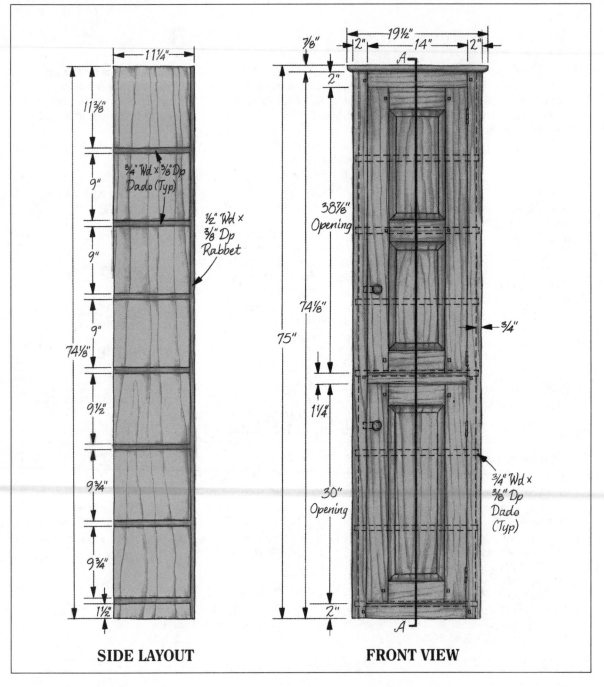

SIDE LAYOUT

FRONT VIEW

5

Stain the rabbeted edges of the backboards a dark brown or black.

6

Finish sand the parts of the face frame. Glue them together, inserting the tenons in the mortises.

7

Round the bottom portion of the pegs, as shown in the *Peg Detail.*

8

Drill a ¼"-diameter hole through each mortise and tenon in the face frame. Drive a peg into each hole to secure the tenon in the mortise, then cut off the peg flush with the inside surface of the frame.

9

Finish sand the remaining parts of the case and assemble them in the following order:

- Glue the shelves to the sides and reinforce the joints with 6d square-cut nails.
- Glue the assembled face frame to the case. Reinforce it with 6d nails.
- Attach the top to the face frame and sides with glue and 6d nails.
- Attach the backboards to the sides, top, and shelves with 4d nails. Do *not* glue the backboards in place.

As you work, sand all joints clean and flush. Set the heads of the nails. If you wish, cover the heads of the nails in the sides and front with putty.

PEG DETAIL

(Make from *very* hard wood.)

SECTION B

SECTION C

SECTION D

FACE FRAME JOINERY DETAIL

TOP VIEW
BACKBOARD JOINERY DETAIL

3/8" Wd × ¼" Dp Rabbet

6" (Typ)

½"

½" Wd × ⅜" Dp Double-Blind Rabbet

19½"

17 ¼"

1⅛"

12¾"

TOP LAYOUT

PLAN OF PROCEDURE

10

Cut the joinery needed to assemble the doors:

- ¼"-wide, ³⁄₈"-deep grooves in the inside edges of all door rails and stiles, as shown in the *Door Frame Joinery Detail*
- ¼"-wide, 1"-deep, 2¼"-long mortises in the inside edges of the door stiles
- ¼"-wide, 1"-long tenons on the ends of the door rails

11

Notch the tenons in the rails as shown in the *Door Frame Joinery Detail,* creating a haunch in each tenon and fitting it to its mortise.

12

Raise the door panels, beveling the edges and ends to fit the grooves in the rails and stiles, as shown in *Section A.*

DOOR FRAME JOINERY DETAIL

PANEL PROFILE

SECTION A

13

Drill a ⁹⁄₁₆"-diameter hole in each left door stile for the door latch assembly, as shown in the *Top Door Layout* and *Bottom Door Layout*.

14

Finish sand the door parts and assemble the rails and stiles with glue. Put the panels in place as you glue up the door frames, but do *not* apply glue to them. The panels must float in the grooves.

15

Reinforce the mortise-and-tenon joints in the door frames with pegs, as you did on the face frame.

16

Mortise the door stiles and face frame stiles for hinges, then mount the doors to the case.

TOP DOOR LAYOUT   **BOTTOM DOOR LAYOUT**

PLAN OF PROCEDURE

17

Turn the door pulls as shown in the *Door Pull Layout*. Finish sand the pulls on the lathe.

18

Drill a ½"-diameter hole through each door latch, ½" from one end, as shown in the *Door Latch Assembly Detail*.

19

Bevel the end of each latch opposite the hole you just drilled. Also, cut a taper in the wedge.

20

Insert a door pull through the hole in each left door stile. Glue the latch on the pull shaft. Don't press the latch too tightly on the shaft — the pull must turn freely. Drill a ¼"-diameter hole through the latch and pull, and glue a pin in the hole.

21

Experiment with the position of the wedges on the inside face of the left face frame stile. Temporarily tape each wedge in place with double-faced tape. When you turn the pull counterclockwise, the beveled edge

of the latch should contact the wedge, holding the door closed. When you find the proper position, glue the wedge to the inside surface of the stile.

22

Remove the doors and the hardware from the case. Do any necessary touch-up sanding, then apply a finish to the completed chimney cupboard. Finish *all* sides of the project — inside and out, top and bottom. Then mount the doors to the case.

**DOOR PULL
LAYOUT**

**DOOR LATCH
ASSEMBLY DETAIL**

HANGING CORNER SHELF

Corner furniture — triangular shelves, cupboards, tables, and chairs designed to fit in a corner — was popular in country homes. Eighteenth- and nineteenth-century rural cabins and houses tended to be small, while families were large. Consequently, folks couldn't afford to waste an inch of space. So when the walls and floors filled up with furniture, they began to use the corners.

This small shelving unit was designed to hang in a corner, possibly filling the space above a table or chair. Shelves of this size were usually more decorative than practical — this unit has just three small shelves, of three different sizes. When every inch counts, however, three shelves of any size can be a welcome addition.

EXPLODED VIEW

BILL OF MATERIALS

WOODEN PARTS/*FINISHED DIMENSIONS*

A.	Right side	3/8" x 8 11/16" x 24 3/4"
B.	Left side	3/8" x 8 5/16" x 24 3/4"
C.	Top shelf	3/8" x 3 1/8" x 3 1/8"
D.	Middle shelf	3/8" x 4 3/4" x 4 3/4"
E.	Bottom shelf	3/8" x 8 5/16" x 8 5/16"

HARDWARE

4d Square-cut nails (16–18)

PLAN OF PROCEDURE

1

Plane, rip, and cut the parts to the sizes shown in the Bill of Materials.

2

Lay out and cut the shape of the sides, as shown in the *Side View Pattern*.

3

Cut the curved edges of the shelves, beveling the top and middle shelves at 45° and the bottom shelf at 84°, as shown in the *Shelf Edge Profiles*.

4

Finish sand the parts of the corner shelf, and assemble them with glue and square-cut nails. Set the heads of the nails.

5

Drill a 1/4"-diameter hole through the project, near the top where the two sides meet.

6

Do any necessary touch-up sanding and apply a finish to the completed project.

7

Drive a nail in the corner where you want the shelf. (The head of this nail must be less than 1/4" in diameter, so it will fit through the hole near the top of the piece.) Hang the finished shelves from the nail.

TOP VIEW

45°

TOP AND MIDDLE SHELF

84°

BOTTOM SHELF

SHELF EDGE PROFILES

SIDE VIEW PATTERN

PLATE SHELF

Families once kept all their dinnerware on racks like these. To save space, they made the shelves very narrow. The plates stood on edge, leaning against a rail at the back of the shelves. A shallow groove or a small molding running the length of each shelf prevented the plates from slipping off. Sometimes the craftsman added pegs or hooks underneath the shelves to hang cups and other eating or cooking utensils.

Today, most families couldn't fit their dinner service on a small rack. Plates and cups are easier to come by — and more numerous — than they once were. However, the old racks are still useful. They make good places to display collections of small items — keepsakes, boxes, dolls, old tools, and (of course) plates.

The rack shown is a small set of hanging shelves, with several pegs below the bottom shelf. The sides are shaped slightly at the bottom, and the edges of the top are molded, adding just a little decoration to an otherwise utilitarian design.

EXPLODED VIEW

BILL OF MATERIALS

WOODEN PARTS/*FINISHED DIMENSIONS*

A.	Top	$1/2$" x $5^3/4$" x $35^1/2$"
B.	Sides (2)	$1/2$" x 5" x $32^3/4$"
C.	Shelves (2)	$1/2$" x 5" x $33^1/2$"
D.	Valances (2)	$1/2$" x $2^1/2$" x 34"
E.	Stretchers (2)	$1/2$" x $2^1/2$" x 33"

F.	Plate rails (2)	$1/2$" x $3/4$" x 34"
G.	Pegs (5)	$7/8$" dia. x $3^1/2$"*

*Make the pegs at least this long, then cut them to length
after you install them.*

HARDWARE

4d Square-cut nails (16–20)

PLAN OF PROCEDURE

1

Plane, rip, and cut the parts to the sizes shown in the Bill of Materials. You can purchase pegs from most woodworking suppliers. If you plan to turn them, cut the pegs about 1" longer than specified.

2

Cut the joinery necessary to assemble the project:

- 1/2"-wide, 1/4"-deep dadoes in the sides, as shown in the *Side Layout,* to hold the shelves

SIDE LAYOUT

SIDE VIEW

- ½"-wide, 2½"-long notches in the upper ends of the sides, to hold the valances

- ½"-wide, ¾"-long notches in the back edges of the sides to hold the plate rails

3 Lay out and cut the shape of the sides, as shown in the *Side Layout.*

35½"

¾"

½"

33"

¾"

½"

2½"

10⅛"

2½"

12⅝"

3½" Lg x ⅞" Dia Pegs
(5 Req'd)

1¼"

2½"

6½"

5½"

5½"
(Typ)

FRONT VIEW

PLAN OF PROCEDURE

Rout or cut the molded shapes:

- 3/16"-diameter beads in the lower front of the front valance and both stretchers, as shown in the *Stretcher/Valance Profile*
- 1/8"-radius cove in the front and ends of the top, as shown in the *Top Edge Profile*
- 1/4"-wide round-bottom groove in the top surface of the shelves, as shown in the *Plate Groove Detail*

If you're turning your own pegs, turn them to the profile shown in the *Peg Detail*.

Drill 1/2"-diameter holes through the bottom stretcher to hold the pegs, as shown in the *Front View* and *Side View*.

Finish sand the parts of the plate rack and dry assemble them to check the fit of the joints. Reassemble the parts with glue and square-cut nails. Set the heads of the nails.

8

Do any necessary touch-up sanding and apply a finish to the completed project.

9

Hang the finished plate rack on the wall by driving screws or Molly anchors through the back top valance.

PLATE GROOVE DETAIL

PEG DETAIL

TOP EDGE PROFILE

STRETCHER/ VALANCE PROFILE

WARDROBE

There were no closets in early American country homes, so craftsmen built large cupboards in which to store clothes and linens. Cupboards first appeared in Europe in the early seventeenth century, and immigrants brought many different designs to America. Some were made in one piece (as shown), others were small cupboards stacked on larger ones, or large cupboards stacked on chests of drawers. They were called by many different names, depending on who made them. The Germans called a storage cupboard a *Schrank* and the Dutch, a *kas*. The French term was *armoire*, and the Spanish, *trastero*. The English had several different names — *clothespress, linen press,* or *wardrobe*.

This wardrobe is based on English-derived pieces, although it's a little deeper than most. It also has several adjustable shelves — most had fixed shelves only. This extra depth and movable shelving make it more useful in a contemporary setting. It will hold a 27" television as well as smaller audio and video components. You can use it as an entertainment center to hide modern electronics from view and preserve the country look of a living room or den.

EXPLODED VIEW

**DOOR
EXPLODED VIEW**

BILL OF MATERIALS

WOODEN PARTS/*FINISHED DIMENSIONS*

A.	Sides (2)	$3/4$" x $21^{1}/4$" x 55"
B.	Top	$1/2$" x $25^{3}/8$" x $48^{3}/4$"
C.	Backboards (7)	$1/2$" x $6^{5}/16$" x $53^{3}/4$"
D.	Fixed shelves (2)	$3/4$" x $20^{3}/4$" x $41^{1}/4$"
E.	Face frame stiles (2)	$3/4$" x 3" x 55"
F.	Top face frame rail	$3/4$" x $5^{1}/2$" x 38"
G.	Bottom face frame rail	$3/4$" x 2" x 38"
H.	Front top molding	$3/4$" x $4^{7}/16$" x $48^{1}/4$"
J.	Side top moldings (2)	$3/4$" x $4^{7}/16$" x $25^{1}/8$"
K.	Front base molding	1" x $5^{1}/2$" x 44"
L.	Side base moldings (2)	1" x $5^{1}/2$" x 23"
M.	Glue blocks (4)	$3/4$" x $3/4$" x $4^{1}/2$"
N.	Door stop	$1/2$" x 1" x $40^{1}/2$"
P.	Door stiles (3)	$3/4$" x 3" x $47^{3}/8$"

Q.	Left inside door stile	$3/4$" x $3^{3}/8$" x $47^{3}/8$"
R.	Door rails (6)	$3/4$" x 3" x $13^{15}/16$"
S.	Door panels (4)	$1/2$" x $12^{1}/2$" x $19^{7}/8$"
T.	Door catch	$3/4$" x $3/4$" x $1^{1}/2$"
U.	Pegs (18)	$5/16$" x $5/16$" x $1^{1}/4$"*
V.	Adjustable shelves (1–3)	$3/4$" x $20^{5}/8$" x $40^{3}/8$"

*Make the pegs at least this long, then cut them to length
after you install them.*

HARDWARE

$1^{1}/2$" x 2" Butt hinges and mounting screws (3 pairs)
Door latch
4d Square-cut nails (48–60)
#8 x $1^{1}/4$" Flathead wood screw
$1/4$"-dia. x $3/4$" Metal pins (4 for each adjustable shelf)

PLAN OF PROCEDURE

1

If necessary, glue up stock to make the wide parts — sides, shelves, top, and door panels. Plane, rip, and cut the parts to the sizes shown in the Bill of Materials, except the moldings and door parts. Don't cut the door parts yet; wait until you've built the case. Cut the moldings to the proper thickness and width, but leave them longer than specified.

2

Cut the joinery needed to assemble the case:

■ 3/4"-wide, 3/8"-deep dadoes in the sides to hold the fixed shelves, as shown in the *Front View*
■ 1/2"-wide, 3/8"-deep rabbets in the sides to hold the backboards
■ 1/2"-wide, 3/8"-deep, 41 1/4"-long double-blind rabbet in the back edge of the top, as shown in the *Top Layout/Bottom View*
■ 1/2"-wide, 1/4"-deep rabbets in *both* edges of the middle backboards, and *one* edge of the right and left backboards, as shown in the *Back Joinery Detail*

■ 3/8"-wide, 3/8"-deep, 1 3/4"-long mortise in the middle fixed shelf for the door catch, as shown in the *Fixed Shelf Layout*
■ 1/4"-wide, 1"-deep, 4 3/4"-long mortises in the inside edge of each face frame stile near the top end, as shown in the *Face Frame Assembly Detail*

■ 1/4"-wide, 1"-deep, 1 1/4"-long mortises in the inside edge of each face frame stile near the bottom end, as shown in the *Face Frame Assembly Detail*
■ 1/4"-wide, 1"-long tenons on the ends of the face frame rails

TOP LAYOUT
BOTTOM VIEW

BACK JOINERY DETAIL

FRONT VIEW

PLAN OF PROCEDURE

**FACE FRAME
ASSEMBLY
DETAIL**

FACE FRAME LAYOUT

3

Notch the shoulders of the tenons in the face frame rails to fit the mortises.

4

Drill 1/4"-diameter, 1/2"-deep holes in the sides to support the adjustable shelves, as shown in *Section A*.

5

Lay out and cut the shapes of the shelves, as shown in the *Adjustable Shelf Layout* and *Fixed Shelf Layout*. Sand the sawed edges.

6

If you plan to use this project to hold audio, video, or other electronic equipment, drill six to eight 1"-diameter ventilation holes in the top and in each shelf, near the back edge. Also drill a ventilation hole in each backboard, near the top end.

7

Stain the rabbeted edges of the backboards a dark brown or black.

SECTION A

PLAN OF PROCEDURE

8

Finish sand the parts of the face frame. Glue them together, inserting the tenons in the mortises.

9

Round the bottom portion of the pegs, as shown in the *Peg Detail*.

10

Drill a $5/16$"-diameter hole through each mortise and tenon in the face frame. Drive a peg into each hole to secure the tenon in the mortise, then cut off the peg flush with the inside surface of the frame.

SECTION C

SECTION D

SECTION E

$5/16$" $5/16$"

C — C

D — D

E — E

$1\frac{1}{4}$"

PEG DETAIL

(Make from *very* hard wood.)

$40\frac{3}{8}$"

$1\frac{3}{4}$"

$45°$ Miter for Cords

$1\frac{3}{4}$"

$20\frac{5}{8}$"

ADJUSTABLE SHELF LAYOUT

$1\frac{3}{4}$"

$45°$ Miter for Cords

$1\frac{3}{4}$"

$20\frac{3}{4}$"

$\frac{3}{8}$" Wd x $\frac{3}{8}$" Dp x $1\frac{3}{4}$" Lg Mortise on Middle Shelf Only

$\frac{3}{8}$" $\frac{3}{8}$"

$18\frac{1}{4}$"

$1\frac{3}{4}$"

$41\frac{1}{4}$"

FIXED SHELF LAYOUT

Finish sand the remaining parts of the case and assemble them in the following order:

- Glue the shelves to the sides and reinforce the joints with square-cut nails.
- Glue the assembled face frame to the case. Reinforce it with nails.
- Attach the top to the sides with nails. Don't drive these nails all the way in, in case you have to shift the position of the top when you attach the moldings.
- Nail the backboards to the sides, top, and shelves. Do *not* glue the backboards in place.

As you work, sand all joints clean and flush. Set the heads of the nails. Cover the heads of the nails in the sides and front with putty.

Fit the base moldings to the case, mitering the adjoining ends at 45°.

Lay out and cut the shapes of the base moldings, as shown in the *Front View* and *Section A*. Sand the sawed edges.

14

Finish sand the base moldings. Attach the front base molding to the case with glue and nails. Attach the side base moldings with nails only — do *not* glue them. Reinforce the joints with the glue blocks shown in the *Front View*.

Cut the 45° bevels in the top moldings, as shown in the *Molding Detail*.

Fit the top moldings to the case, compound-mitering the adjoining ends at 45°.

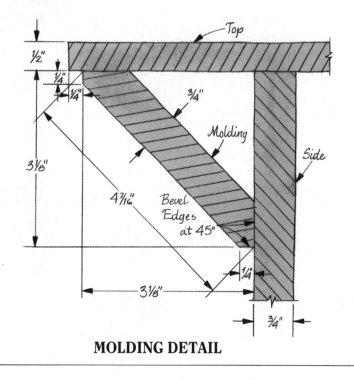

MOLDING DETAIL

PLAN OF PROCEDURE

17

Finish sand the top moldings. Attach the front top molding to the case with glue and nails. Attach the side top moldings with nails only — do *not* glue them in place. If necessary, shift the position of the top to center it over the moldings. Set the nails in the top and cover the heads with putty.

18

Measure the door opening and make any necessary changes in the dimensions of the door parts. Cut the door parts to size, then cut the joinery needed to assemble the doors:

- 3/8"-wide, 3/8"-deep rabbets in the adjoining edges of the inside door stiles
- 1/4"-wide, 3/8"-deep grooves in the inside edges of all door rails and stiles
- 1/4"-wide, 1"-deep, 2 1/4"-long mortises in the inside edges of the door stiles, as shown in the *Door Assembly Detail*
- 1/4"-wide, 1"-long tenons on the ends of the door rails

LEFT DOOR LAYOUT

19

Notch the tenons in the rails as shown in the *Door Assembly Detail,* creating a haunch in each tenon and fitting it to its mortise.

20

Raise the door panels, beveling the edges and ends to fit the grooves in the rails and stiles, as shown in *Section B.*

21

Finish sand the door parts and assemble the rails and stiles with glue. Put the panels in place as you glue up the door frames, but do *not* apply glue to them. The panels must float in the grooves.

DOOR ASSEMBLY DETAIL

Haunch (Typ)

2¼"

¼" Wd × ⅜" Dp Groove (Typ)

2¼"

¾" ¼"
¼" ⅜"

¼" Wd × 1" Dp × 2¼" Lg Mortise (Typ)

2¼"

⅜"

3"

2¼"

3"

⅜"

⅜"

2¼"

3"

⅜"

1"

⅜"

SECTION B

3"

¼" Wd × ⅜" Dp Groove

Panel

3⅜"

⅜" Wd × ⅜" Dp Rabbet

¾"

15°

Stile

Rail

⅛"

1¼"

Left Inside Door Stile

3"

PLAN OF PROCEDURE

 22

Reinforce the mortise-and-tenon joints in the door frames with pegs, as you did on the face frame.

 23

Mortise the door stiles and face frame stiles for hinges, then mount the doors to the case. Mount a commercially made door latch on the outside surface of the left door.

 24

Cut the shape of the door catch, as shown in the *Door Catch Detail*. Attach it to the inside face of the left inside door stile with the flathead wood screw. The catch must turn freely on the screw. When it's vertical, the end of the catch must rest in the mortise in the middle shelf.

 25

Remove the doors and the hardware from the case. Do any necessary touch-up sanding, then apply a finish to the completed wardrobe. Finish *all* sides of the project — inside and out, top and bottom. Then mount the doors to the case.

 26

Insert metal pins into the holes in the sides where you want to position the adjustable shelves and rest the shelves on the pins.

DOOR CATCH DETAIL

WHALE SHELF

To add decoration to racks and shelves, country craftsmen often shaped the sides. Some of these contours were simple geometric patterns, laid out with a compass and a rule. Others mimicked the prevailing furniture styles or incorporated traditional folk patterns. Still others were flights of individual fancy.

During the mid-eighteenth century — the Queen Anne period — craftsmen began to incorporate flowing S-curves (also called cyma curves or *ogees*) into their furniture designs. Small sets of shelves with delicate ogee supports became very popular and continued to be made into the early nineteenth century. These shelves are an example of this motif. Folks called them "whale-end shelves" or simply "whale shelves," because the sides looked like silhouettes of surfaced whales. The shelves were cut and attached to the whale shapes so each shelf was a different width and each compartment a different height.

EXPLODED VIEW

BILL OF MATERIALS

WOODEN PARTS/*FINISHED DIMENSIONS*

A. Sides (2) $1/2" \times 7" \times 33 1/4"$
B. Top shelf $1/2" \times 4 1/2" \times 41 1/2"$
C. Top middle shelf $1/2" \times 2 3/4" \times 41 1/2"$
D. Bottom middle shelf $1/2" \times 4 1/2" \times 41 1/2"$
E. Bottom shelf $1/2" \times 5 1/2" \times 41 1/2"$

HARDWARE

4d Square-cut nails (16)
Leather thong (12")

PLAN OF PROCEDURE

1

Plane, rip, and cut the parts to the sizes shown in the Bill of Materials. Bevel the front edge of the top, bottom middle, and bottom shelves at 65°, as shown in the *Shelving Profiles*.

2

Cut ½"-wide, ¼"-deep dadoes in the sides, as shown in the *Front View* and *Side Pattern*.

— 4½" —

65°   ½"

TOP SHELF

— 2¾" —   ½"

TOP MIDDLE SHELF

65°   ½"

— 4½" —

BOTTOM MIDDLE SHELF

3

Lay out the *Side Pattern* and cut the shape of the sides. Sand the sawed edges.

4

Drill a ³⁄₁₆"-diameter hole through each side, near the top end, as shown in the *Side Pattern*.

5

Finish sand the parts of the whale shelf and dry assemble them to check the fit of the joints. Reassemble the parts with glue and square-cut nails.

6

Set the nails and cover the heads with putty.

— 5½" —

65°   ½"

BOTTOM SHELF

SHELVING PROFILES

7

Do any necessary touch-up sanding and apply a finish to the completed project.

³⁄₁₆"
Dia
Hole
Thru

1 Square = 1"

SIDE PATTERN

PLAN OF PROCEDURE

8

Cut two 6" lengths of leather thong. Insert a thong through the hole in each side, as shown in the *Thong Detail*. Tie a knot to secure the thong.

9

Drive nails or install Molly anchors in the wall where you want to hang the shelf. Paint the heads to match the wall, then suspend the shelf from the nails or anchors, looping the leather thongs over them.

6" Lg
Leather
Thong

3/16" Dia
Hole Thru

Side

THONG DETAIL

Leather Thong
(2 Req'd)

4½"

6¼"

½" Wd x ¼" Dp
Dado (Typ)

8¼"

33¼"

½"
(Typ)

12¼"

½" Wd x ¼" Dp
Rabbet

½"

½"

42"

FRONT VIEW

STEP-BACK CABINET

In the sixteenth century, Europe began to import fine porcelain from the Orient. So folks could display these treasures in a protective enclosure, joiners developed a cupboard with glass doors. The French called this a *cabinette* (which the English shortened to "cabinet"), after the word cabin, a one-room house with windows.

The techniques needed to make cabinets were more difficult than those required to make other pieces of furniture. Joiners who possessed these skills advertised themselves as "cabinetmakers." The term quickly became synonymous with makers of fine furniture.

Although American craftsmen were advertising themselves as cabinetmakers in the early 1700s, cabinets were rare in the colonies until much later. Glass was a luxury. But as America began to industrialize, it became less expensive and cabinets more common. By the nineteenth century, many country homes had glass-front cabinets in which to display their china.

There were many different styles of cabinets, but one of the most popular was this "step-back" cabinet. It's actually a cabinet top on a cupboard base. The top isn't as deep as the base, so the cabinet seems to "step back" from the wider cupboard.

**BASE
EXPLODED VIEW**

BILL OF MATERIALS

WOODEN PARTS/*FINISHED DIMENSIONS*

Base

A.	Base sides (2)	3/4" x 17¹/4" x 34¹/4"
B.	Counter	3/4" x 19" x 50"
C.	Base shelf	3/4" x 16³/4" x 47¹/4"
D.	Base backboards (7)	¹/2" x 7¹/16" x 29"
E.	Base face frame stiles (2)	3/4" x 4" x 34¹/4"
F.	Top face frame rail	3/4" x 2" x 42"
G.	Bottom face frame rail	3/4" x 1" x 42"
H.	Base door stiles (3)	3/4" x 3" x 26¹/8"
J.	Left inside base door stile	3/4" x 3³/8" x 26¹/8"
K.	Top door rails (2)	3/4" x 3" x 15¹⁵/16"
L.	Bottom door rails (2)	3/4" x 4" x 15¹⁵/16"
M.	Base door panels (2)	¹/2" x 14¹/2" x 19¹³/16"

N.	Door catch	5/8" x 1" x 1¹/2"
P.	Pegs (12)	¹/4" x ¹/4" x 1¹/4"*

Cabinet

G.	Bottom face frame rail	3/4" x 1" x 42"
K.	Top door rails (2)	3/4" x 3" x 15¹⁵/16"
L.	Bottom door rails (2)	3/4" x 4" x 15¹⁵/16"
N.	Door catch	5/8" x 1" x 1¹/2"
P.	Pegs (14)	¹/4" x ¹/4" x 1¹/4"*
Q.	Cabinet sides (2)	3/4" x 11¹/4" x 48¹/2"
R.	Top	¹/2" x 15³/8" x 54³/4"
S.	Cabinet shelves (3)	3/4" x 10³/4" x 47¹/4"
T.	Cabinet backboards (7)	¹/2" x 7¹/16" x 48³/4"

**CABINET
EXPLODED VIEW**

U.	Cabinet face frame stiles (2)	3/4" x 4" x 481/2"
V.	Top cabinet face frame rail	3/4" x 61/2" x 42"
W.	Front molding	3/4" x 47/16" x 541/4"
X.	Side moldings (2)	3/4" x 47/16" x 151/8"
Y.	Cabinet door stiles (3)	3/4" x 3" x 347/8"
Z.	Left inside cabinet door stile	3/4" x 33/8" x 347/8"
AA.	Sash stiles (2)	3/8" x 5/8" x 277/8"
BB.	Sash rails (8)	3/8" x 5/8" x 621/32"
CC.	Top/bottom vertical glazing bars (4)	1/4" x 3/8" x 95/16"
DD.	Middle vertical glazing bars (2)	1/4" x 3/8" x 91/4"
EE.	Horizontal glazing bars (4)	1/4" x 3/8" x 147/16"

HARDWARE

11/2" x 2" Butt hinges and mounting screws (4 pairs)
Door latches (2)
Door pulls (2)
6d Square-cut nails (36–42)
4d Square-cut nails (36–42)
#8 x 11/4" Flathead wood screws (12)
1/8" x 77/16" x 93/16" Glass panes (12)

*Make the pegs at least this long, then cut them to length
after you install them.*

PLAN OF PROCEDURE

To help this project progress smoothly, build it in two parts. First build the base, then the cabinet to sit on top of the base.

Making the Base

1

If necessary, glue up stock to make the wide parts of the base — sides, shelf, counter, and door panels. Plane, rip, and cut the base parts to the sizes shown in the Bill of Materials, except the door parts. Cut these after you've built the base case.

2

Cut the joinery needed to assemble the base:

- ³/₄"-wide, ³/₈"-deep dadoes in the sides to hold the shelf, as shown in the *Base Side Layout*
- ½"-wide, ³/₈"-deep rabbets in the back edges of the sides to hold the backboards
- ½"-wide, ³/₈"-deep, 47¼"-long double-blind rabbet in the back edge of the counter, as shown in the *Counter Layout,* to hold the backboards

- ³/₈"-wide, ¼"-deep rabbets in *both* edges of the middle backboards, and *one* edge of the right and left backboards, as shown in the *Back Joinery Detail*
- ¼"-wide, 1"-deep, 1¼"-long mortises in the inside edges of the base face frame stiles, near the top ends, as shown in the *Face Frame/Cabinet Door Joinery Detail* and *Base Face Frame Layout*
- ¼"-wide, 1"-deep, 1"-long mortises in the inside edges of the face frame stiles, near the bottom ends
- ¼"-thick, 1"-long tenons on the ends of the face frame rails

BASE SIDE LAYOUT

COUNTER LAYOUT

FRONT VIEW

SIDE VIEW

PLAN OF PROCEDURE

3

Notch the tenons of the top base rail to fit the 1¼"-long mortises.

4

Drill screw pockets with ³/₁₆"-diameter pilot holes in the sides, as shown in the *Counter Joinery Detail*. Make 3 pockets in each side, near the top end. The placement of these holes is not critical, but they should be evenly spaced along each side.

BACK JOINERY DETAIL

7¹/₁₆"
³/₈"
Backboard
³/₈" Wd × ½" Dp Rabbet
³/₈" Wd × ¼" Dp Rabbet (Typ)
Side

COUNTER JOINERY DETAIL

Counter
#8 × 1¼" FHWS
Screw Pocket
¾" Dia C'Bore &
³/₁₆" Pilot Hole
Side

BASE FACE FRAME LAYOUT

³/₈"
1¼" ³/₈"
2"
26¼"
34¼"
42" (Typ)
1"
1"
8" Rad
1" 4"
5"
2"
4"
40"
2"
4"
48"

5

Lay out and cut the shapes of the sides and face frame stiles, as shown in the *Base Side Layout* and *Front View*. Chamfer the outside corners of the stiles, stopping 2" from the top ends and 5" from the bottom ends. Sand the saw and mill marks smooth.

6

Stain the rabbeted edges of the backboards a dark brown or black.

FACE FRAME/ CABINET DOOR JOINERY DETAIL

7

Finish sand the parts of the face frame. Glue them together, inserting the tenons in the mortises.

8

Round the bottom portion of the pegs, as shown in the *Peg Detail*.

9

Drill a 1/4"-diameter hole through each mortise and tenon in the face frame. Drive a peg into each hole to secure the tenon in the mortise, then cut off the peg flush with the inside surface of the frame.

 SECTION D

 SECTION E

 SECTION F

(Make from *very* hard wood.)

10

Finish sand the parts of the base case and assemble them as follows:

- Glue the shelf to the sides and reinforce the joints with 6d square-cut nails.
- Glue the assembled face frame to the case. Reinforce it with 6d nails.
- Attach the counter to the sides with screws.
- Nail the backboards to the sides, top, and shelf with 4d nails. Do *not* glue the backboards in place.

As you work, sand all joints clean and flush. Set the heads of the nails. Cover the heads of the nails in the sides and front with putty.

PEG DETAIL

PLAN OF PROCEDURE

11

Measure the door opening and make any necessary changes in the dimensions of the door parts. Cut the door parts to size, then cut the joinery needed to assemble the doors:

- 3/8"-wide, 3/8"-deep rabbets in the adjoining edges of the inside door stiles
- 1/4"-wide, 3/8"-deep grooves in the inside edges of all door rails and stiles
- 1/4"-wide, 1"-deep, 2 1/4"-long mortises in the inside edge of each door stile, 3/8" from each end
- 1/4"-thick, 1"-long tenons on the ends of the door rails

12

Notch the tenons in the rails as shown in the *Base Door Frame Joinery Detail,* creating a haunch in each tenon and fitting it to its mortise.

13

Raise the door panels, beveling the edges to fit the grooves in the rails and stiles, as shown in *Section B.*

**BASE
DOOR FRAME
JOINERY DETAIL**

14

Finish sand the door parts and assemble the rails and stiles with glue. Put the panels in place as you glue up the door frames, but do not apply glue to them. The panels must float in the grooves.

SECTION B

15

Reinforce the mortise-and-tenon joints in the door frames with pegs, as you did on the face frame.

16

Mortise the door stiles and face frame stiles for hinges, then mount the doors to the case.

17

Chamfer the top corners of the base door catch, as shown in the *Base Door Catch Detail*.

18

Using a wood screw, attach the door catch to the inside surface of the left inside base door stile (as you face the assembly), near the top end. The catch must turn freely on the screw. When turned so the chamfered end is up, it should overlap the top base face frame rail.

19

Mount a door latch on the outside surface of the left inside base door stile and a door pull on the right inside base door stile.

BASE LEFT DOOR LAYOUT

BASE DOOR CATCH DETAIL

PLAN OF PROCEDURE

Making the Cabinet

20

Plane, rip, and cut the cabinet parts to the sizes shown in the Bill of Materials, except the door parts. Cut these after you've built the cabinet case.

21

Cut the joinery needed to assemble the cabinet:

- 3/4"-wide, 3/8"-deep dadoes in the sides to hold the shelves, as shown in the *Cabinet Side Layout*
- 1/2"-wide, 3/8"-deep rabbets in the back edges of the sides to hold the backboards
- 1/2"-wide, 1/4"-deep, 47 1/4"-long double-blind rabbet in the back edge of the top, as shown in the *Top Layout*, to hold the backboards
- 3/8"-wide, 1/4"-deep rabbets in *both* edges of the middle backboards, and *one* edge of the right and left backboards, as shown in the *Back Joinery Detail*
- 1/2"-wide, 3/8"-deep dovetail notches in the front edges of the top and middle shelves, as shown in the *Cabinet Shelf Layout*, to hold spoons

- 1/4"-wide, 3/8"-deep, 1 3/4"-long mortise in the middle shelf for the cabinet catch
- 3/8"-wide, 3/8"-deep grooves in the shelves, 1 1/4" from the back edges, to hold plates
- 1/4"-wide, 1"-deep, 5 3/4"-long mortises in the inside edges of the face frame stiles, near the top ends, as shown in the *Face Frame/ Cabinet Door Joinery Detail* and *Cabinet Face Frame Layout*
- 1/4"-wide, 1"-deep, 1"-long mortises in the inside edges of the face frame stiles, near the bottom ends
- 1/4"-thick, 1"-long tenons on the ends of the face frame rails

CABINET SIDE LAYOUT

TOP LAYOUT

CABINET SHELF LAYOUT

³/₈" Wd × ³/₈" Dp Groove

³/₈" Wd × ³/₈" Dp × 1³/₄" Lg Mortise (Middle Shelf Only)

Optional ¹/₂" Wd Dovetail Notch (Top and Middle Shelves Only)

1¹/₄"

³/₈"

10³/₄"

21¹/₄"

³/₈"

³/₈"

10°

9⁵/₈" 2" 4⁵/₈" 2" 10³/₄" 2" 4⁵/₈" 2" 9⁵/₈"

47¹/₄"

CABINET FACE FRAME LAYOUT

³/₈"

5³/₄"

³/₈"

6¹/₂"

35"

48¹/₂"

42" (Typ)

1"

1"

1"

5"

6"

12" Rad

2"

4"

40"

48"

2"

4"

PLAN OF PROCEDURE

22

Notch the tenons of the top cabinet rail to fit the mortises.

23

Lay out and cut the shapes of the face frame stiles, as shown in the *Front View*. Chamfer the outside corners of the stiles, stopping 6½" from the top ends and 3" from the bottom ends. Sand the saw and mill marks smooth.

24

Finish sand the parts of the face frame. Glue them together, inserting the tenons in the mortises. Reinforce the mortise-and-tenon joints with pegs.

25

Finish sand the parts of the cabinet case and assemble them as follows:

- Glue the shelves to the sides and reinforce the joints with 6d square-cut nails. (The plate grooves in all the shelves and the mortise in the middle shelf must face up.)
- Glue the assembled face frame to the case. Reinforce it with nails.
- Attach the top to the sides with nails. Don't drive the nails all the way in, so you can adjust the position of the top later.

26

Cut the 45° bevels in the moldings, as shown in the *Molding Detail*.

27

Fit the top moldings to the case, compound-mitering the adjoining ends at 45°.

28

Finish sand the moldings. Attach the front molding to the case with glue and nails. Attach the side moldings with nails only — do *not* glue them in place. If necessary, shift the position of the top to center it over the moldings.

29

Stain the rabbeted edges of the backboards a dark brown or black.

30

Nail the backboards to the sides, top, and shelves with 4d nails. Do *not* glue the backboards in place.

MOLDING DETAIL

PLATE GROOVE DETAIL

31

Sand all joints clean and flush. Set the heads of the nails. Cover the heads of the nails in the sides and front with putty.

32

Measure the door opening and make any necessary changes in the dimensions of the door parts. Cut the door rails and stiles to size, then cut the joinery needed to assemble the door frames:

- 1/2"-wide, 3/8"-deep rabbets in the adjoining edges of the inside door stiles
- 1/4"-wide, 1"-deep, 2 1/4"-long mortises in the inside edge of each door stile, 3/8" from each end
- 1/4"-thick, 1"-long tenons on the ends of the door rails

33

Notch the tenons in the rails as shown in the *Face Frame/Cabinet Door Joinery Detail*, fitting each tenon to its mortise.

34

Finish sand the door parts and assemble the rails and stiles with glue. Reinforce the mortise-and-tenon joints with pegs.

35

Rout a 1/4"-wide, 3/8"-deep rabbet all around the inside edges of the cabinet door frames. Square the corners where the rabbets meet with a chisel.

TOP LEFT DOOR LAYOUT

SECTION A

PLAN OF PROCEDURE

36

Cut and install the sash rails, sash stiles, and glazing bars, following the procedure in Installing Glass in Cabinet Doors. Sand all the joints clean and flush.

37

Mortise the door stiles and face frame stiles for hinges, then mount the doors to the case.

38

Taper one end of the cabinet door catch, as shown in the *Cabinet Door Catch Detail*.

39

Using a wood screw, attach the door catch to the inside surface of the left inside cabinet door stile, just above the middle shelf. The catch must turn freely on the screw. When turned so the tapered end is down, it should rest in the shelf mortise.

40

Mount a door latch on the outside surface of the left inside cabinet door stile and a door pull on the right inside cabinet door stile.

Finishing Up

41

Remove the doors from the base and cabinet and remove all the hardware from the doors. Do any necessary touch-up sanding, then apply a finish to the base, cabinet, and doors. Coat all wooden surfaces — inside and out, front and back.

42

Put the cabinet on the base. Replace the hardware, then hang the doors.

43

Install glass panes in the cabinet doors, holding the glass in place with glazing compound. Mix paint or stain with the compound to match the finish.

CABINET DOOR CATCH DETAIL

Door Gap
Left Door
Middle Shelf
#8 × 1¼" FHWS
1⅞"
⅝"
1"
⅞"
⅞"
7⁄16"
⅝"
1½"
Door Catch
Round Over End
¼" Wd × ⅜" Dp × 1¾" Lg Mortise for Door Catch

SECTION C

Sash Rail
Glass
⅝"
3⁄16"
¼"
5⁄8"
⅜"
Glazing Bar
Glazing Compound

SASH RAIL/ SASH STILE/ GLAZING BAR ASSEMBLY DETAIL

¼" Wd × ⅜" Dp Rabbet

COUNTRY CRAFTSMAN'S KNOW-HOW: INSTALLING GLASS IN CABINET DOORS

Country craftsmen never mounted large panes of glass in their cabinets, for a very good reason: There weren't any available. The technology needed to cast large, flat panes wasn't developed until the late nineteenth century, well after the country furniture era. Instead, when they wanted to make a large glass cabinet door, they arranged several smaller panes in a delicate wooden frame usually in multiples of 3 or 4. This framework was called sash work or *glazing*.

There is no one way to make glazing. The glass panes can be configured many different ways, and the wooden parts can be lapped, mitered, mortised, or simply butted together. Country craftsmen, as you might expect, usually kept the glazing simple. They configured the glass in a simple grid, often in multiples of three or four. Four-, nine-, and twelve-pane doors were the most common. This, in turn, simplified the joinery. The glazing shown is assembled with ordinary butt joints.

1 This glazing consists of three parts: The vertical outside moldings are called *sash stiles (a)*, the horizontal outside moldings are *sash rails (b)*, and the narrow, inside strips that actually support the glass are *glazing bars (c)*. These are set into an ordinary door frame consisting of *rails (d)* and *stiles (e)*.

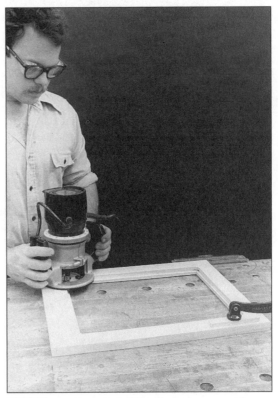

2 Before you can install the glazing, you must have something to set it in. Make a door frame, then rout a deep rabbet all around the inside. Square the corners of the rabbet with a chisel.

(Continued)

COUNTRY CRAFTSMAN'S
KNOW-HOW: INSTALLING GLASS IN CABINET DOORS — *CONT.*

3 Carefully measure the inside dimensions of the frame, then cut the sash stiles, sash rails, and glazing bars to fit it. The sash stiles should span the opening from top to bottom. The sash rails, because they are interrupted by the stiles, will be somewhat shorter. Likewise, the horizontal glazing bars span the opening from side to side, and the vertical bars will be shorter. These parts must fit snug, but not so tight that they bow.

4 Some craftsmen prefer to lap the sash rails and stiles — or vertical and horizontal glazing bars — for extra strength. If you choose to do this, you must measure the position of these lap joints very precisely.

5 Rest the frame on its front surface. Dry assemble the parts in it. Carefully arrange them so the openings in the grid are the sizes required. (In most projects, the grid openings should all be the same size.) Mark the locations of the parts on the door frame and each other, then remove the parts.

6 Glue the horizontal glazing bars in the frame first. Apply the glue generously, and wipe away any that squeezes out with a wet rag. The inside edges of the bars must be flush with the inside surfaces of the door frame.

7 Next, install the sash stiles, gluing them to the door rails and the glazing bars. Check that all the parts are square to one another and properly positioned — the outside surfaces of the sash stiles must be flush with the outside surfaces of the door frame. Let the glue dry completely.

8 Glue the vertical glazing bars to the door frame, sash stiles, and horizontal bars. Make sure the bars are centered on the sash stiles.

9 Finally, glue the sash rails to the horizontal glazing bars, sash stiles, and door frame. Once again, make sure the sash rails and bars are centered — this will create many small ledges and lips in which to rest the glass panes.

10 Complete the cabinet and apply a finish. Then install the glass panes in the door, holding them in place with glazing compound. Mix this compound with paint, stain, or dye to match the finish on the cabinet.

Note: For an accurate country reproduction, use "antique" glass. This glass is cast with imperfections to mimic old-time glass. It's available through most glass shops.

PIPE BOX

Although we remember these small, hanging boxes as "pipe boxes," they weren't originally intended to hold pipes. Most country gentlemen had only one or two pipes — hardly enough to fill a box — and those usually had short stems. Only in taverns and inns, where the proprietor kept a selection of long-stem clay pipes for guests, did pipe boxes really hold pipes.

Originally, these boxes had another purpose altogether — and another name. Folks built them to hold "candles" — not the wax candles we think of, but slender sticks of candlewood (resinous pine) or lengths of dried, pithy rush soaked in tallow. Wax candles were a luxury in colonial America; common people usually burned these strips of pine and rush for light at night. Because they burned quickly — each candle lasted no more than fifteen or twenty minutes — folks had to keep a large supply at hand. They filled their "candle boxes" before dusk each day.

The box shown is an original design, but it's typical of early American candle boxes — or pipe boxes, if you prefer. A deep bin, open at the top, held the candlewood or rush. A small drawer at the base held flint, an iron striker, and "punk" to help light the candles.

EXPLODED VIEW

BILL OF MATERIALS

WOODEN PARTS/*FINISHED DIMENSIONS*

A.	Back	$3/8"$ x $4 1/4"$ x $16"$
B.	Front	$3/8"$ x $4 1/4"$ x $9 3/4"$
C.	Sides (2)	$3/8"$ x $2 7/8"$ x $12 5/8"$
D.	Bottom	$3/8"$ x $2 7/8"$ x $3 1/2"$
E.	Bin bottom	$3/8"$ x $2 1/2"$ x $3 1/2"$
F.	Drawer front	$3/8"$ x $2 13/16"$ x $3 7/16"$
G.	Drawer sides (2)	$3/8"$ x $2 9/16"$ x $2 3/4"$
H.	Drawer back	$1/4"$ x $2 9/16"$ x $2 11/16"$
J.	Drawer bottom	$1/4"$ x $2 3/4"$ x $3 7/16"$

HARDWARE

$1/2"$ Brass knob

$7/8"$ Wire or "headless" brads (30–40)

PLAN OF PROCEDURE

1

Plane, rip, and cut the parts to the sizes shown in the Bill of Materials.

2

Cut 3/8"-wide, 93/4"-wide notches in the sides, as shown in the *Side View*.

3

Lay out and cut the shapes of the back and front, as shown in the *Front View*.

FRONT VIEW

SIDE VIEW

4

Finish sand the parts of the pipe box that you have made so far. Assemble them with glue and wire brads. Set the heads of the brads.

5

Cut 3/8"-wide, 1/4"-deep rabbets in the ends of the drawer front, as shown in the *Drawer Detail/ Top View.*

6

Lightly sand the drawer parts, then assemble them with glue and brads. Set the brads.

7

Finish sand the drawer front and install a drawer pull. Place the drawer in the pipe box to check the fit, and make any necessary adjustments.

8

Remove the drawer from the box and the pull from the drawer. Do any necessary touch-up sanding and apply a finish to the completed project.

9

Replace the pull on the drawer and rub the bottom of the drawer with soap or wax to help it slide more easily. Replace the drawer in the finished pipe box.

3/8" Wd ×
1/4" Dp ×
Rabbet

1/4"

2 7/8"

3/8" (Typ)

3/8"

2 11/16"

TOP VIEW

2 13/16"

3 7/16"

FRONT VIEW

1/4" Wd ×
1/4" Dp
Rabbet

2 9/16"

1/4"

2 3/4"

2 7/8"

SIDE VIEW

DRAWER DETAIL

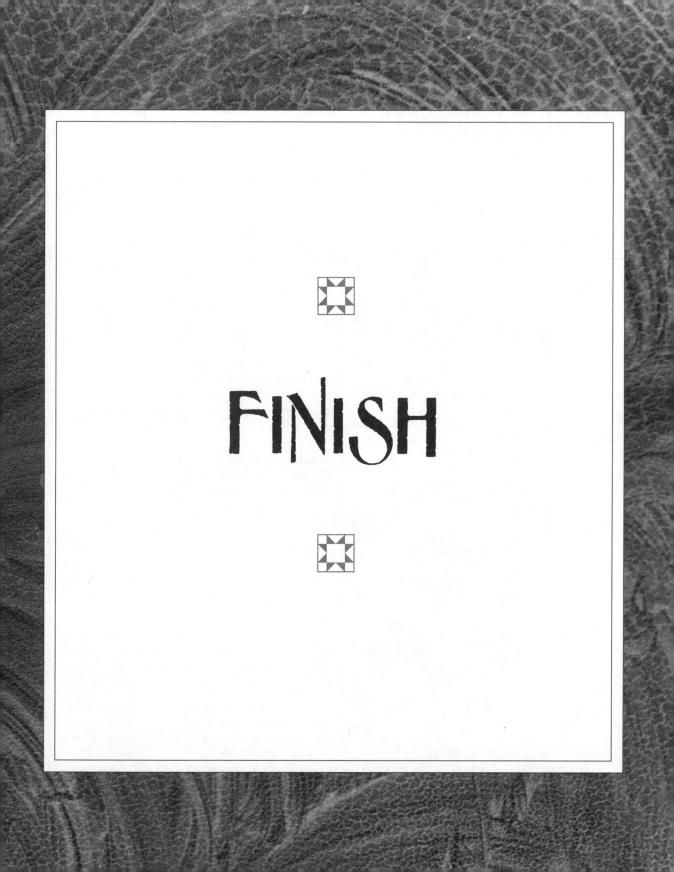

FINISH

FINISHING PHILOSOPHY

Of the three important elements in American country furniture — design, construction, and finish — the finish, most of all, decides the effect that a project has on its viewer. Design and construction determine the purpose of a project, but finish bestows its "look" — the mood, feeling, and ambience of a piece.

To illustrate, imagine that you've made two small cupboards following the same plan. One is built from an elegant hardwood, such as cherry or walnut, and the other from a plainer wood such as poplar. You outfit the fancy hardwood cupboard with brass hardware and the other with iron. Finally, you apply a natural finish to the hardwood piece, and paint the plain piece.

Even though these two cupboards are designed and constructed identically, they will have different effects on an observer. The naturally finished piece will look much more sophisticated. The painted piece will have a down-home, utilitarian appearance. The fancier piece would best be placed in a formal dining room or living room, while the plainer one would look more at home in a kitchen or family room.

Before you finish a country piece, consider the effect or look you want — *how you want it to appear to a viewer* — then choose from the many different finishes available to you. Choose carefully! You can ruin days, weeks, even months of work by applying the wrong finish to properly designed and constructed furniture.

NATURAL VERSUS ARTIFICIAL AGING

Perhaps the most important question you must answer when choosing a finish is whether or not you want it to look aged immediately upon finishing it. There are two schools of thought on this question.

The first maintains that historical and historically inspired furniture should be finished in a *traditional* manner and allowed to age naturally. Apply old-time country finishing materials using country methods, appropriate to the same period in which the furniture would have been built. Then let the piece develop a natural patina over many years — just as an antique would have aged.

The second (and currently most popular) school holds the opposite view: An antique reproduction ought to look like an antique. Use both traditional and modern finishing materials and methods to create an artificial patina, complete with dings and scratches. A finish that successfully imitates the natural aging process is sometimes called a *museum-quality* finish.

The finishing philosophy that's right for you will depend on your tastes and the look you want your project to have. You might even switch philos-

These two sofa tables are similar in size and design. However, they were finished differently. One was stained and lacquered, the other grain-painted. This gives them a completely different look. The stained piece appears reserved and formal, the painted piece festive and folksy.

ophies now and again, depending on what you build and how you use it. The Workshops is best known for the museum-quality finishes that they apply to their furniture, but they sometimes apply a traditional finish on request.

EXPERIMENTATION AND EXPERIENCE

No matter what effect you're after, whether you use a clear, natural varnish or paint the wood, whether you let the piece age naturally or age it artificially, every finish requires a singularly important first step: You must experiment with the planned finishing procedure and the materials *before* you apply the finish to the completed project. This may save a great deal of refinishing later on.

As you build, save the larger scraps from your project. Finish sand these at the same time you sand the other parts, then set them aside. When you've completed the project, get out the scraps again. Use them to experiment with finishing materials. If you're undecided as to what look you want, finish several different scraps using different methods. If you've never tried a finish technique before, practice on a scrap to gain experience.

These practice runs are especially important if you decide to apply a museum-quality finish. Artificially aging a project generally requires several different materials and methods — more so than other finishes. Some materials may be incompatible, causing a chemical reaction that could ruin your project. Or you may have unanticipated problems with your equipment. Unless you're an experienced finisher, always try the finish on a scrap first.

Both of these salt boxes have milk paint finishes. One, however was painted with an old-time recipe and will age naturally. The other was finished with more modern materials and aged artificially.

This scrap was used to experiment with grain-painting techniques. In each experiment, the craftsman used the same tool and the same colors; he just applied them differently. As you can see, a little change in finishing technique can make a big difference. If you're in doubt as to how the finish will turn out, practice first on a scrap.

TRADITIONAL FINISHES

You might expect that the choice of finishes in eighteenth- and nineteenth-century America was more limited than it is now, but this was not the case. Although country craftsmen didn't have ready-mixed finishes as we do, they had plenty of ingredients for mixing their own. Furthermore, they often experimented with different mixes before settling on something they liked.

As a result, there were no truly "traditional" finishing materials. Each craftsman had one or more mixtures that he preferred, and these were as unique as his own signature. There were, however, several finishing methods that became popular during the Country era (1690 to 1860) in America. It's these techniques that we remember as traditional country finishes.

A BRIEF HISTORY OF FINISHING

Finishing was a relatively new practice among American *country* craftsmen. Furniture finishing, of course, had begun with furniture making. The Egyptians, Greeks, and Romans used a variety of materials to protect the surface of their furniture and enhance its appearance. These included varnishes (a mixture of resins and oils or spirits) and paints (pigments suspended in oils). However, all but the most basic finishing techniques were forgotten in Europe during the Dark Ages. For over 1,000 years the sparse, crude furniture of the medieval era was either painted or left unfinished.

As Europe climbed out of the Dark Ages and furniture styles once again began to evolve, so did finishing techniques. During the Gothic period, joiners began to polish the surface of their furniture by rubbing it with a liquid or semi-liquid material such as linseed oil, walnut oil, or a mixture of turpentine and beeswax. The harder they rubbed, the more oil or wax built up on the sur-

face of the wood. After a lot of elbow grease had been expended, the surface became smooth as glass. This painstaking rubbing technique was the first to be called *finishing*. By the sixteenth century, finishing had largely replaced painting on stylish European furniture, although most country pieces were still painted.

With the Renaissance, European craftsmen experimented with dozens of new finishing materials and techniques. They rediscovered varnishes, which quickly replaced oils and waxes as the preferred finish on quality furniture. Varnish, they found, preserved the wood better and held its gloss longer than previous materials.

Trade with the Orient introduced Europe to many exotic varnishes, most importantly lacquer. Lacquer was made from the resin of the Chinese sumac tree, *Rhus verniciflua*. Although it needed special conditions to harden (it was often applied in a damp basement or cave), it dried quickly and allowed the craftsmen to build up many layers in a short time. Oriental craftsmen used this property to build up three-dimensional pictures on the lacquered surfaces of their furniture.

European cabinetmakers began to imitate this technique, but true Chinese lacquer was rare. They invented several substitute finishes such as *gesso*, a mixture of plaster of paris and sizing. Gesso could be applied much thicker than lacquer; the surface built up much more rapidly. However, if skillfully done, the result was very similar to true lacquer. The art of applying three-dimensional, pictorial finishes with gesso and other lacquer substitutes became known as *japanning*, since most lacquered furniture was imported from Japan.

During the late Renaissance, France began to import another varnish finish, *shellac*. Shellac was the resinous excrement of the lac bug, an insect native to India and Ceylon. When dissolved in alcohol, the mixture dried so quickly that multiple layers could be built up in minutes. French cabinetmakers took advantage of this property and developed the *French polish.* Use of shellac quickly spread to other countries.

This was the state of the finishing art as Europe began to colonize America. Cabinetmakers were in the midst of an explosion of new finishing materials and techniques, although much of this was confined to city craftsmen. Most country furmituremakers continued to use hand-rubbed oil or that ancient stand-by, paint. But a few had begun to experiment with innovative varnish mixtures. They brought all of these ideas, both old and new, with them to the New World. By the time of the American Revolution, country craftsmen were using most of the same techniques as their counterparts in the city.

DUPLICATING TRADITIONAL FINISHING MATERIALS

Perhaps the most difficult task in duplicating a traditional country finish is obtaining the same materials a country craftsman might have used. However, you can find most of these if you look around — consult the Sources section for names and addresses.

You also have to know what you're looking for. For example, most eighteenth- and nineteenth-century varnishes were made from *copal* resin. Copal was extracted from the copa tree, a variety of cedar that grew in Central America and Africa. You can't use modern varnishes for a traditional finish. Most of these are distilled from flax seed or the tung tree.

Paints, too, have changed. To make old-time paints opaque, craftsmen added *lime paste* (hydrated or "slaked" lime and water) to their paint recipe. Today, paint manufacturers use titanium dioxide and silicates for the same pur-

pose. However, several finishing companies still sell powdered mixes that use lime.

A few traditional finishes, such as hand-rubbed oils and shellac, haven't changed in 200 years. You can purchase these right off the shelf in most paint or hardware stores. And you can come close to re-creating others by making them from scratch.

APPLYING TRADITIONAL FINISHES

Hand-Rubbed Oil — The most common material used for hand-rubbed oil finishes was boiled linseed oil. (The oil was boiled to prevent it from going rancid.) However, cabinetmakers also employed walnut oil, cottonseed oil, and other plant oils. Add 2 tablespoons of japan drier per pint of oil.

1 Carefully remove all mill marks and other evidence of power tools, then finish sand the surface to 220#.

2 Apply a generous coat of oil and rub into the wood with your hands. (The warmth of your hands helps the oil to penetrate deeply.) Allow it to soak in for a few hours, then wipe off the excess.

3 Apply yet more oil and polish the wood with 320# wet/dry paper. (Old-time craftsmen used sharkskin.) The sandpaper will create a fine sawdust, which mixes with the oil to make a paste. This, in turn, fills imperfections in the wood and creates a glass-smooth surface. Wipe off the excess.

4 Allow the oil to dry overnight, then apply another coat. Rub it in vigorously with a clean cloth.

5 Allow the second coat to dry overnight, and repeat as needed until you build up the gloss you want.

Hand-Rubbed Beeswax — You can purchase beeswax from dental supply outlets, crafts stores, and some hardware stores. Cut or break the beeswax into small chunks, pack it into a jar, and add just enough turpentine to cover the wax. You may also want to add a small amount of carnauba wax to make the finish harder. Allow the mixture to sit overnight. In the morning you'll find the beeswax has turned into a soft paste. If the paste is too stiff, add more turpentine; if it's runny, add more wax. (If you add carnauba, gently warm the mixture in a pan of water over an electric burner to melt the two waxes together. **Warning:** Do *not* use an open flame.)

1 Carefully remove all mill marks and other evidence of power tools, then finish sand the surface to 220#.

2 Apply the beeswax paste to a small area with a soft cloth, rubbing vigorously.

3 Allow the wax to set for a few minutes, then polish it with clean cheesecloth. Continue rubbing until you remove all the streaks and the wax is buffed to a high gloss.

4 Repeat, applying wax to just one small area at a time until you've finished the entire project.

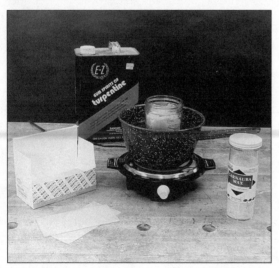

When mixing waxes for a hand-rubbed wax finish, melt them together in a water bath over an *electric* burner. Do *not* use an open flame.

Brushed-On Varnish — Varnishes are more finicky than most finishes and require the proper conditions. The finishing room must be relatively free of dust, and the temperature should be between 65° and 85°F. Use a good animal bristle brush and prepare it by soaking the brush in turpentine for a day or so. Just before you use it, remove the brush from the turpentine and wipe it clean on a rag or paper. This will remove any loose bristles.

1 Carefully remove all mill marks and other evidence of power tools, then finish sand the surface to 220#.

2 "Fill" the brush by dipping half the length of the bristles into the varnish. Do *not* wipe the brush on the sides of the container.

3 Let the varnish "flow" onto the surface of the wood, wiping the brush *across* the grain until the bristles are fairly dry.

After you apply the varnish across the grain, smooth it with just the tip of the brush, wiping with the grain. Hold the brush nearly vertical as you do this.

4 Repeat, starting the next set of brush strokes 1"–2" inside the area you covered with the first set. Wipe toward the unvarnished area. Continue until you've covered the entire surface.

5 While the varnish is still wet, smooth it with the very tip of the brush, wiping *with* the grain.

6 Allow the first coat to dry completely (usually 6–12 hours). The varnish will look awful. There will be dimples, specks, and other marks, but this is normal. Sand out the imperfections with wet/dry 320# sandpaper. To prevent the sandpaper from loading, dip it in linseed oil from time to time as you work.

Note: Be careful not to sand through the varnish at the edges and corners. Use a sanding block to apply even pressure over the entire surface.

7 Repeat Steps 2 through 6 to build up several coats of varnish.

8 Rub out the last coat with linseed oil and pumice stone. Fold a soft, clean cloth into a pad and soak it in oil. Press the pad into the pumice, then rub the varnish vigorously. Replenish the oil and pumice on the pad as needed. Periodically, wipe away the grime from the surface to check your progress. Continue until the varnished surface has a smooth, even sheen.

9 Apply a paste wax, such as a beeswax/carnauba mixture, to the varnished surface and buff it.

French Polish — You can apply shellac with a brush in a similar manner as varnish. However, many country craftsmen preferred to apply it with a pad, using a technique known as French polish. To make this polish, purchase orange shellac flakes — these are available from some paint stores and many mail-order woodworking suppliers. Mix 5 ounces of flakes with 1 cup of denatured alcohol for a "5-pound cut." Then fold a clean, soft cloth around a wad of cotton balls to make an egg-sized pad.

1 Carefully remove all mill marks and other evidence of power tools, then finish sand the surface to 220#.

2 Sprinkle a few drops of alcohol on the pad and work it in with your hand. Next, add a few drops of shellac, followed by a few drops of linseed oil. The pad should feel moist to the touch.

3 Begin rubbing the surface of the wood in a circular or figure-8 pattern. This pattern should be about 12" across.

4 Refill the pad with alcohol and shellac as needed. If the pad begins to stick to the surface, add a few more drops of linseed oil to lubricate it.

5 In a short time, the finish will begin to accumulate on the surface as you rub. Cover the entire surface, building up the finish to the desired depth.

6 Shake a few drops of alcohol onto the pad and wipe the finish in the direction of the grain. This will remove any circular marks.

7 Allow the finish to dry overnight, then rub it out with linseed oil and pumice stone.

8 Apply paste wax to the surface and buff it to a high gloss.

To build up a French polish, rub a thick (5-pound cut) shellac onto the surface in a circular or figure-8 motion. Keep the shellac from drying on the pad by sprinkling it with alcohol now and then. Lubricate the pad with linseed oil to prevent it from sticking to the surface.

Staining — Old-time craftsmen often stained their furniture for effect. They stained light woods, such as oak and maple, dark brown or black. Even darker woods, such as walnut, were sometimes stained a bright red color known as "Dragon's Blood." These stains were either thinned varnishes tinted with colored resins, or "spirit stains" — vegetable dyes dissolved in alcohol, turpentine, or oil.

1 Carefully remove all mill marks and other evidence of power tools, then finish sand the surface to 220#.

2 Wipe the varnish, oil, or spirit stain on the surface with a cloth or brush, then wipe off the excess with a clean cloth dipped in thinner. Take care to coat the wood evenly. If any areas appear darker than the others, apply a little extra thinner to the clean cloth and rub until the wood lightens.

3 If you want a darker stain, wait a few minutes before you wipe the excess stain off, or apply successive coats.

When sanding a stained, varnished, or shellacked surface, be careful not to sand through the finish to the raw wood, especially at the edges and corners. Use a sanding block to apply even pressure over the entire surface.

4 If you want to apply varnish or shellac over the stain, seal the stain with a "wash coat" of shellac. Mix 2 ounces of shellac flakes in 1 cup of alcohol (to make a 2-pound cut) and brush this over the stain. Lightly sand with 220# paper, then apply a "top coat" of varnish or shellac as you would normally. The wash coat prevents the stain from bleeding into or clouding the clear top coat.

Note: When sanding stained, varnished, or shellacked surfaces, be careful not to sand through the finish to the raw wood. You may choose to ignore this advice when applying museum-quality finishes, however. You may *want* to sand through the finish in certain areas to simulate wear.

Milk Paint — One of the most popular country finishes was milk paint, which came into general use in the last half of the eighteenth century. There were many different recipes for milk paint, but most combined skim milk, lime paste, linseed oil, and pigment. (Sometimes cottage cheese was substituted for milk.) The casein in the dairy product bound the pigment to the wooden surface, producing a hard, waterproof finish. The milk paint finish on some historical country furniture — particularly Shaker furniture — has lasted for almost 200 years with no noticeable signs of fading or wear!

Today, several manufacturers offer powdered milk paint that you simply mix with water. These can be purchased at most paint and craft stores. The choice of colors is limited, but you can combine colors to get different hues. You can also mix white milk paint with fresco colors or water-soluble aniline dies to produce your own colors.

When you mix milk paint, be careful to mix only as much as you need. It will keep in your refrigerator for a few days, but not much longer than that. Before using the paint, strain it through a cheesecloth or nylon stocking to remove any lumps of undissolved powder.

1 Carefully remove all mill marks and other evidence of power tools, then finish sand the surface to 150#.

2 Dampen the surface of the wood with a wet rag. This will help the paint adhere to the surface of the project.

3 Apply a coat of milk paint with a brush. Put the paint on thickly if you want the finish to have some texture; use less if you want it to be smooth.

4 Allow the first coat to dry (usually 4–8 hours), then apply a second. You don't need to sand the surface between coats.

5 Allow the second coat to dry overnight, then sand with wet/dry 320# sandpaper to smooth out the brush strokes. As you work, wet the paper with water to prevent it from loading.

6 Mix a teaspoon of japan drier to a pint of linseed oil, and apply this mixture to the painted surface. Allow the oil to soak in for a few minutes, then wipe away the excess with a soft, clean cloth.

7 Allow the oil to dry overnight. If you want a glossy finish, apply a coat of paste wax and buff.

Note: You can make a semi-opaque paint stain or "wash" by mixing milk paint with more water than the recipe calls for. Apply this wash as you would a spirit stain, using water as the thinner. If you want to apply clear varnish or shellac over the wash, seal it with thin (2-pound cut) shellac.

Grain Painting — In the late eighteenth century, as classic furniture styles began to incorporate exotic woods with highly figured grains, many country cabinetmakers began to "grain" their furniture with paint. Ostensibly, this grain painting was intended to imitate expensive woods and hide inferior materials. However, the technique soon evolved into a folk art form. Many "grainers" applied bold patterns and colors — fanciful caricatures of wood grain. This became known as *faux bois,* French for "false wood."

To grain a piece of furniture, you need a special tool (or combination of tools) to either apply the paint or partially wipe it off. The sorts of tools used by grainers are as fanciful as their work. In addition to a variety of "graining combs," you can also use brushes, feathers, putty, corncobs, sponges, a wad of newspaper, almost anything.

1 Carefully remove all mill marks and other evidence of power tools, then finish sand the surface to 150#.

2 Apply a "base coat" of paint. This can be any color, light or dark.

3 Seal the base coat with a wash coat of shellac (2-pound cut).

4 Fill the bottom of a bowl with a small amount of mineral spirits or varnish. On the edge of the bowl, put a small amount of an artist's oil color. This color must contrast with the base coat. Mix the color and the spirits — you must experiment to get just the right mixture.

5 At this point, you have two choices: (1) Apply the color/spirits mixture with your graining tools, creating a pattern, or (2) paint the mixture onto the surface, covering it completely. Before it dries, wipe part of it off with the graining tools, exposing the base coat and creating a pattern.

6 Let the grain painting dry completely. Then seal it with a wash coat of shellac.

7 Follow with more coats of shellac or a coat of varnish. This will protect the grain paint from wear.

You can use many, many different tools to grain paint, and with each tool you can achieve different effects. This shows just one of the many possible effects of traditional graining combs.

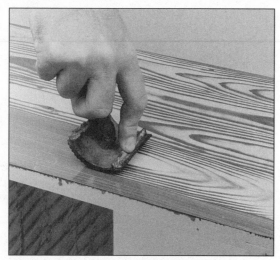

You can paint realistic wood grain with a molded rubber "grainer" — these are available at most crafts stores. Rock the tool back and forth as you drag it through the wet paint.

Use a feather to imitate the grain pattern of a crotch burl. Swirl the feather through the wet paint, drawing parallel arcs.

Not all grain paintings imitated wood grain. Some were fanciful patterns that were invented by the finisher. This half-moon pattern was used on several historical pieces. It's applied with a brush.

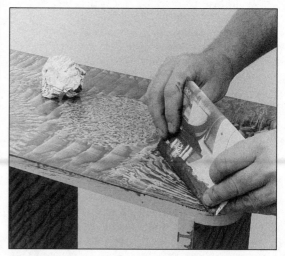

One of the most versatile graining tools is a piece of newspaper. Crumple it into a ball and dab it into the wet paint to mimic burls. Or fold it so you have a straight edge and make a series of parallel dabs to imitate curly grain. You can also dab in quarter-circles or half-circles to create fan shapes.

MUSEUM-QUALITY FINISHES

In a museum-quality finish, the effect — the antique look — is more important than the materials you use. The final finish must protect the surface of the wood, but you can use any material, traditional or modern, that correctly simulates the effects of age. At the Workshops, the finishers commonly use latex paints, aniline die stains, and spray lacquer. (Contemporary lacquer bears little resemblance to old-time Chinese lacquer. The resin is made from nitrocellulose, and many of the vehicles are distilled from petroleum products.) Yet the final effect is almost indistinguishable from traditional materials that have been naturally aged.

To achieve the right effect, you must first understand the natural aging processes. The wood, the finish, and the hardware all show their age in different ways. The surface of the wood changes color and collects chips and dings. Traditional finishes dry out, shrink, and become discolored and scratched. Hardware rusts or tarnishes.

Think about each detail of your project. If it *had* been built during the Country era, what would have happened to it over the centuries? If you want, make up a history — whom it belonged to, how it was used, where it was kept. Create 150–200 years of fictional use and abuse. This fantasy will help you to build a believable *surface history*.

ARTIFICIAL AGING

There are many different processes that affect the appearance of every antique. For each process, there are one or more ways to simulate its effects on a reproduction:

Patina — Wood reacts with both light and air. When the surface is exposed to sunlight, it often changes color. It may also oxidize in the open air, which also alters the hue. Each wood changes in a different way. Most species become darker; walnut becomes lighter. This color shift happens, for the most part, only on the surface of the wood. This layer of exposed dark (or light) wood is called the *patina*.

To discover how the patina of a particular wood develops, study antiques that were built from this species. Purchase or mix a stain that simulates the color of this patina. In some cases, you may be able to create an artificial patina by treating the wood with chemicals. Cherry, for example, will darken when you apply ammonia. Pine, poplar, and maple develop a patina when you paint them with diluted (10 percent) nitric acid, then gently warm the surface with a heat gun. To simulate the patina of walnut, lighten it with wood bleach.

Accumulation of Dirt and Grime — Although a piece of furniture may be periodically cleaned and waxed, dirt eventually becomes ground into the surface. The dirt may also mix with oils on the surface to become grime. This grime accumulates

To simulate dirt and grime, apply a dark glaze and wipe most of it away before it dries. Leave the areas that would have accumulated more dirt a little darker than the rest of the project.

in cracks and crevices, and around door pulls and latches. Where the wood is unfinished, dirt collects in the pores of the wood, staining it a brownish gray. You can duplicate all of these effects by wiping the finished surface with glaze — a thick, dark stain.

There are several commercial glazes available, but you can easily make your own. Mix 2 ounces of Burnt Umber and 2 ounces of Burnt Sienna artist's oil paints with 8 ounces of turpentine, 3 ounces of boiled linseed oil, and 1/4 ounce of japan drier. Apply the glaze with a rag or brush, let it soak into the wood for a few minutes, then wipe it off. Wipe away as much glaze as possible in the center of broad areas, but leave some at the edges. (More dirt and grime accumulate at the edges than in the center.) When properly glazed, a surface should be lighter at the center, then darker and darker toward the edges.

Rounding — As a piece of furniture is used, the hard edges wear and round over. This doesn't happen evenly. For example, if you study an antique cupboard door, you'll find that the edges are worn more in the vicinity of the latch or pull. The corners of tabletops, top edges of drawer fronts, front edges of shelves and chair seats, inside edges of doors, and bottom ends of legs are all areas that wear faster on most furniture. Round over or "break" most of the hard edges and corners on an antique reproduction with sandpaper. Then use a rasp and file to round over and remove stock from the areas that would have seen the most wear.

Many of the edges on a piece of country furniture will become rounded with normal use. Identify these areas, decide how much they would have worn, then round them over with a rasp, file, or sandpaper.

Make a distressing tool by wiring 30–40 keys to a wooden handle. (Most hardware stores will be glad to give you their mis-cut key blanks.) *Lightly* beat the surface with the keys to create dents and scratches.

Distressing — Although wooden furniture is durable, the surface is not particularly resilient. It shows every dent and scratch. Over the years these accumulate, especially in the areas that see the most wear — around feet or legs, on tabletops, chest lids, shelves, and the seats of chairs. You can duplicate these marks by lightly beating the surface of a reproduction with a small ball peen hammer, a light chain, or a collection of keys. Be careful not to leave too many marks or make them too deeply; it's easy to over-distress a surface. Remember, the wear and tear should be believable.

Chips, Gnaw-Marks, and Other Damage — Occasionally, the wood is damaged rather than just dented or scratched. The corner of a drawer or the tip of a pendant may break off. Cabriole legs sometimes crack at the ankles. Rats and mice gnaw the backs of drawers, particularly if those drawers were used to hold foodstuffs or clothes. You can simulate all of this damage with a hammer, chisel, rasp, or other suitable tool. Once again, don't overdo it. Country furniture should look worn, but not as if it's been through a war.

Worn Finish — Just as the corners and the edges of wood wears, so will finish. Most antiques show areas where the finish has worn away completely, showing the bare wood underneath. These areas are the same as mentioned previously under "Rounding" — the surfaces around door pulls and latches, corners of tabletops, front edges of shelves and chair seats, and so on. To simulate this wear, sand away the finish on these areas with 320# wet/dry sandpaper. Wet the sandpaper with water or linseed oil to prevent it from loading.

Discolored and Cracked Finish — As a finish ages, it often darkens. Sometimes, it becomes stained, mildewed, or collects "fly specks." Old varnish and paint often become brittle, shrink, split, and appear "crackled."

To darken or stain a finish, wipe it with a dark glaze, let the glaze set a few minutes, then wipe it off again. If you want it darker yet, repeat. To add fly specks, dip a toothbrush in the glaze. Hold the brush about 12" from the surface of the wood and run your thumb through the bristles, spattering the surface of the project. Don't overdo this — a few fly specks go a long way.

There are several ways to simulate a crackled finish. The easiest, perhaps, is to apply a base coat of ordinary lacquer, then spray this with special "crackle lacquer." The crackle lacquer is a chemical agent that cracks the lacquer coat directly underneath it, showing the wood, stain, or paint beneath that. You can control the crackling effect (making larger or smaller cracks) by varying the amount of crackle lacquer you apply or by mixing it with varying amounts of thinner.

Note: Crackle lacquer *must* be applied over clear lacquer, tinted lacquer, or lacquer paint. For the best effect, seal the wood, stain, or paint you want to show through the cracks with clear lacquer or a wash coat of shellac. Apply the lacquer you want to crack over the sealant, then apply the crackle lacquer.

Crackle lacquer is especially formulated to react with the lacquer coat immediately underneath it and cause it to crack. It's normally applied with a spray gun, but you can also use a spray bottle.

You can also achieve a crackle finish with latex paint. Apply a base coat of latex and cover this with a thin, even coat of hide glue. Let the glue dry completely, then paint over the glue. As the second coat of latex dries, it will begin cracking. You can control the crackling by thinning the paint or covering the crackled latex with enamel. "Set" the cracks by covering the paint with clear shellac or varnish.

Finally, you can purchase several different types of "crackle paint" at most crafts stores. They may also have chemical agents to crack acrylic paint. These work well for small projects, but they're not economical for large ones.

Accumulated Layers of Finish — Many antiques are finished several times during their lifetimes. A typical early nineteenth-century Windsor chair,

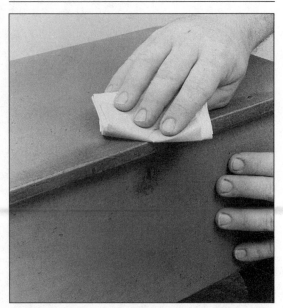

Antique furniture often accumulates several layers of paint. Each of these may be worn or chipped, showing the bare wood or colors underneath. To duplicate this effect, apply several coats of contrasting paint. After applying each coat, sand it or chip it away in the areas that would have seen the most wear.

for example, might have been finished with a thin, green milk paint when it was first made. Later in the century, it could have been covered with the black lacquer that was so popular in Victorian decor. In the 1920s or 1930s, it might have been painted once more with colored enamel. Each of these layers would have worn away partially, revealing bare wood or the colors underneath them.

To simulate this history, you must apply successive layers of paint. Sand and chip away a layer in the areas that are prone to wear, then wipe it with glaze to discolor it. Repeat for each layer. This is a painstaking process, but there are no good short-cuts for simulating this particular type of aging.

Liming — Country furniture made in the mid-Atlantic and southern colonies was often finished with an inexpensive whitewash, a mixture of lime paste and salt. As this whitewash wore off, the wood showed through, looking as if it had been stained white. To duplicate this look, mix oil-based white paint with mineral spirits to make a semi-transparent stain. Use this stain as you would a glaze — wipe it on the wood, allow it to set a few minutes, then wipe it off again.

Rusting and Tarnishing — Hardware also shows its age. Iron rusts, brass tarnishes. Pins, pivots, and other working parts come loose. Cast metal may break — it's very common to find old willow-and-bail pulls with one or more of the points missing.

To age iron hardware, including screws and nails, dip the metal in a 30 percent solution of nitric acid for 10–15 minutes. (**Warning:** Do this *outside,* wear rubber gloves and eye protection, and be careful not to breathe the fumes.) This will remove the rust-resistant zinc chromate coating. Rinse the hardware in distilled water. Dip it in gun bluing for 2–3 minutes, or until the surface turns black. Allow it to dry overnight — don't blot it dry. The metal will look used and worn, and there will be a thin layer of rust in the crevices.

To age brass hardware, first soak it in lacquer thinner. This will remove the lacquer coating that most hardware manufacturers apply to keep the brass bright. Blot the hardware dry. Make a salt water solution, adding 2 tablespoons of salt to 1 cup of water. Also, fill an old coffee can ⅓ full of ammonia. Dip the hardware in salt water, then suspend it *above* the ammonia on a string or in a wire basket. (Do *not* dip it *in* the ammonia.) Put the lid on the can, and gently warm it with a heat gun. As the ammonia fumes accumulate inside the can, the brass will begin to darken. (**Warning:** Do this *outside,* and avoid breathing the fumes.)

As soon as the darkening stops (in one or two minutes), repeat — dip the hardware in salt water and suspend it over the ammonia again. After several repetitions, the brass will be almost black. Dip it in salt water one final time and let it dry. Buff the flat areas bright with #0000 steel wool,

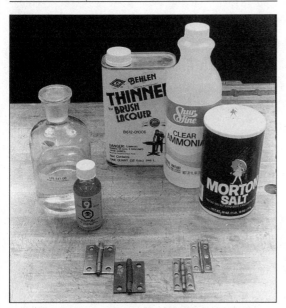

To artificially age iron hardware, strip the protective coating off with nitric acid, and apply gun bluing. For brass, strip it with lacquer thinner, and tarnish it with salt water and ammonia. All of these chemicals are available from hardware stores, grocery stores, or chemical supply houses.

allowing the tarnish to stay in the crevices.

If you decide to break off a portion of a brass pull or escutcheon, remember that the wood underneath the brass will likely be lighter than the rest of the surface. Also, the outline of the brass will be defined by a thin line of accumulated grime. To duplicate this, fasten the brasses in place, and lightly score the finish around them with a scratch awl. Wipe a glaze over the project, including the brasses. Before the glaze dries completely, remove the brasses and wipe them clean. Break off a *few* small pieces from one or two brasses. When you replace the brasses, the broken pieces will be outlined in simulated grime. Furthermore, the wood will be a shade lighter where the brass had covered it.

STICKING TO HISTORY

Although there are a lot of processes that age a piece of country furniture, none of them is complex. They can all be duplicated simply, using a few special techniques and a lot of horse sense. There are only two tricks: First, come up with a finishing plan that includes all the details. Second, arrange the various steps of this plan in the *proper chronological order.*

This chronology is extremely important! For the aging to appear authentic, you must carry out the simulation just as it might have happened in history. For instance, when you distress the wood, do so *after* you have applied a finish. If you're applying several layers of finish to build up a paint history, do a little distressing after each layer. This is the way it would have happened in real life.

The following procedures are outlines of finishing plans that are commonly used at the Workshops. The steps are arranged so the work flows easily, but they add the effects of age in the same order that history would have done so.

Museum-Quality Natural Finish — This finish is appropriate for formal furniture made from hardwoods such as walnut, cherry, and maple. It's transparent, so you can enjoy the wood grain. If your project is made from figured woods, you can take advantage of optional procedures to enhance the grain pattern.

1 Carefully remove all mill marks and other evidence of power tools, then finish sand the surface to 220#.

2 If the wood is figured, stain it a dark brown. Let the stain dry, then sand the surface again with 220# paper. Figured wood normally presents a swirl of end grains and long grains on its surface. Where the stain penetrates the end grain, the wood will remain dark. The long grains, which absorb less stain, will be lighter after sanding. This duplicates the way in which the end grains would have absorbed oil, wax, and grime over the years, growing darker than the long grains. It also accents the figuring.

3 Apply the "patina" stain — the color that the wood would otherwise achieve over time with exposure to sunlight and air. Note: If you're using a chemical stain, such as ammonia or nitric acid to create a patina, switch Steps 2 and 3.

4 If you want a crackle finish, first apply a coat of ordinary lacquer to seal the stain. This lacquer may be clear or tinted with aniline dyes. Then apply crackle lacquer to crack the ordinary lacquer.

5 Allow the lacquer (or the patina stain, if you skipped Step 4) to dry completely. Then do the rounding, distressing, and re-create any other wear and tear that might have happened to the wood or finish over time. As mentioned previously, be careful not to overdo this step.

6 Apply glazing to the surface, allow it to set for a few minutes, then wipe it off. Let it dry for at least 6 hours.

7 Apply the "top" coat — clear lacquer, shellac, or varnish.

8 Fasten the hardware in place, then rub out the finish with #0000 steel wool and oil soap. You may substitute dark paste wax for the soap, if

you wish. Buff the surface until you get the sheen you want.

Museum-Quality Painted Finish — This finish is best suited for informal projects made from utilitarian woods such as poplar or for folk designs that are meant to be painted. You can also use it to disguise the grain of projects made from several different wood species.

1 Carefully remove all mill marks and other evidence of power tools, then finish sand the surface to 150#.

2 Apply a base coat of latex paint, milk paint, or lacquer paint.

3 Seal the base coat with clear shellac, varnish, or lacquer.

4 For a crackle finish, apply a coat of lacquer paint that contrasts with the base coat, then apply crackle lacquer over that. This second coat will crack, letting the base coat show through the cracks.

5 If you want to "grain paint" the project, skip Step 4. Apply the graining, let it dry thoroughly and seal it with a clear finish. (If you want to crack the grain painting, seal the graining with clear lacquer, then apply crackle lacquer.)

6 Allow the previous finish or sealer to dry completely. Then do the rounding, distressing, and re-create any other wear and tear that might have happened to the wood or paint over time. Be careful not to overdo.

7 If you want to build up multiple layers of paint, repeat Steps 2, 3, 4, and 6 as desired.

8 Apply glazing to the surface, allow it to set for a few minutes, then wipe it off. Let it dry for at least 6 hours.

9 Apply a final coat of clear lacquer, shellac, or varnish.

10 Fasten the hardware in place, then rub out the finish with #0000 steel wool and oil soap. Substitute dark paste wax for the soap, if desired. Buff the surface.

SOURCES

If you need sources of country furniture supplies — tools, hardware, finishes, or other materials — here's a list of companies and the products they provide:

COMPANY	PRODUCT
Ceramichrome, Inc. Arts and Crafts Division Stanford, KY 40484	Finishes
Chroma Acrylics, Inc. P.O. Box 510 Hainesport, NJ 06036	Finishes
Connecticut Cane & Reed Co. P.O. Box 762 Manchester, CT 06040	Seating materials
Constantine's 2050 Eastchester Rd. Bronx, NY 10461	Wood, tools, general woodworking supplies
Country Accents P.O. Box 437 Montoursville, PA 17754	Tin
Craftsman Wood Service 1735 W. Cortland Ct. Addison, IL 60101	Wood, tools, general woodworking supplies
Eisenbrand Hardwoods, Inc. 4100 Spencer St. Torrance, CA 90503	Wood
Garrett Wade 161 Avenue of the Americas New York, NY 10013	Tools, hardware, finishes, general woodworking supplies
Horton Brasses Nooks Hill Rd. P.O. Box 120V Cromwell, CT 06416	Brass hardware
Leichtung Workshops 4944 Commerce Parkway Cleveland, OH 44128	Tools, hardware, general woodworking supplies

COMPANY	PRODUCT
Mohawk Finishes Route 30 North Amsterdam, NY 12010	Finishes
Native American Hardwoods 6570 Gowanda State Rd. Hamburg, NY 14075	Wood
Olde Mill Cabinet Shoppe 1660 Camp Betty Washington Rd. York, PA 17402	Finishes
Shaker Workshops P.O. Box 1028 Concord, MA 01742	Seating and finishing materials
Tremont Nail Company P.O. Box 111 Wareham, MA 02571	Nails
The Wise Company 6503 St. Claude Ave. Arabi, LA 70032	Brass and iron hardware
Woodcraft 10 State St. P.O. Box 4000 Woburn, MA 01888	Tools, hardware, general woodworking supplies
Wood Finishing Supply Co. 100 Troop St. Palmyra, NY 14522	Finishes
The Woodworker's Store 21801 Industrial Blvd. Rogers, MN 55374	Tools, hardware, general woodworking supplies
Woodworker's Supply 5604 Alameda Place Albuquerque, NM 87113	Tools, hardware, general woodworking supplies
The Workshops of David T. Smith 3600 Shawhan Rd. Morrow, OH 45152	Hand-forged iron hardware

REFERENCES

Should you wish to know more about the history of country furniture or want additional references for design ideas, here is a suggested reading list.

BOOKS

- **American Antiques from Israel Sack Collection, Volumes 1 through 7,** Highland House Publishers, Inc., 1981
- **American Country Furniture 1780-1875,** Ralph and Terry Kovel, Crown Publishers, 1965
- **American Furniture,** John S. Bowman, Exeter Books, 1985
- **American Painted Furniture 1660-1880,** Dean A. Fales, Jr., Bonanza Books, 1986
- **The American Shakers and Their Furniture,** John G. Shea, Van Nostrand Reinhold Co., 1971
- **Antique Country Furniture of North America,** John G. Shea, Van Nostrand Reinhold Co., 1975
- **Decorated Furniture of the Mahantongo Valley,** Henry M. Reed, Bucknell University Press, 1987
- **Fine Points of Furniture — Early American,** Albert Sack, Crown Publishers, 1950
- **The Furniture of Historic Deerfield,** Dean A. Fales, Jr., E.P. Dutton & Co., 1986
- **Hispanic Furniture,** Sali Katz, Architectural Book Publishing Co., 1986
- **Illustrated Guide to Shaker Furniture,** Robert F.W. Meader, Dover Publications, 1972
- **The Knopf Collector's Guides to American Antiques: Furniture, Volumes 1 and 2,** William C. Ketchum, Jr., Alfred A. Knopf, Inc., 1982
- **Neat Pieces, The Plain-Style Furniture of 19th Century Georgia,** Atlanta Historical Society, 1983
- **New Mexican Furniture 1600–1940,** Lonn Taylor and Dessa Bokides, Museum of New Mexico Press, 1987
- **The Pennsylvania German Collection,** Beatrice B. Garvan, Philadelphia Museum of Art, 1982
- **The Pine Furniture of Early New England,** Russel Hawes Kettel, Dover Publications, 1956
- **Religion in Wood, A Book of Shaker Furniture,** Edward and Faith Andrews, Indiana University Press, 1971
- **The Shaker Chair,** Muller and Rieman, The Canal Press, 1985
- **Shaker Design,** June Sprigg, Whitney Museum of American Art, 1980
- **Shaker Furniture,** Edward Deming Andrews, Dover Publications, 1950
- **The Windsor Style in America, Volumes 1 and 2,** Charles Santore, Running Press Book Publishers, 1981
- Several additional books are listed on page 39.

MAGAZINES

- **Antiques,** Old Mill Rd., P.O. Box 1975, Marion, OH 43085
- **Antiques and The Arts Weekly,** The Bee Publishing Co., 5 Church Hill Rd., Newtown, CT 06470
- **The Antique Review,** P.O. Box 538, Worthington, OH 43085
- **The Maine Antiques Digest,** 71 Main St., Waldoboro, ME 04572

INDEX

CREDITS

A friend of ours who has written several enormous books once observed: "Authors often write acknowledgments that go on for pages, and you wonder whether it's necessary. Well, it is. All those thank-you-kindly's are well-deserved. No one person can write a book; no *two* people can write it. The task is too mind-boggling. A good book is *always* a team effort."

This book is no different. It has been a mind-boggling task, and we would never have finished it without the help of many good people. We have a lot of thank-you-kindly's to deliver, so bear with us. In particular, we have relied on the craftsmen, craftswomen, and other folks at The Workshops. We have been awed by their artistry, enlightened by their woodworking savvy, and genuinely astonished by their patience. But most of all, we have been warmed by their good company. Thank you, Clare Allen, Kent Allen, Joe Bradley, John Buchanan, Ed Campbell, Jerry Cook, Kelly Cook, Loretta Cooper, Patty Cramer, Cathy Gatch, Eric Hancock, Kelly Holliday, Larry Hough, Todd Hough, Cathy McFarland, Walt Miller, Elzo Morgan, Dawn Morningstar, Jerry Parker, Harold Pauley, Jerry Ratliff, Bobby Rooks, John Rose, Dixie Rose, Marilee Rose, Rex Rose, Troy Sexton, Greg Shooner, David T. Smith, Grace Smith, Jason Smith, Julie Smith, Lora Smith, Mary Spellmire-Shooner, Beth Stephenson, Susan Swearigen, Tom Thompson, Chris Woods, Luke Woods, and Warren Young. Whew!

But wait, there's more! We have also depended on many other people, organizations, and institutions who've tracked down historical trivia, lent photographs, checked woodworking procedures, and have helped us with the thousands of details that make up this book. Many thanks to Rich and Sue Burmann, Thomas Clark, Jane Sikes Hageman, Gordon Honeyman, Tom Kuhns, Bob Menker, Mary Myers, Larry Owrey, Ruth Penewit, Tom and Ann Workman, Ohio Historical Society, Warren County Museum, and Winterthur Museum.

And special thanks to that one person whom we probably forgot to include in these acknowledgments but will remember (never to forget again) two days after this book goes to the printer.

ABOUT THE AUTHORS

Nick Engler is an experienced woodworker and woodworking writer. He worked as a luthier making traditional American musical instruments, founded *Hands On!* magazine, and has published 20 books on the wood arts. Nick is a contributing editor to *American Woodworker* magazine and teaches woodworking at the University of Cincinnati.

Mary Jane Favorite is a prolific folk artist, woodworking designer, and illustrator. She is accomplished in several crafts, but is best known for her whimsical wood carvings and whirligigs. Mary Jane's drawings frequently appear in publications such as *American Woodworker* magazine. She has co-authored four woodworking books and has contributed project designs to many others.

Rodale Press, Inc., publishes AMERICAN WOODWORKER™, the magazine for the serious woodworking hobbyist. For information on how to order your subscription, write to AMERICAN WOODWORKER™, Emmaus, PA 18098.